D1568260

"Nick Weber's memoir is replete with stories of an extraordinary individual's dedication, innocence and experience. His long, sometimes bumpy, road to becoming and being a Jesuit, a clown and a family member reveals a lifelong dedication to fairness, dignity, equity and love."

—Jennifer Williams, International Futures Forum, London, UK

The Circus That Ran Away With a Jesuit Priest
Memoir of a Delible Character

By
Nick Weber

1317. Confirmation, like Baptism, imprints a spiritual mark or indelible character on the Christian's soul...

1582. The sacrament of Holy Orders, like the other two [Baptism and Confirmation], confers an indelible spiritual character...

The Catechism of the Catholic Church, United States Catholic Conference, 1994

First published by Dog Ear Publishing
4010 W. 86th Street, Ste H
Indianapolis, IN 46268
www.dogearpublishing.net

dog ear
PUBLISHING

ISBN: 978-1-45750-978-0

This book is printed on acid-free paper.

Printed in the United States of America

DEDICATION

From its inception this book has been intended as a tribute to the scores of troupers who made the Royal Lichtenstein Circus what it was, and to the memory of the one who trouped farther and faster than any of us, Mitchell Jerome Kincannon.

Contents

Preface

Ordinary people like me are not usually so self-inflated as to write memoirs. Not in the wildest world imaginable could I consider myself possessed of anything like an iota of wisdom to share with a reader. I have, nevertheless, decided to publicly render what I can recall of my experiences. With luck, some might dare to imagine new and possibly healthier routes for themselves. Others, startled in the frightening fancy of an adventure with me as a shotgun-navigator, might resolve to remain more alert to their own maps. Minimally, some might be amused by a "good read" as they while away the slow rain of a cool and cloudy afternoon.

Some of the dialogues I record here I can repeat verbatim; others I've had to re-construct, approximating the best words I can fit into meetings I otherwise remember well.

A comic working title for this project was *If You Can't Say Something Nice About Someone, Don't Mention Their Name.* With few exceptions that became a governing maxim and anonymity was the operative mode in most of such scenarios. In the detailing of other components of the story, I and others judged that the use of pseudonyms was appropriate. Also, I have omitted the characteristic "S.J." ("Society of Jesus") after Jesuit names. Assume clerics associated with a Jesuit institution are Jesuit. All others, especially in my youngest years, are either diocesan clerics or members of other religious communities.—Not all of the dedicated performers who helped realize the achievements of the Royal Lichtenstein Circus could be mentioned by name in the body of this project. Consequently, an inclusive chronology is included at the end. With that I incur two risks: despite meticulous effort, someone might have been omitted; the few performers whose stay with us was less than happy may wish they hadn't been listed. For both disappointments, I apologize at the outset.

An early working subtitle for the memoir described it as *distracted.* Distraction remains a theme especially in the recounting of my Jesuit training. In those years there were hosts of sidetracks warring with my focus, and I yielded. I wrote about many of them. Even in my writing there are distractions. Like Shakespeare, a late-life hobby. So poor old Hamlet and friends pop up from time to time, all haphazardly cited from my tattered 1969 edition of the *Pelican Complete Works*.

Finally, there are things polite people, even friends, don't talk about. They agree not to bring up such subjects. One of those subjects is politics (at root the same word as *polite*); the other is religion. In this telling of my story I am half polite: I don't discuss politics. But there is no way I cannot discuss where my religious quest has brought me. And if surprise might be seen as somehow salvific, this book's trek along not over-trod roads just might be sacred.

1.

Arrows

But then begins a journey in my head,
To work my mind, when body's work's expired;
For then my thoughts, from far where I abide,
Intend a zealous pilgrimage to thee.

—W. Shakespeare, Sonnet XXVII

High noon. Thursday, September 10, 1987. Yale University's central lawn above the undergrad library. If you are a Yalie cutting across campus through that area, you have already noticed the mild warmth of an abundant fall sun that seems to dare all the planted campus areas to remain the right shade of green. What isn't right is the sound carrying beyond the lawn area. As you approach, almost orchestrated laughter betrays the presence of a crowd, an audience.

It is an utterly exotic apparition without excuse or explanation. Centered on the span of lawn is a tiny circus: shrilly-striped ring, flags everywhere—even atop the trapeze rigging—a tightwire, and two white-faced clowns engaging that audience, several hundred students seated on the grass, some right at the edge of the ring. There is attention in the air. These Ivy Leaguers are sitting at the feet of clowns. Of course there is attention. The students know they are students and the clowns know they are clowns. Full circle. Complete consciousness. Open and free.

A Chief Clown is setting a table with dishes. Like his huskier companion he wears a crisply tailored tunic in the style of a very trim Elizabethan doublet. What hair he has left is shoulder length and matches his reddish blond mustache and goatee. He is almost skinny, and completely intense in every gesture. In the charged silence of very focused pantomime, he makes it more than clear

1

that he can pull a checkered tablecloth out from under the dishes he has set on a table. His partner encourages him with the dare of a child. No reference has to be made to the welfare of the dishes. Everyone knows what is not supposed to happen. Everyone also knows that buried somewhere in this so crude playlet is something they don't know. That's clown comedy. That's the anticipated surprise that conjures attention in circus entertainment. Both these guys move with a bravado and surety that immediately reveals the hundreds of times they've done this for audiences they still hear laughing. They are also deceived, willingly, by the self-trickery that allows actors to believe in utter nonsense.

The setup complete, the audience complies with a silent request to provide a massive drum roll, infusing textbooks and backpacks with new usefulness. Utter nonsense. The cloth is pulled and the dishes remain in their respective, expected positions. From somewhere behind a large backdrop there is a mighty alarm of simultaneous whistles as the clown takes his bow and accepts ready applause—even from his accomplice. Too good. Everyone knows they are supposed to be suspicious. Nonetheless, Chief Clown begins to speak, professorially, chest out. Get ready to take notes.

"Just when—"

And just then it happens.

The accomplice nonchalantly picks up the table. And in tipping it to carry it out of the ring, he reveals that all the dishes are tied in place. Explosive laughter covers the professor's opening phrase. No matter. Oblivious to anything out of order in the ring, he pursues his topic, knowing full well he will repeat the opening structure on his way to a revelation: the nonsense just enacted was not only innocent but cathartic. It contrasts with a much larger arena of nonsense that has pervaded the atmosphere of our lives.

> "…machine-gun fire fugues have out-cadenza'd all the possible logic of your favorite computer concerto…
> Just when the haughty *entrechat* of well-timed lies has outdanced the delicate but oh-so-muscled *pas de deux* of heart and truth…
> Just then, between reports of last shell emptied and falsehood delivered,
> Hope finds even in the geography of today, promise for tomorrow.
> Now then, with you we enter this just-then now-space to stretch and breathe.
> In this humble ring, the logic of the snare drum and the clumsy dance of clowns and dogs
> Seize our sense of time, till 'just when' waltzes 'just then' to 'just now.'
> And suddenly all of the truly exciting things all of you—even you.—could be doing right now…
> Give way to the bold and gold, round and red, totally-useless-somehow-necessary world of— THE CIRCUS."

And the mighty whistle alarm loads the ring with three more clowns, all speaking at once with such diction and pressure that although they are each saying something different, you know they are making even syntactical sense. And so begins fifty-five minutes of rapid-fire entertainment that is really a hybrid of theater and the rarefied repertoire of circus. It is a seamless parade of juggling, balancing, parables and acrobatics that only a trained ensemble including four men, two monkeys, a dog, a prancing miniature horse, and a waltzing bear could muster.

The audience can't be more present to this brash and humble ceremony. Of course there is the conventional punctuation of applause, laughter, and downright cheering. But there is more. On both sides of the ringed performance space there seems to be an almost tangible thrall. Unspoken, there flashes in everyone's eyes an acknowledgement of presence, of all to all. *I see you. I see you seeing me. I am so happy to be here.* And so it goes. Of course it ends. The central lawn empties. By late afternoon it is bare. Till next year.

That was over thirty years ago.

I never got to see what those students saw. I saw those students, though. I was that Chief Clown. The Royal Lichtenstein Circus was the bold and risky realization of a vision I'd had in the late Sixties. It lasted for twenty-two years of performing throughout most of the United States in shopping centers, on college campuses, in high school and elementary school gyms, and church halls. That circus meant I went to Yale for five years. I also went to Princeton, Cornell, Beloit, UCLA, Emory, Purdue, Tulane, Louisiana State and Stanford. I never managed to graduate from any of them because I couldn't stay long enough. But I reaped the treasure of a priceless education.

Retirement is also priceless. The distance of time and the perspective of finally staying in one place have been additional gifts. For what it's worth, I think that little circus was the best thing I ever accomplished. That may or not be true. It may only be a biased guess. No matter. What does matter is my rock solid conviction that those twenty-two seasons, that circus, and that day at Yale University would never have happened had I not been both a practiced circus clown and an ordained Jesuit priest. Finding such an electric amalgam, trouping through its best and worst energies, and arriving at late life's more challenging horizons is the story of this book.

*   *   *

Not very far from where I am writing, a few hundred people, mostly younger and with families, are huddled under a broad span of vinyl against the light rain of a cool afternoon. They are not gathered there because of the weather. They are focused on a tightly disciplined group of performers, some human and some animal, who leap, twirl, dance and strut—but most of all surprise. An intricate series of whistles, drum rolls, and the heady-if-predictable rhythms of galops, waltzes, and marches cue a succession of images unique to this ritual. When the ritual succeeds the hundreds gasp, applaud, and laugh, amazed at what these performers have imagined and found possible. It only happens that it is raining; the vinyl encloses and comforts a very special assembly who have chosen to pay their admission and see a circus.

Four blocks from that field, another few hundreds of all ages and social tiers are gathered in a building as gray as the afternoon sky. They too are focused on a heavily disciplined ritual, this one with far fewer performers. They sing, speak, and gesture a set of very ancient images, already known to the crowd, and cued by printed rubrics only the performers see. Since it is a high holiday, the lead performer uses incense profusely, the heady vestige of a similar ritual's onetime need to cover the odor of slaughtered animals. Truth to tell, surprise would be suspect here. When this ritual is successful, most of the attendants very silently feel a private expansion, a sacred sense of connection with a transcendent source and target. Perhaps most immediately they experience a heightening of their sense of self-worth and that of the persons around them. It only happens that they are in a building; even were they out under the afternoon's gray sky, no enclosure would be required to identify them as a very chosen assembly who are attending church.

As history has it, that circus is one of the few remaining American tented circuses still traveling with trained animals and a live brass band. And that church is Roman Catholic, one of the few in its metropolitan area that has not been downsized or eliminated.

To a sociologist, the two gatherings I have described might be seen to depend upon or emerge from two different cultures. To those who find themselves in either the bleachers or the pews, or at different times in both, the gatherings seem to inhabit two very different worlds.

I grew up in both those worlds at the same time. Insofar as I might ever have grown up, I even worked as a professional in both of those worlds, simultaneously. As an ordained Roman Catholic priest of the Society of Jesus—a Jesuit—I was a performing clown, animal trainer, and executive producer of the Royal Lichtenstein Circus. During those years, that unique circus was an official ministry of the California Province of the Jesuit Order. Sharing such a story is a frightening project, fraught with risks—but so is any good circus. Insofar as the story is revelatory, it should be a heightening project, even punctuated with self-disclosure—and so is any apt religious ritual.

*   *   *

For dozens of generations now, circuses have found their daily way to odd lots, fairgrounds, city parks, and fields with the help of what the business calls the "24-Hour Man." This individual staples or tapes dozens and dozens of paper arrows to mileage markers, highway route signs, and phone poles, signaling every turn of the way to a show's next lot. Those frail paper messages begin appearing as the rigs leave the field that was their home yesterday, and continue meticulously until the weary early-morning drivers pull their exotic wares onto a new lot. Thus it goes, day in and day out, for an eight-month season until the very last set of arrows indicates the long-awaited turn into winter quarters and the chance to rest, repaint, and rehearse before next spring's leave-taking.

The arrows are vital if everyone is to arrive on time. But fatigue and distraction sometimes interfere with the process so that drivers and their "shotgun" riders doubling as navigators don't see the arrows. Miss a set of arrows and you may be in for a dangerous lane shift, U-turn, or a complete lack of arrows. You will have "blown the arrows," as showpeople say.

I am no longer on the road. I did not "blow the arrows." I consciously chose, on different occasions, not to follow them.

2.

The Things of a Child

"We are such stuff as dreams are made on."
—Shakespeare, *The Tempest, IV.i.156-7*

Yuba City, California. The southeast corner of Plumas Street and Colusa Highway. September 18, 2011, 6:15 pm PDT.

It's a Tesoro filling station now. Nevertheless, had you been in exactly the right spot on this corner seventy-two earlier, you would have heard a gasping yell. It would have been by one of the latest hitchhikers to thumb a lift from planet Earth whirling through its late summer journeys around itself and the sun.

I was lucky to catch that ride. I didn't deserve it and I hadn't done much to get ready for it. Everything sort of fell—or shot—into place. I certainly don't remember preparing. But I must have been ready. I have lasted through a good many years, wrecks and breakdowns, successes, losses and wins on four continents and counting.

The first miles? Took about three years or so. Zip memories. Bits and pieces, maybe. Some guys have tried to convince me I can pull up more than that, but it's all guesswork on my part. After four years, bingo. Lights on. Adventureland.

I'll conjure with those bits and pieces first. High ceilings. Unpaved basement with a dirt floor and musty smells. Gravel driveways. Bamboo hedgerow. Freckles on Mom's hands and arms. Front bedroom crib. Palm trees out front on a busy street. Balancing on the edge of the bathtub. The silver half-dollar with mushrooms in the frying pan. Screened porch in back. Threats about bamboo spankings. Fireplace in living room.

Complete sentences? There are only a couple of them left. Those palm trees had a bark I could pull small pieces from and toss into the street—until a kind police officer brought me into the house suggesting it was an unsafe place for me to be. I'm thankful for the benevolence of that first cop contact, because I would be out of place all my life. It's a professional hazard for a circus man, and some of the police who discovered me weren't so nice.

Also, the Japanese were the reason I couldn't get pants with two back pockets. Those folks had assumed a lot of influence on our lives in those days, but that even seemed extreme to me.

Early clown props

And I was balancing on that bathtub without a net. I slipped, and my foot connected with the space heater nearby. The only relief from the pain came from across the gravel driveway. My grandmother Elsie arrived and made a bowl of vinegar water and plunged my foot into it. (She would later teach the family doctor the wonder of mustard plasters.)

Oh, and one more. This had to have been pretty close to when the lights came on, because this one is a little technical. I was with another little boy, a neighbor or relative. We were out front next to one of those date palms. We had gotten some cigarette papers and matches. You can put it together. What we didn't put together was the tobacco with the rolled paper. That detail we had either forgotten or never noticed. We just rolled and lit, and puffed like mad, until the flame touched our lips. It was too hot for us to look cool. Luck again. I had only seen my dad rolling his own. I hadn't yet seen a fire-eater.

Concentrating on one's early experiences is one thing; recalling them accurately, quite another. Remembering what happened over six decades in the past can be an exercise in foggy exploration. But then there appear those select faces, settings, smells, sounds and feelings that emerge quite clearly.

One thing's for sure: I hate beer. Always have. (I have double-locked my apartment door as I write this here in Milwaukee.) But I owe the intensity of my early inventiveness and creativity to beer. Not that I'm all that inventive or that creative, but I am intense. I can at least concentrate *until* I imagine or invent something. Beer made that happen. No, really. It's not what you think.

My paternal grandfather sold beer. Nicholas J. Weber II (I'm Nicholas J. Weber IV—we concentrate more than we invent) sold groceries and bottled soft drinks before I knew him, but by the time I came along, he sold beer; and my dad, Number III of course, worked for him. What was important for me was that my grandfather's house and my house both backed onto a large piece of property whose gravel driveways led to a motley collection of buildings. My grandfather's real estate comprised a third of our block in the little northern California town of Yuba City. As far as I ever knew, this landscape well-served a thriving beer distributorship in the mid-1940's.

The buildings were of various ages and styles, some open sheds, some rickety, and one an overwhelming metal warehouse structure known in our family as "the plant." Just west of this large structure, my grandmother tended a small garden of iris and tiger lilies. Two sides of this garden were hedged with, well, hedges. And along the north side, extending out from the plant was my own personal laboratory, studio, and shrine: a one-time chicken coop, now a toolshed. It was never designated for me; I just discovered it. It comprised two shabby sections of unpainted wood with a tin roof. Garden tools lined the walls of one section, and a third of the north wall of the other was still poultry netting. The outer section had a dirty glass window, and the crude plank door was never locked. Here was the exclusive and hidden atmosphere that conjures a young boy's images of "fort," "hideout," and "clubhouse." For me it was all that and more.

Perhaps a chief engine in a child's imagination is the need to somehow repeat in a reduced and artificial way the behavior patterns and rituals he observes in the adult activity around him. This dimension of play is acting, and it is self-conscious. The child knows it is acting. Such self-consciousness can sometimes feel acutely risky. And a valuable function of a hideout or clubhouse domain is the assurance of privacy and focus. That beer distributorship with its cluttered sheds and buildings afforded me such assurance.

In such a place, playtime, variously rehearsal and performance, allows fantasy to soar. That's why after all these years of professional rehearsal and performance, I can remember that long-ago shed as my first studio. Away from the glare of so-called reality and the limited vision of preoccupied adults, I could imagine and practice. Typically, my experiences in the adult world fed this elemental and crude mimesis. And even in the small-town Forties, there was a lot for a little kid to experience. But it was not long, maybe unusually soon, before I found worlds of my own inside the real world's grown-up happenings around me.

They were worlds. I did find them. But in the oblique light at the other end of my life's day, I can see that they were at once valuable and dangerous. I learned to mimic, even the sacred, and I unwittingly exploited the so-close relationship of stage and sanctuary. I discovered and perfected skills with balance and fire. I began honing the magician's art of misdirection. Those protean creative gestures would develop to carry me through most of my professional life. And I couldn't have indulged them without the near-secrecy of that early rustic studio.

The danger was not in the seclusion exactly; it was in the control I had. Even when I chose to populate those quiet spaces because I needed acolytes or roustabouts and performers, I chose people I could control in a game I designed. That may be why I was never interested in team sports; I couldn't control them. I strenuously appropriated not only the environment of control, but the dimension of graceful, even social manipulation native to each of the worlds I had discovered. Because even in the rubric of service pursued by the rituals of religion and creative entertainment, performers control. In the noble enterprise of esoteric study and ascetic training, they achieve, albeit for the good of one's fellows, a controlling aesthetic. My journey to such an aesthetic began in a discarded toolshed.

The beer distributorship was successful and busy. My shed went largely unnoticed. But I was not unnoticed. I was everywhere on that property when I wanted to be, and lived as much at my grandparents' house as my own. I was sometimes too present. Sometimes my grandfather (I called him "Pabst" because of a beer he sold) came up from the plant to discuss something with Gramma Elsie that he didn't want me to hear. He would tell me that if I went down to a certain faucet near a black-walnut tree along the main driveway, I'd find a dime. I was gone.

Such memories are richly populated with the three chief characters in the drama that was becoming my life: Pabst, Gramma, and Beth.

Beth, my father's slightly younger sister, was a bright business-minded woman who kept herself informed with constant reading. She was not a healthy person, constantly in need of medical care. She went to her death in her thirties, unmarried, and a victim of cancer. But she loved me with the strength, moral guidance, persistent protection and readiness to instruct that very few experience even with parents. We were very close, always. Everyone else in our family knew this. I'm the one who took forever to realize and admit it.

Gramma was from the big Tull family, a farm girl who had relocated from the countryside north and west of town where one of her brothers was still farming. She told me and all the family stories about her mother, of course. But the one that really carries punch in my later life is one about her own grandmother, whom I never knew. Gramma Beebe had told my grandmother that she remembered from her childhood waking up in the back of a Conestoga wagon to see her father paying off an Indian to let them pass.

Gramma used to joke that she was part Indian (as in Native American, as in Cherokee to be exact). At least I thought she was joking. But in a non-joking way, she had dropped remarks about the family coming from Arkansas.

These days there are colleges all over Arkansas. No, I don't think any of my ancestors would have attended. But thirty years after hearing Gramma's stories, I found some of those colleges. Among hundreds of colleges all over the country that became repeated venues for the Royal Lichtenstein Circus, there were half a dozen campuses scattered near the middle of Arkansas. So it was that after a show at Arkadelphia's Ouachita Baptist College we headed along U.S. 270 for an appearance at the University of Arkansas in Pine Bluff and saw the directional sign for state 290 into Tull. And after that show? (No, you're there too early.) Up I-65 through Little Rock and then I-40 past the intersection to play two dates in Conway: the University of Central Arkansas, and Hendrix College. Then back to Little Rock to pick up westbound I-40 toward West Memphis passing the junction of S.R. 31 north to Beebe. The Indians? Go ahead and check it out. Cherokees alright, but I probably even have some Osage in me, too.

The heartbreak for me now is that I didn't ask for more stories. From everybody.

Elsie Rose Weber, "Gramma Elsie"

In 1945, my world, at 618 Shasta Street and around the corner at my own house on Bridge Street, consisted of wooden houses with high ceilings, sets of long wooden stairs, large screened-in porches, and my mother, aunt and grandmother busy and content with the constant routines of housekeeping and home-making. Though I lived in and around these routines, they couldn't command much of a youngster's attention span. But outside, I ruled in a kind of kinder-kingdom: a landscape of gravel and dirt, storage sheds (including my very own), parked delivery trucks, and house-high stacks of empty beer cases. Here, a five-year-old imagination, in very active solitude, could reinvent whatever world or galaxy it chose to engage.

It wasn't only solitude. Gradually our neighborhood began to speak to me in the energetic voices of kids older, younger, and my age. They lived on four sides of that corporation yard. Representing all middle and lower class strata, we became an unselfconscious collective single-mindedly exploring the tiny part of the world available to us, and fantasizing the part that was not. Since Pabst owned a sizeable chunk of Yuba City's world, my kingdom behind 618 Shasta Street soon became a modest hub for the meeting, dreaming, and clumsy dancing of a tribe of little boys.

But once a week, I exchanged that kingdom and my tribe for a dramatic excursion with Pabst and Aunt Beth across our Feather River Bridge to Marysville's Saint Joseph Catholic Church and Sunday morning Mass. There is almost nothing in that period of my life that has tattooed my memory and emotions more effectively than the hours I spent in Saint Joseph's.[1] The very first trip was an overload of sensory surprise.

Scale, if not simply threatening, probably commands a child's attention before anything else. And there, where it had been for nearly a century, at the corner of Seventh and C streets in Marysville, was a church whose broad and steep array of front steps would hypnotize even an adult. Halfway up the climb of those steps, our simple ascending rhythm almost evolved into a march as we were accompanied by the grand, repeated two-strike peal of a huge bell hidden somewhere above the main door. By design, the faux Gothic doorframes and the one hundred foot steeple would impel a kid's perception, if not his thoughts, aloft, so that by the time he entered the church proper, he would be certain that something was *up*.

Surprise. Inside Saint Joseph's, the largest enclosure I had ever entered, dwarfing even the plant at home, some*one* was up. Several *someones*. Up there. On the ceiling. Never mind that I had given up my outside kingdom and come indoors with grownups. Now, forty feet above me, there were seas of rolling clouds where all manner of great loving folks swam and watched over me.

But there was also silence. After the bell, as soon as we entered the doors, silence. Pabst and Aunt Beth and the other people around us had lost their voices. So other senses took over, and not only sight. I could smell the dark wood pews and blonder wood floors, varnished and over-cleaned since long ago. They smelled cold and hard, unlike the people who used them. Some

[1] Gramma was never with us at Mass in those days. She was a non-practicing Methodist. I surmised that from the few remarks she ever made about religion before Pabst died. After his death, she converted to Catholicism, "because that is what Dad would want." At that time, Yuba City didn't have a Catholic parish of its own; it was a "mission" of the larger church in the older and larger community across the river in Marysville.

places on the rounded top of the pew-back in front of us were grimy to the touch, while other places were worn smooth.

What dim light there was conspired with the silence nudging my attention back to those people above. As the questions about who they were, what they were doing, and what they thought of me roiled up, the bell sounded again and I was startled quite a lot as everyone in the church stood. I was aware, perhaps only for the second time, that I was surrounded by people. Then I noticed that in front of us but on the other side of the center aisle there were two rows of black statues. They were all facing forward, posed to look like they were focusing ahead of them. And their focus pulled my own up to the front of this huge room for the first time.

There was more light up there now, and it couldn't all be coming from the gigantic candles I hadn't noticed before. Everything up there seemed white and decorated, like a birthday cake to hold the candles. And there were people moving up there: one tall and two short, themselves decorated, so they could be on the cake. But one thing was sure. These people were like the ones above me because they, too, floated. From place to place they floated, all over the giant cake.

Whatever they were doing was important because then everyone knelt down before them even though they had their backs to us. Aunt Beth made me kneel between her and Pabst on the little low wood bench I had been standing on. When I got settled, I discovered something frightening: the statues were also kneeling. And the three people up front were talking but not to each other because they never looked at each other. Even when I could hear, I couldn't understand what they were saying. They just seemed to mumble fast, all the while looking straight ahead at the cake. I gave up and returned to the folks up above. At least they were looking at me and at each other.

Then I was startled again because everyone around me sat. How did they know they all wanted to sit down at exactly the same time? Even the statues. The tall one was now on top of the cake reading from a huge book. Then a short one floated the book to the other side of the cake and everyone stood, at exactly the same time of course. There was more mumbled reading from the same book, and occasionally the tall one's voice seemed to thunder. It might as well have been thunder, because I still couldn't understand what he was saying. And like thunder, it scared me a little. The tall one scared me. Why did he make the short one move that book if he was just going to keep reading from it?

Then the tall one floated up to a tree house near the cake and I could see his long, skinny face clearly. He looked down at us but very soon began reading again. Now I could understand what he was saying, but the story he was reading didn't sound like stories at home. There was still some thunder, and now I could hear a strange clicking in his speech. When he was through reading, everyone sat down. He was talking to us, but still there was thunder and clicking, so I went back to my friends floating above me.

Suddenly, from behind me there was music. I had only heard music on the radio or when Dad played "Margie" on the piano. But this was loud and rumbly and sweet. When I looked back, I saw grownups high above me, but not as high as the floaters on the ceiling. They all held books and were singing. Behind them, the wall was decorated, like another cake, with huge unlit candles. In front of the singers, a lady sat at a large dressing table looking at herself in a little mirror. Aunt Beth didn't want me looking at the music people so I was again looking at the front. But I could still hear the music, and sometimes it made my seat shake.

And so it went. Floating and mumbling and reading and up and down. And there were special bells from the cake, and shiny gold things for the tall one to drink out of, and then Pabst and Aunt Beth and many other grownups (even the statues) went up front and knelt and the tall one floated very near them and mumbled. When they came back, they held their hands together in front of them and were very, very serious. What did the tall one do to them? After the statues went up front and turned around to come back, another surprise: they were not all black. They had a patch of white above and below what looked like people faces. They were even more serious than Pabst and Aunt Beth.

We left. The huge bell rang as soon as we were on the steps outside and everyone could suddenly talk again. The harsh daylight and simultaneous conversations, all mumble-free, thunder-free, and click-free, jarred me. However, they didn't shake me enough to dislodge the mysterious images I silently and carefully harbored as we descended the expanse of brick steps to my grandfather's maroon Chrysler sedan.

On our way back through Marysville and across the Fifth Street Bridge to Yuba City and home, a private and rich silence completely distracted me from the adult exchange in the front seat. Almost. Even though they didn't mumble, thunder, or click, they used a new word, very foreign to my world. *Monsignor*.

By the time we parked I knew without asking that *Monsignor* was the tall one's name.

* * *

"Ad Deum qui laetificat juventutem meam."[2]
—Psalm 42

Of course those eye-widening experiences and wonderful musings repeated themselves week after week, and they are now recognizable as my very important introduction to the world of mystery, spirit, and above all, the sacred.

---

[2] These words were the first altar boy response in the Latin Tridentine Mass: "To God who gives joy to my youth."

Most folks didn't think of preschool in those days. Your first formal schooling was—well, in the first grade. The adults in my life then were Pabst, Grandma Elsie, my teachers, and above all, Aunt Beth. It was World War II. Dad was in Lawrence, Kansas, studying electronics for the Navy and was eventually stationed in Pearl Harbor.

My mother, Doris, disappeared. Until I was in my thirties, most of what I would remember of her is what Aunt Beth told me when I was five. It is a stark, bare memory. Beth held me in her arms in Gramma's kitchen and said that my mother no longer wanted me or my dad. Noticing my welling tears, Beth offered, "It's okay. You can cry, honey." I did. And then, impossible as it seems, it was over. I would not revisit the event till twelve years later. (Actually, it revisited me one night while I was falling asleep in my senior year of high school.)

Now, in the little I remember of that moment in my fifth year, I'm sure it was then that two very important traits established themselves as part of my hard wiring for life: the determination to take control of things myself, and the hiding of very real anger when things got beyond my control. Even of that emotional catastrophe, I took control: what was left could leave. What angers can be left. To leave is to control. That is the only way I can explain the ease with which I have so dispassionately moved on through so many of my life's configurations.

Nonetheless, everyone who has heard me tell more than a few stories knows that I have continued to take Aunt Beth's "permission" seriously all my life.[3] No matter who or where listeners are gathered, no matter what the subject, the tears can well up and there's little I can do but ride out the wave. These days, the autumn of a very full life, I can risk admitting that through all those cool separations—even from my family—*I* was being controlled.

For a little kid, any trauma has to share his attention with the myriad experiences the world offers him as he continues to meet so much of it, and control it, for the first time. Life continues, and personalities develop, no matter what. Vast amounts of data need to be absorbed and processed as the brain marches insistently through the twenty or more years it needs to develop. There will be more tears, more injuries and more bad news all suffered in the heat of a distracting series of adventures called growing up.

*   *   *

Fortunately some of the more startling elements of my early worship were explained away. The moving black statues turned out to be the loving

---

[3] At my seventieth birthday party I was reminded of a very popular birthday party clown I hadn't thought of in years. Describing one of his routines, I caught myself saying, "I'm going to tear up telling this, but it's okay," and continued. Don't get me started on Hamlet remembering his birthday party clown. Alas, that's what launches the Yorick speech.

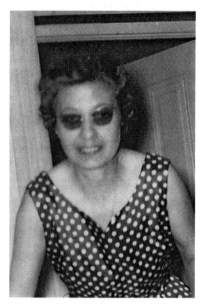

**Rose Elizabeth Weber,
"Aunt Beth"**

and disciplined Sisters of Notre Dame de Namur who would soon be my teachers. They were a congregation of religious women founded in France and missioned to this educational ministry in early post–Gold Rush northern California. Monsignor was our pastor, Right Reverend Thomas E. Horgan. He would continue thundering years later even when handing out our report cards in the classroom. The clicking, really just a sharp rolling of his *r*'s, was a characteristic of his very Irish brogue. He floated in function of his elegant posture and a very well-tailored and pleated flowing cassock under his Mass vestments.

Monsignor's shorter partners would soon include me and my best friends as we donned less elaborate cassocks and learned the Latin and rituals required of altar boys. The tree house was the pulpit, and the cake was the altar for the "unbloody sacrifice of Calvary" reenacted in the Mass. Of course the lady at the dressing table was at the choir loft's organ console following the ceremony in a rearview mirror as she faced the giant candle-like pipes of the organ itself. The gold on the altar was the priest's chalice, paten and the ciborium.

And so it was that the small boys of our tribe, Catholic or not, played in a backyard toolshed, converting scraps of burlap fabric, wooden slats, and pieces of cardboard into the paraphernalia of rehearsed and memorized ceremony. With an empty beer case as a tabernacle, and an endless pursuit of what could be imagined as holy, an almost forgotten storage area was constantly reinvented as sacral. This humble enclosure, dusty, hot, and still smelling of poultry and soil, harbored the precious processes of holy intention. Steeled with concentrated preparation, the rituals might lead outside into sweltering Sacramento Valley heat, as a mystical cross was carried in procession to be buried under the odd orange tree. Robed performers trudged through the gravel of the corporation yard to a weed-filled abandoned dog pen surrounding the tree. Such public pageantry was of course a call for an audience, at once desired and feared. (The occasional customer, truck driver, or member of the Weber family was always a possibility.) But the fear was mostly that we would forget some detail, never that some adult would find us ridiculous.

Years later, I was coaching young priests who wanted to improve their presiding style. I described their task as that of rendering their personal faith vis-

ible. I demanded they show me what they believed rather than just tell me—
the same challenge laid down in every theatrical rehearsal hall. They had an
advantage over actors, of course; they'd spent lifetimes believing the truth of
their faith. Actors had to come to the truth of their characters only indirectly.
But in both professions, the performers, whether liturgical presiders or stage
actors, really had to believe what they professed. Even as boys, our toolshed
ventures were always pervaded by intense belief. After a life of teaching and
performing, I am humbled by the profound importance of the universal human
capacity to *make* believe.

Across the street from Saint Joseph's Church, I would spend seven years at
Notre Dame Elementary School, where my sense of the spiritual and sacral
would be carefully honed between lessons in reading, arithmetic, history, and
geography.

As an unwitting baby I had been baptized at Saint Joseph's. As a second
grader, after my first go with the frightening sacrament then called penance, or
confession, I would join the grownups in their walk up front to receive communion. And five years later, in the seventh grade, I would be confirmed. In all
I received four sacraments at Saint Joseph's.

As a young Catholic schoolboy I would be well trained in the practices of my
faith, for which I held not only a deep respect and love, but an instinct as well.
Pabst, Aunt Beth, Saint Joseph's Church, and the Sisters of Notre Dame de
Namur would help me embrace a sacred world with plenty of room for mystery and spirit. The privileged perspective of hindsight suggests that long
before the first grade, I developed the two most important reflexive skills of my
life: reading, and paying attention to paying attention.

In a sense, focus has been my lifelong preoccupation. Contriving focus is the
consuming quest of every artist: the unrelenting pursuit of designs that compel a public to visit new experiences. And there in Saint Joseph's, I very early
found myself engaged by an architectural style that enjoyed over a millennium
of careful refinement with a congregation's focus as its chief objective. As
important, my human "floaters" in their own architecturally determined space
were actors, supported by a mostly memorized script, lighting, décor, costume,
and musicians, who also enjoyed an architecturally determined space. This was
truly my first experience of theater.

3.
Fields

"A pied piper whose magic tunes lead children of all ages into a tinsel and spun candy world of reckless beauty and mounting laughter, of whirling thrills, of rhythm, excitement and grace, daring, blaring and dance."

—C. B. DeMille, *The Greatest Show on Earth*, Paramount Pictures, 1952

It took me twenty-five years to figure out the recipe for the smell. There is nothing like it anywhere else on earth. The ingredients turned out to be fresh-cut grass or hay, popping corn (especially with commercial flavoring additives), horse manure, tiger or lion sweat, cotton candy being spun, and most importantly, the "essence of elephant." There was only one event that could muster such an exotic concoction wherever it happened to occur: the traditional American tented circus.

The recipe is demanding. The cotton candy must be "in process." Hot, spinning flavored sugar is the key; anything already swathed in plastic won't cut it. Popping corn with the additive is also an advantage. When it comes to concession products, every butcher who's worked in the "blues"[4] knows what many a concession manager has forgotten: "They smell it—you sell it."

Why tents? Tent fabric, even modern-day vinyl hauled into the air directly from flatbed trucks, absorbs the "essence of elephant" and preserves it far longer and more intensely than air-conditioned buildings can. And the chief ingredient of the recipe is that "essence." Too romantic to be credible? Just visit such a circus with an old-timer who's been away for awhile. All bets are on

---

[4] Those pesky salesmen with huge racks of cotton candy who invariably stand in front of you during a performance are called "butchers." In traditional circus seating chairs were painted red in the better sections, and the higher cheaper benches were painted blue.

that it will only take moments before the aged trouper takes a deep breath and sings out something like "Home!"

Why American? All the ingredients are usually on a tented European circus lot. Often the acts are of a superior quality. But just as often, the menagerie is tucked away in the backyard so that the elegant aromatic mixture is not available out front where the spectators arrive, and where the "floss and corn"[5] are working their magic. Historically, American circuses have carried exotic traveling menageries and proudly displayed their animals near the front of the lot before, during and after performances.

If we were lucky when I was a kid, either Marysville or Yuba City got that heady fragrance once a year. In Marysville during August of 1944, we got lucky. My mom and Aunt Beth took me to an evening performance of the Cole Brothers Circus. It must have been too much for me because I remember only a few mercilessly edited details of that very first visit to a circus.

My family survived the Depression and the fallout to follow, and they were hardworking, productive citizens with their emotional feet on the ground. But when it came to matters of the circus, they took pride in knowing something about this pied piper that lifted their dreams beyond Yuba City and small-town commerce.

There was family warmth in Gramma's appreciation of the circus. When she told of making sure that Dad and Beth got to the circus yearly as they were growing up, it was a report on educational responsibility. There was detail and care and respect when she recalled favorite memories of dancing elephants and clowns.

These were memories garnered from the much colder ones of stressful times when middle- and lower-class America sacrificed a little more to be sure their kids got to the circus. Everyone inside and outside the circus business knew that for even the major cities, the circus was among the chief entertainments of the year. In towns like Marysville and Yuba City, everything stopped on the day one of these canvas behemoths trouped into town and paraded up main street.[6] By the end of the second performance at a typical edge-of-town field, virtually every citizen had seen the big show and when it all stole away in the night it took with it half the hearts in town. One day it would steal away more than my little boy's heart.

Of the performance itself, I can only recall the classic clown firehouse gag: a "real" conflagration of a small prop house with a clown fire department rescuing clown residents, who always included a very amply bosomed-and-bottomed

---

[5] Circus people call cotton candy "floss." It was invented for the Saint Louis Exposition in 1904 and sold as "Fairy Floss."

[6] In a lyric of Irving Berlin's iconic "There's No Business Like Show Business," circus people recognize the detail of modernization that would eventually cost them their beloved street parades: "Everything the traffic will allow."

matron throwing her baby to the firemen and then threatening to jump from the roof. Stock clown repertoire, this routine is seldom produced anymore. It demands a sizable contingent of professionally trained clowns, a fire engine, controlled pyrotechnics, and lots of water. I have only seen it a few times in my life.

From my 1944 initiation, besides the clown gag and the pervasive rich smell, I recall that the sidewall of one of the tents was red and white striped, and that I tripped over a tent stake as we were leaving the grounds. I recovered from the tripping, but what I never ever got over was my mother's telling me that nothing of what I had just experienced would be there in the morning. After their one day with us, these exotic people were moving their wonderful array of tents, animals, music, light and smells south to Fresno.

That was powerful magic and my first encounter with what show people matter-of-factly but affectionately call "the road." By 1973 I would think nothing of driving 14,000 miles during an eight-month circus season comprising two cross-country treks. So I once bristled overhearing a brother Jesuit wearily mention that he'd been "on the road" for two whole months. (I knew he had been "in the air" flying around the country recruiting for a university.)

The day-in, day-out demands of taking a rig down the highway are replete with adventure and surprise. It is always an ordeal but essential to the life of every traditional circus and its performers. As a pervasive and very physical privilege, it is embraced in a relationship of fear and respect. To this day, when performers from different circuses take leave of each other, they do not say goodbye. They say, "See ya down the road." or just "Down the road."

After my first circus, the roads of gravel leading to my shed carried a different tribal energy, and it threatened Gramma's flowers and lawn. Surprisingly or not, at the beginning the emphasis was on stuff, not skills—stuff that had to be set up on the little patch of lawn outside the shed and surrounded by the flowerbeds. We developed a plywood frontispiece that was our marquee, located at the edge of the lawn. This blazoned the word *CIRCUS* in bright cheap enamel, and it prevented people who hadn't "entered" from seeing the performance. Admission was free at the start, but eventually we got brave enough to ask for a few cents from each spectator.[7]

Emphasis was on comedy, so props were easy to come by. Anyone who has ever wondered why the great clowns can amuse you with just a chair, a broom, and a newspaper or bucket has not spent time putting a circus together. Those items are always close to hand around a show. But in the ceremony of performance, the same humble objects are sacred props, their ordinariness notwithstanding. As

---

[7] Once we even had a concession. It was obvious that we had been planning a performance with an admission fee. Unannounced, Aunt Beth suddenly appeared with ice cream cones for everybody. (She probably correctly suspected our audience wouldn't get its money's worth.)

such, they must appear and disappear on cue. Here we labored as diligently as we did with the routines themselves. The actual running of the show was more important to us than the routines themselves.

Time, not necessarily *timing*, was critical. There were more than artistic reasons for this. Just as the Cole Brothers Circus had to be in Fresno the next day, our circus had to be all torn down and stashed in the shed before Aunt Beth called me for supper. There was pride in leaving the lawn as though nothing had happened. And if Gramma found a trampled tiger lily the next morning, there was no sign of our stuff. Here this afternoon, gone this evening. Magic. Naturally, Gramma knew very well what was up.

What she didn't know was that I was even then risking the bulk of my creative life on a clumsy, noisy ritual. Forty-five years later, even after decades with my priestly ministry that was the Royal Lichtenstein Circus, I was still in the grip of that risk, and I had determined to test it in the rough commercial firing oven of large American tented circuses.

*   *   *

Forty-five years and my own circus later, my version of Monsieur La Plume

My passport to the rough and real deal was Monsieur La Plume, the all-white clown I had helped a young college grad develop for the 1984/1985 season of our more modest show. Since I still had the costumes, I packed up a season's supply of clown white, eyebrow pencils, moist rouge, and cold cream to repeat the journey I had asked so many young performers before to make: I joined out with the circus.

And I arrived late. The live band had already moved on. So I found my way into the rhythms I loved with only the help of a drum machine and recorded, thinly orchestrated approximations. I knew I could find the real music where I always had: in the eyes and hearts of the audience. I paid attention. Soon I realized that much of the audience had also moved on. Very seldom did a town stop what it was doing and make time for us. There was too much else to do.

Even at the circus there was too much for some of the audience to do. I can remember the first time I saw a person talking on a cell phone in the seats. I was honestly shocked that anyone or anything could be so important. Silly me. Of course I was being paid for my own silliness, so I very seriously got the person's attention.

"Tell her I'm working right now, but I should be home by seven, and ask her if there's anything I should pick up for dinner."

It got a nice laugh in that section, even from the person with the phone. Now he had something important to tell the person on the other end and I had a ready mini-routine for the heavily cell-phoned audiences of the immediate future. Gradually I found a place for my kind of clown. I knew some circus history—enough to recognize in the photos of circus crowds from half a century before a true cross-section of American society. I also knew that in the past even my style of clown spoke. And if there was one thing I could do it was talk.

*   *   *

On most shows, the clowns are to greet the spectators before the show in a time zone known as "come-in." That became my most comfortable function. Here I was able to be as creative as I had ever been. Props and gags almost invented themselves: a huge cotton candy cone with a pair of sunglasses stuck in it, apparently left by an overeager sampler; an invisible trained dog introduced as an Airedale; a candied apple with a pair of dentures embedded. These, along with some of my old routines kept up my supply of material.

More than anything, the atmosphere of an old-fashioned traditional circus fed my imagination and my wit. One day, the revered owner-founder of Carson and Barnes Circus, Mr. D. R. Miller, overheard me pitch one of my stock lines to some arriving guests.

"Come right on in, everybody. There's plenty of room in the tent today; the fat lady quit in yesterday's town."

Months later, I didn't know he was sitting behind me on a very slow day. The crowd was not even trickling in the front door. I heard my name.

"Nick. Where's the fat lady today? We need her."

I loved teasing teenagers who were obviously preoccupied with how to look cool being approached by a clown at the circus. Only if they were both good looking would I use a line I adapted from Jackie Mason's Broadway show. I addressed the girl.

"Are you with him?"

If they got that far with me and giggled a little and looked at each other, even a little bit of a blush wouldn't stop me from finishing the gag, again to the girl but pointing at the guy. "You can do better than that."

It was a compliment to both of them of course, and only once was the guy threatened. I never got hit, though.

Seasonal temperatures provided opportunities. On really hot afternoons I would walk up to some little kids and very seriously ask a merchandising question. "Excuse me. Would you be interested in a nice hot steaming cup of chocolate?" If it was bitter cold, I would proclaim a sale in the snow-cone department.

Teasing little kids was especially fun. They really do want to believe adults can play as well as they can. I would catch them talking about our zebras, and interrupt. "*Shh*. Don't tell anyone but that's not a real zebra."

"Yes, it is."

"No it's no-ot. It's just a horse with Venetian blinds."

Or when I encountered them coming out of our chemically hopeful Porta Potties I'd ask them a once private question. "Did you flush?" They'd have to think about it. Then they'd realize that you don't flush those toilets.

*   *   *

Throughout the best of five years on the road with larger circuses, a vast array of evidence brought reality to most of the dreams from my youth and maturity. But it was a tempered reality that forced me to admit America's affair with the traditional circus was growing more and more tentative.

My onetime student and survivor of the Royal Lichtenstein Circus's first national tour John MacConaghy said it first. He was speaking only of our tiny show and especially our show's ability to present animals on college campuses. But what he said I now know applies to circuses in general.

"I think there was a window of opportunity which allowed us to get away with it. Now it wouldn't work."

That opportunity fed needs and capacities now filled otherwise. Painful as such an admission is, and impossible as it is to fix or even justify blame, history bears it out. I once gave a speech to the national convention of the Circus Fans Association of America during a San Francisco meeting. It was a clever and nostalgic talk titled "It's Not Over Till the Fat Lady Sings." Even then I knew very well that quite literally the fat lady had sung long ago. But I needed to believe it was all still possible.

Such belief pales with even a glimpse of what the American circus was and what it accomplished. Since such illustrative glimpses succeed best when they seize on the most striking of examples, I use images and impressions drawn from the history of the Ringling Brothers and Barnum and Bailey Combined Shows in its tours during the first half of the twentieth century.

This was a gigantic amalgam of the great individual circuses whose names it bore. Physically it was a vast tented city that included restaurants, a blacksmith shop, myriad dressing enclosures, horse stables, a menagerie of seven hundred animals, a museum of freaks and human oddities, and a gigantic tented arena seating ten thousand people for the feature performance. Transported on four separate customized trains, the uncanny outlay was also carried on the working backs of 1,500 personnel. During an eight-month season crossing the United States playing mostly one-day stands, the show typically gave a late morning parade on a city's main street and an afternoon and an evening performance before heading for the next day's town.

The performance itself included not only the age-old menu of acrobatics, unusual manipulative skills, comedy and trained animals. It had borrowed heavily from the opera and ballet theaters their penchants for settings, costumes, music and movement. To describe it as a grand panoply is understatement. It truly was "The Greatest Show on Earth."

Even in 1944, I inherited only the vestige, the faithful remnant of magic chemistry this once universally embraced cultural icon brewed. Nevertheless, even this reduction held identity and power. Years with my own circus capped by my years on much larger shows have helped me uncover an almost genetic makeup of this wonder that answered my own vital needs and perhaps those of a seemingly distant culture.

The most easily understated characteristic of such a long ago form of entertainment might be the easiest to overlook. The circus was real, not in the current sense that distinguishes live performance from recorded. It was present: it to me and I to it. I could actually touch so much of it; I could smell all of it. And unlike the theater, it did not imitate anything. It was itself.

For an afternoon and a night, this huge import to our town called all of us to a field for a mighty picnic with friends and relatives and strangers we had only seen a few times. School kids saw each other in an entirely different setting. Everybody was talking and holding their breath and clapping and laughing. At the picnic and for days after, there was a new subject of conversation.

And for all our socializing with each other through an afternoon or evening, we knew not one of the folks who gave us this good time. We didn't know our hosts. No one we knew owned the circus. It didn't belong to any of us. But because we knew it came from some other town and moved on to Fresno, we counted those populations as lucky as we were. And if we fantasized a little, we knew we had connected with at least both those towns, even physically.[8] Did the circus take something of us with them? Of course. Fantasies aside, this is the privilege of traveling entertainment. I am certain that our own tiny Royal Lichtenstein Circus brought something of Portland State University to Kansas State University and that both of those campuses affected what we brought to Atlanta's Emory University. Given the tracery bred into our memories and apperceptive nervous systems it could not be otherwise.

Like all picnics, the circus—even what's left of it today— is a relentless interface with nature. Tents themselves were called into being by nature and even when they enclose us we know that they are among our most frail interactions with the elements. Inside the tent, there is earth beneath our feet and everything earth brings with it: mud and dust and grass and weeds and bugs. At

---

[8] Very often, even in my adult years, I have caught myself wondering how many people in far-away cities had sat on the same bleacher stringer or chair that I was using or touched the rail that I was touching. It was not at all an antiseptic concern; it was very much a social one.

the same time, wonderfully, the circus is not like all picnics. Here, there is something like a land-bound Noah's ark of our neighbors, animals from near and far. If we're fortunate, nature is allowed to display just how fragile she can be. We might be addressed by an elegant and charming "armless wonder," a handsome giant, pixie midget, or comic three-legged man. Often these performers could be philosophical. Even dispassionately so. But whether they said the actual words or not, such special people would dynamically remind us that we are all odd and how tricky our own bout with birth was.[9]

The feature displays of this grand picnic compel us to enjoyment for its own sake, while all of us eat and talk and laugh. As in few other of life's moments we cannot escape the joy in image after image unloading this parade of exquisite human beings and animals. Our focus is galvanized by nothing less than the power of beauty's constant capacity for surprise.

Seeping through all of our apertures for awareness is the subtle integrating perception of unity. Friends and neighbors and strangers feel safe and empowered with the right to quietly exult or erupt in laughter. Performers trust far beyond the margins of our own experiences of dependency, and trust we will be appreciative. Animals trust in their rights to imitate us and their masters never hesitate to talk with them. And lest any of this stellar exhibition of human capacity seem a ceremony too distant from us, the clown reminds us that it's okay to be a clumsy acolyte at the ritual, that ordinariness is appropriate. It is then that we realize our own limitations themselves bring perspective to our applause. Just when we remember that every single one of us, spectator and spectacle, is embraced by gravity, the clown falls (or his pants do) and we know for certain that what we remember is right.

That's when it all works. For me, it has only worked that way a handful of times. Those were enough times to justify holding my hand out and my breath in for just one more time. Once more unique power and promise just might culminate within the delicate architectural membrane of a tent beyond which is tomorrow and a slightly different forever.

I cannot for a moment doubt that my approach to that power and promise began in a small-town backyard while I was playing with my friends. I can't remember there ever being fights. We played strenuously, but the only rule of our games was that anything could be anything as long as it was something.

---

[9] I consider myself indeed lucky to have met some of these marvelous human oddities, been reminded of my own dance with fate, and overwhelmed with the gratuity of nature in blessing such sideshow attractions with the happiness they share with me. I have frankly grown tired of the sanitized pity being extended to this entire population of circus performers now. Some performers were unhappy and mistreated. (So were wire-walkers and jugglers and animal trainers and clowns.) Many, if not most, found in the circus a happy and productive home that too many lived to see taken away from them by a population over ready with some vague "sensitivity" and institutions of "mercy."

That meant the only competition was to make the most believable "something." All of us were ready to be audience or performers, and that developed in us a ready, rustic benevolence. We needed to perform, and performers need audiences. In our clumsy aping of religious ritual, simple circus routines and the elemental effects of stage magic, there were in our small hands and skinny arms the very veins and ligaments of all theater. Years later, through some lucky artistic calculus, I would turn that anatomy inside out and use circus as a way to celebrate theater. Unsurprisingly, the venues would often be as impromptu as that privileged backyard.

Exactly two weeks before this towheaded little Yuba City kid saw his very first circus only to hear that it would disappear, there was an even greater vanishing act on the other side of the world. It was partly because guys like Dad had been attacked a few years earlier in Pearl Harbor. A scientific trick with Uranium cynically named "Little Boy," obliterated the city of Hiroshima and tragically altered world history forever.

It's worth recalling that all this happened before single-piece telephone handsets, ubiquitous orthodontics, blister packaging and commercial jetliners; before black and white cinema became just a special effect, and the word *gay* sadly lost its first meaning, and when all popular music was heard on *The Arthur Godfrey Show* or the *Lucky Strike Hit Parade*; before credit cards, fast food, American pizza, the freeway system, and canned drinks or six packs of anything; before Catholics would fight over how Mass was to be celebrated and northern U.S. whites cared about segregation; before shopping centers and malls, and the end of double features and newsreels; before NAFTA, NASCAR, NASA, and NATO; before professional sports became industries and the Ringling Brothers and Barnum and Bailey Circus rolled up its tents for the last time; before American English became the series of pauses between "whatever," "y'know," "What can I say?" and "like"; before animal rights activists worked so hard against any animal's right to work; before television and my first day of school.

*   *   *

Not long before I started school, Pabst brought our family through a major horizon shift. An hour's drive in mountains north northeast of Marysville, he had purchased two hundred acres on which he built ranch houses for the family and caretakers, and barns and corrals for livestock. It was property possessed of abundant water and wooded with oak, cedar, and pine.

Sulphur Springs Ranch was to be something of a hobby away from the concrete, gravel, and trucks of the beer distributorship in town. But with the success of livestock breeding, especially cattle, it too took on the feel and fever of a business. Gramma would live at the ranch for weeks at a time while Aunt Beth and Pabst maintained the operation in the flatlands. On the weekends they would escape to the ranch and all of us would be together. However, that development of an additional property began for me a life of shifting homes and a sometimes city/sometimes country domicile roulette that would last for over twelve years.

Along with the mere expanse of our land with readily explorable creeks, woods, and ponds, there were animals and barns. Besides the cattle, we also raised hogs, goats, horses, chickens, ducks, rabbits and pigeons. From the start, animals were prominent in our concerns. They weren't members of the family, but some of each species were closer to us than others, almost pets. Most of them were sold for slaughter or slaughtered for our own use. But we lived surrounded by animals and their concerns. Our relationships with them were at once exploitative and caring in a managed mutuality: we supported them so they could support us. Probably there could not have been a better preparation for the coming two decades of my adult life spent caring for a menagerie of domestic and exotic animals in a much more intense mutuality of support.

Our hired hands were the first people I ever heard speak a language other than my own outside of church. That too was apt preparation. I have spent a lifetime respecting the skill, determination and loyalty of Mexican immigrants, legal and illegal. And with very few exceptions, I have no idea or concern who of my friends possessed papers allowing them to sweat on the soil of El Norte to make our projects succeed.

It would be a few years before I was old enough to venture off the property and meet kids my own age, so compared to Yuba City, Sulphur Springs Ranch was active solitude in spades. I spent most days exploring, wondering, and working out with an aggressive imagination.

But it seemed like Gramma just plain worked. She knew farm and ranch life. Even in Yuba City, turning out the wash was an all-day operation of loading, wringing, rinsing (and bluing), re-wringing, carrying, and hanging out to dry on multiple clotheslines. The ranch wash was no exception. And in the beginning we didn't even have electricity. "Coal oil" powered hurricane lamps. The kitchen stove, including the oven, depended on wood that had to be carried in. Behind the woodshed was the toilet: an outhouse furnished with a sack of lime. For awhile even water was carried into the house from an outdoor well. Gradually, electricity, plumbing, and gas stoves found us. But there were still buckets of raw milk to pasteurize and skim for butter, killed chickens to dress, fruit and vegetables to can, and meals to prepare. We were farm folks; the main meal was at noon, "dinner." At night we ate supper. I was admonished more than once not to "call what I cook for dinner *lunch*."

Gramma looked like a farm girl. She always had a ruddy pink fresh-scrubbed face that I cannot imagine ever to have known cosmetics. Ready to laugh, she was also serious, probably the most serious of all her older siblings. I got the impression that as the baby of their family and then in her marriage with Pabst, she might have been protected all her life. And in those years she was raising me, I knew her as mostly separate from the on goings of the outside world around her. Making her family's home was her life.

The bombing of Hiroshima and then Nagasaki ended the war, of course. About a week later everyone on the ranch migrated across the road to the southern end of my Uncle Frank's property. There a middle-aged character known to everyone as "Ol' Hoffman" had his shack. He also had a shortwave radio. It seemed to be the only way anyone could figure out how to hear Hirohito's announcement that Japan was surrendering. I'm sure there was simultaneous translation of some caliber.

I didn't pay attention. I was distracted because Ol' Hoffman hadn't bothered to hide his ample collection of pinups. I was fascinated. It was my first cheesecake, and it was captivating for my very young eyes. Shortly after that, in our living room at the ranch, Gramma noticed my fascination with a photo in the *National Geographic* and proved herself the gentle and timely teacher she was. It was then that I was invited to appreciate the female breast in a disarmingly poetic light.

I only remember words like "in the springtime" and "the mother" and "takes out" and "to feed milk to her baby." Taken together, those simple words, especially, "in the springtime," elevated and illuminated my experience at Ol' Hoffman's. Problematically, I was born in late summer, Gramma was born in late fall, Dad in early fall, and Beth in winter. And we all somehow got nursed. But the poet in her wanted to make a point with "springtime"; I got that point, gently.

Of all the memories from those early days on the ranch, probably the most powerful and dramatic was the night Dad came home from the war. Ol' Hoffman also had a phone and that's probably how Gramma found out Dad was in Yuba City and headed up to us. I do remember that when she heard the news, she cried aloud. Until then, I didn't know grownups did that. She didn't want me to know that either and hurried to another part of the house where her muffled sobs weren't muffled any longer. I watched the headlights come up the long driveway from Willow Glen Road. Then it was my turn to cry.

But when he got there Nick J. Weber III, Gramma's "Nickie," turned his homecoming into a party. He had been stationed with the Navy's submarine division in Honolulu, so the first thing he did was present his amply figured mom with a grass skirt. I thought that was the funniest thing of the night. Gramma was a Lane Bryant woman and almost always corseted. Just imagining her in a grass skirt, never mind the hula, was too much. Then he sat me in the middle of the living room floor and tipped his duffle bag upside down in front of me. Out cascaded a huge jingling assortment of his collected odd change. It was more money than I'd ever seen. Pieces of coral and seashells of all sizes and shapes and textures tumbled out among the coins.

Laughter and good partying and a kid's new presents can be distractions. To this day, I cannot remember what my sailor dad looked like that night. The years, especially mine, would tell that tale by the time I was his age when he was discharged. And we still looked alike holding each other's hands on his deathbed sixty-three years later.

4.

Steps

Dad. Nick J. Weber III

The ranch for me was a summer and weekend venue, an exotic promise of continuing adventure away from all the trouble my imagination engaged in town. While school was in session Dad and I lived in Yuba City with Pabst and Gramma and Beth at 618 Shasta Street. As he had from the time he was in high school, Dad worked for his dad, and I began what would become thirty-five years of going to classes.

In September of 1945, accompanied by a neighbor boy who was already in the seventh grade, I took the city bus from Bridge Street across the Feather River to Notre Dame School in Marysville, where Pabst, Dad and Aunt Beth had gone.

What a first day that was. Three of us boys immediately struck up a relationship that continued so steadfastly we gained a second-grade moniker as the "Three Musketeers." John would leave the trio when his family moved during our fourth year. But Douglas and I remained best friends all the way through high school.

To others, our relationship must have seemed improbable. He took care with every move he made. He was the best groomed kid in our class with a head of straight black hair perfectly parted on the left side and the front combed up a bit and back in the moderate pompadour style of the day. Delicately featured, there were very few times when any of us saw his face break into a free and wide laugh. Smiles and chuckles yes. He had a sense of humor, but his reaction to a joke or a prank was controlled. And when he spoke, the syllables were exact, his voice modulated well in advance of his years.

"Maybe we could try—" and he would humbly express an insight none of us saw coming. I cannot recall ever hearing him raise his voice. He could be intense, but his tone, like everything about him was careful. He was the first one to be on top of any year's yo-yo season. Other guys would brag "Hey, I can do 'Rock the Cradle.'" Doug would quietly ask if I'd ever seen "Rock the Cradle" and then execute the move perfectly. Not for a crowd. Just for me.

Doug rode a bike before I was ever allowed to think of such a skill. For sports, he was built to be a shortstop and enjoyed it; I would rather work up a sweat putting on a show. Typically he would practice catching, throwing and batting while I would balance the bat on my chin. He was good at team projects and I wasn't. I was splash and he was focus. If I was a magnifying glass, he was a microscope. But we got along famously. We harbored each other's secrets and there were very few we didn't share.

I made other friends of a very different caliber. We became intensely intimate even though they were often uncomfortably clingy and demanding. I doubt it is possible to recall when or from whom I first heard their names but from the start they had me dancing and I let them take my hand in far more than a young boy's awkward handshake. I don't think there can be a more effective gesture than manually tracing the sign of the cross on the upper body to the rhythm of the most sacred names in the Christian story. Long before liturgical renewal, it was this simple and sacred dance that identified folks like me.

Of course sometime earlier I was learning about God, and more humanly, about Jesus. But "Father," "Son," and "Holy Ghost," the rhythmic words to my sacred dance immediately began a conversation with these important friends. I was taught that such chats could negotiate and settle very important, very personal accounts. Most wonderful of all, these friends were empowering and they were mine and I could access them as though they couldn't help responding. Even in the context of all their might and magnificence, they were available. I was learning their rules and their rights over me, but I could talk back just by tracing our danced sign and starting in. Even when I knew we disagreed and closed the session and went my way, they were there, waiting. They were my guys. We were close. I am confident this was the ground floor of whatever spirituality I achieved in life.

But it was a ground floor served by two different elevators and I spent most of my life indiscriminately—and unwittingly, using both of them.

First of all everything valuable was "up." I had already succumbed to what I would one day recognize as set design, blocking, orchestration, oral interpretation and role playing and my very emotional goals had fixed on my friends "up there" on the ceiling of Saint Joseph's. I didn't know their names, but I knew they were good and that if I trafficked in whatever was going on with Monsignor and his helpers, I could be that good. I was drawn. I felt *invited* by such folks who would even run the elevator car for me.

Second, I was becoming aware of a self-help plan, meticulously spelling out what I could do to just about ensure my success in arriving "up there" with my friends. There was even bookkeeping so I could test my early schoolboy math: numbers of days and years attached to various prayers. There were bargain days when bonuses multiplied. There were new names, more potential friends who had made it and would help me get there. And from my teachers there were downright awards for learning the names and the prayers. Stepping onto this elevator, I felt completely in charge, and pushed the buttons myself.

Dangerously simple? Undoubtedly. Yet this alternate embracing of an invitation and a drive to save myself became the characteristic movement of my religious life. I suspect I have not been alone in this. In an extreme form, the self-help elevator might have been labeled "Works" as far back as Martin Luther's day.

Long before I did, Doug began piano lessons independently of school and achieved a skill that I admired and envied. Eventually I persuaded Aunt Beth and Gramma to let me enroll for lessons with one of the Sisters. But it was too late and not meant to happen. Sister led me through the Schaum introductory books but not very effectively. My practice time was limited because the piano disturbed both Aunt Beth and Gramma. And then it was time to transfer to high school and lessons were never again mentioned. I still remember Doug's accomplishments at the keyboard. I will always be jealous.

By the time we began training as altar boys, the simplistic, single-dimensioned relationship we had with God, that private, dedicated connection, had called up a horizontal dimension. It was an easy development. We had friends with whom we talked about our partner/bosses upstairs. We were all in this. Care for me had to involve care for Doug, and John and Dad and... To make it really easy, there were walking and talking professionals who ran nonstop demonstrations of that care, how it worked, how it applied, how it was powerful and attractive and good. The power itself seemed attractive and good. Because of the Sisters, you couldn't miss that for long. But there were priests as well. And altar boys got to be close-up as the priests did their most important caring. Pervading this entire chapter of a Catholic boy's development in the late Forties was the exalted sense of honor and privilege worn by every priest's commitment to care and goodness and the brokering of a mighty power.

In the fifth grade Doug and I confided to each other that we thought we'd like to be priests. We confided everything in each other and everyone knew it. Nor was it a secret how different we were from each other. What was a secret was the shared desire we had for priesthood. In those days quite a few guys thought about committing to priesthood. But you didn't go around talking about it. Even in high school it had nothing to do with today's commonplace concern that you were throwing away your chance at a sex life. Rather, because priests were so respected, it might have seemed presumptuous. In today's parlance that just wouldn't have been "cool."

While school took us from the passions of our freewheeling imaginative play and invention, it truly brought us other loves. Not only did the Sisters shape our rawness with their methodical and disciplined elementary instruction, they captivated our meager and protean capacity for attention. All we could see of them were their faces and hands; their habits were like stencils overlaying everything physical about them except those features most expressive of their personalities.[10] Because of such focus and because these ladies had their pedagogical acts down, the pursuit of reading, writing, and arithmetic was like going to a show long before *Sesame Street*. We loved it.

But there was more than pedagogy and the accident of religious garb. Driving these deft and animated lessons was the bright-eyed dedication of the women themselves. And their eyes *were* bright. What they were doing with and for us was their reason for living. In our early grades they were younger, scarcely out of college, and they were tirelessly concerned with us. They had almost as much energy as we did and all of it seemed bent to the needs of our individual little worlds. So we yielded. We joined them in their efforts to nudge our focal points toward larger contexts. We helped them coax the *I* of each of us toward a capacity for *we*, and subtly merge *our* worlds with *the* world.

And why did we yield? Why did we become complicit in this plot to destroy our perfectly legitimate childhood selfishness? Because underneath the prods, behind the endless rote drills and questions and answers, and even in spite of the stern corrections we brought on ourselves, we sensed a magnetism. In the undaunted efforts of these young women, in their pervasive drive and patient enthusiasm while caring for us, we could detect a quiet compelling power. Till then only experienced at home, taken for granted and accepted as a birthright, this power never really caught much of our attention. But there in the push

---

[10] Who can be sure of the origin of one's idea? Good hunches are more fun. One of my axioms for beginning actors has long been that an actor's most important prop is her face. Her second most important props are her hands. We must easily see them and nothing can be allowed to distract us from seeing them.

and shove of over two hundred kids in eight grades in eight rooms, the Sisters used this power to redeem an otherwise knockabout thrust on the course toward maturity. They loved us.

Which reminds me. Very early in my grade school years, Dad and I fell in love—with the same girl.

I didn't know he was in love, but I enjoyed nothing more than to visit Gracie Bristow's family home, where she would play the accordion for all of us and draw all the Disney characters for me. She was talented and sweet and young and beautiful and I couldn't be around her enough. And then one day, as he was checking my hair and shirt before school, Dad popped the question. To me.

"How would you like to have Gracie for a mom?" It was a slam dunk and he knew it.

Gracie, who became "Mom"

Dad and Grace Minerva Bristow were married in an out-of-town Church of the Nazarene on Valentine's Day and we moved into Alta Park, an apartment complex for veterans. I soon recognized that Gracie worshipped Dad, and she and I continued to fall in love. I don't think we ever stopped amazing each other. One day, after telling me that I was a big reason she married Dad, she gently asked me if I would consider not using her name and calling her "Mom." Another slam dunk.

One morning after breakfast, I took some trash out to the can on our apartment's back porch. The outside air was charged with sounds I had never heard. Jamming the street next to our complex were horses, tractors, and wagons all trying to get onto the field opposite us. A cursory read of the wagon sides told all: the Clyde Beatty Circus was pulling in to be our very own neighbors for a day and the best part of a night. This simply could not be a school day.

Oh yes it could be. And Mom was not feeling as proud of our new neighbors as I was. "They'll all be coming over here for water and bathrooms."

I assured her with all my eight years of wisdom that they had those needs covered. There were tearfully exacted solemn promises that we would attend the show that night. School attendance was a must, though. On the way to the city bus stop, Dad, as curious as I was, stopped at the railroad siding off Bridge Street so we could watch part of the show unload.

I have had the privilege of delivering some wonderful setups and laugh lines over the years. Few held the satisfaction of that morning's explanation to Sister about why several of us were tardy for school.

"And why are you people late?"

"Elephants, Sister."

Dad had gotten me to the bus on time, but elephants are not driven to the show grounds from their railroad cars. They walk. And that day they walked right down Plumas Street in the middle of our town and there was no way the bus could get around them. Of course Sister had no idea the circus was unloading in Yuba City. This was Marysville. So I explained everything to her, except how hard it was to be in school that day.

And that night the show. Oddly I remember more about the sideshow, and what used to be called the "concert" or "after show," than about the main performance. In those less sophisticated days, when the exhibitions of anatomical abnormalities were still accepted as "wonders," sideshows were very popular. They were important staples of a visit to a performance. The "concert" was a wild west enactment of a stagecoach robbery and "battles" between the United States Cavalry and generic "Indians." This all took place where the acts had been in the rings, and you bought a special ticket to remain in the seats for it.

Before the advent of television and a universal indirect knowledge about every possible type of physical entertainment and wild animal behavior, the totality of a circus was exotic. In the middle of a forsaken field any tented soupcon of acrobatic prowess, clever and dangerous animal routines, ribald comedy and rip-roaring band music might logically enough include Indians, sword swallowers, and midgets. Why not? The whole damn thing was impossible—and barely imaginable.

That field across the street from our Alta Park apartment? Years later it became the site of our hospital. It would be where Gramma died on All Saints Day 1975, while I was performing on a stretch of lawn in Texas.

Among the richest memories from my childhood is one that is utterly normal, and, except for being well-nigh miraculous, not at all sensational: the birth of my sister, Susan Mary. She was just a wrinkled baby when she graced my ninth year, but she was mine.[11] For a long while, she would give me my new mom in a new light. Through someone else I would get to revisit a mother's early love. Happy times. I would be in high school before I realized the deep place Gracie was filling in my life. Whatever scenario was planned and executed by the Weber family at my biological mother's disappearance, the excision included some radical emotional surgery—certainly a displacement. For a few years and maybe longer, I was the victim of a total relational eclipse. Now I seemed to be part of a warmer and fuller rhythm.

Dad continued to drive a beer delivery truck and I took the bus back and forth to school. Afternoons there were my hours in the "studio temple" at 618 Shasta Street until Dad got off work. And then there was Susie.

---

[11] *Graced* is used here wittingly as the sacred pun it must be for me.

There was also a puppet theater in my room, and the gang of Alta Park veterans' children I had lassoed into playing circus. Many was the Saturday morning an unsuspecting tenant would look out a front window to see a collection of kids' wagons, cardboard boxes, leashed or caged stray dogs, and pieces of assorted fabric boy-handled into a front lawn performance space only slightly less chaotic than it was primitive.

My sister Susan and I at Sulphur Springs Ranch

Then there was a serious change. Dad and Mom had decided to move with my little sister to the ranch.[12] They were to live in one of the remodeled caretaker's houses. Dad was going to work in the lumber industry and I was to stay in Yuba City with Pabst and Beth so I could continue school at Notre Dame. Weekends and summers we would all be together. Everything around me was increasingly temporary, portable, fluid. That dimension of my personal reality would shape my next sixty years.

Mom's family brought another dimension into my childhood, and it was a gift. There was a profound difference between the Weber household on Shasta Street, where I spent most of my time, and the Bristow household on Franklin Road, west of town. Perhaps the business that sustained us Webers was too close to where we lived. The Bristows were key players in a large equipment company, Marysville Tractor and Equipment Company, way over in Marysville. Whatever may have been the initial religious orientation of various members of the Bristow family, there certainly didn't appear to be conscious and cohesive religious practice of any kind. Of course most of the Weber Shasta Street household was quite consciously and

---

[12] I was already a priest before Dad confided that he had told his father to stick his money where the "sun don't shine." I never knew what the disagreement was over, but it resulted in Dad's leaving the beer distributing job. Our family would be housed on Pabst's ranch.

devotedly Roman Catholic. Even Gramma, who was not raised as a Catholic, supported Pabst and Beth in their observances and revered the practices and devotions of their lives. Dad had pretty much abandoned any practice.

For a little kid, a major discernible difference between the two families hinged on the matter of joyfulness. There was always a gaiety, an atmosphere of fun, teasing, celebration, and some measure of feast on Franklin Road. Shasta Street was a solid and principled environment for a growing kid. But it was solemn most of the time. In spite of the circus in the backyard, things and people were taken seriously. It was a quiet, almost monastic home, and after Pabst died it would become even more so. Gramma would then become Catholic, and with that, her already quiet existence became more like that of a nun. Daily, seated in the same chair at the kitchen table, she dedicated at least an hour to silently recited prayers. I knew when and whether to interrupt her. If she looked up, it was okay.

Poor Dad. He was at heart a Bristow from the time he met Mom. He was a kind of loose cannon that teased Granny Bristow as "Myrt," and razzed Mom's younger sister, Auntie Vern. And there were Mom's dad, Jesse, and Uncle Art Bristow and their friend Charlie Thompson, who would one day marry Auntie Vern. In those guys, Dad had hunting and fishing pals, guys with whom he could talk sports, trucks, and heavy equipment. Bless his heart, my father tried to get me interested in fishing and hunting, but it didn't take. Forget about trucks and machinery.

Once Dad moved up to the ranch, Uncle Art, Mom's older brother, called us the "Okies," thinking of himself as a "flatlander." Dad was "Big Okie" and I was "Little Okie." Art's poised and polite wife, Aunt Nancy, often seemed a tad mortified because there was some real competition between these two guys at several levels. But Dad put up with it all, knowing he could dish it right back to Art. Big Okie would eventually work for the family business, Marysville Tractor and Equipment Company.

Jesse, the Bristow patriarch, was a spirited character who could surprise us all with a detail from history or a *sub rosa* comment about stuff that embarrassed good little Catholic boys. In fact, on Franklin Road, we all played and ate, and the grownups drank, and there was laughter all the time—even before I had younger cousins and a brother and sister of my own to play with. The Bristow place was noisy over things that needed to be enjoyed. The Weber household tended to be quiet with concern for things that just needed to be done.

And Mom? She was a Bristow who loved the Weber Family and adored Dad. She was right smack in the middle, and got away with it. She was always Grace.

*   *   *

My romance with the Sisters of Notre Dame de Namur continued. It was the attention given to individuality that underwrote this love as authentic. In the second grade it was Sister Benedict Julie who spotted the "Three Muske-teers," and in the third grade it was Sister Anthony who suggested that the three of us organize the "Clean-up Club." This was more than a warm recog-nition of our friendship and leadership potential; it was a humble and effective attempt to get the student body to keep a cleaner schoolyard. Typically it would be Doug who, in a moment of school-kid crisis, calmly recommended "We should have a meeting." Then either I or another classmate would announce and run the meeting. When our eighth grade needed funds for our class picnic, it would be Sister Marie Robert who encouraged Doug and me to stage a sideshow attraction as a fundraiser open to the entire school.

The campus for Notre Dame Elementary School was across the street from Saint Joseph's Church, but there was an atmosphere that engulfed both insti-tutions as if they were one. Besides weekend worship with our families, the stu-dent body attended morning Mass every Wednesday. Appropriate behavior (not to say *decorum*) in approaching the church, entering, participating in the ceremony, and returning to school was meticulously burnished week after week.

In a graduate theology course in 1968 I first paid attention to the handy anthropological triad for organizing the elements of any religion: cult, code, and creed.[13] What I had learned by going to church with Pabst or the Sisters would fall into the category of cult: the rituals a group practices about its beliefs. Creed covered the canon of beliefs summarized simply in the Apostles' Creed and more technically in the Nicene Creed recited at Mass. And a group's ethics, its way of behaving derived from its creed, was its moral code. So the task of our Catholic schoolteachers was to develop us as believers who espoused a morality consistent with our beliefs and comfortable enough with our ritual to celebrate our identity as Catholics. For Catholics in the Forties and Fifties, the chief textbook for this task was *The Baltimore Catechism*.

Classroom transitions from a lesson in arithmetic into a unit on religion were seamless and matter of fact. There was nevertheless an atmosphere around religious instruction identifying it as special. This was sacred ground and the students were sacred because the lessons made us initiates into some-thing not everyone possessed. Though this was an atmosphere achieved in the same classrooms used for the other instruction, the material covered was just as meticulous, organized, and seemingly applicable to life as arithmetic, read-ing, and writing.

---

[13] Some add a fourth "c": variously community or *constitution*, both arguably unnecessary as no more than *corollaries*.

It was the structure of *The Baltimore Catechism* that made such a detailed and organized application seem possible.[14] That structure and its dramatic power was the dialogue, used by the Greeks five centuries before Christianity. Set up in numbered questions and answers, the information was packaged and delivered through the illusion of a conversation.

1. Who made us?
   God made us.
2. Who is God?
   God is the Supreme Being who made all things and keeps them in being.

This rhythm marched the young mind through several graduated volumes beginning with the doctrines of the Apostles' Creed, then the Church's dogmas regarding the sacraments, and finally the teachings on Catholic morality. Not only was the coverage extensive, it was precise. More importantly, it was compelling. Questions don't only suppose the possibility of answers; they demand them. And taken in series, the rhythm was relentless: there were 421 questions and answers in the comprehensive book.

Exhaustive and demanding as such a syllabus was, it had the advantages of exactness and apparent finality. It was all there, detailed. And in such nearly mechanical detail, my continued use of the self-help elevator to spiritual success seemed warranted. You knew what you had to know, and because of the questions, you knew what would be demanded of you. The most expansive questions and issues ever to preoccupy centuries of theological discussion were distilled, sliced and diced into a set of questions and answers. From God's will to my will, I knew the possibilities and consequences of any given move by either of us. Bottom line: I could do this. I could push the right buttons myself. I could get myself there.

It was those consequences that most seized the imagination right from page three's "Act of Contrition." As a little boy, I was sure I was sorry for my sins because I dreaded "the loss of Heaven and the pains of Hell." And no matter how loudly I pronounced the archaic King James echo in "because they offend *thee* my God," it was those "pains of Hell" that lurked. And there was no question that the pains stipulated were bodily because the answer to Question 418 referenced bodies still being around at the Last Judgment when we all are supposed to bodily start the long run of eternity.

---

[14] *The Baltimore Catechism* was commissioned by the Maryland Episcopal authority in the 1850's to be an American adaptation and expansion of a sixteenth-century manual, the *Small Catechism* of Cardinal Robert Bellarmine. This brilliant Jesuit who lent his name to my high school alma mater in San Jose was a recognized intellectual powerhouse in the Church. With the sadness so frequently met in history's ironies, one discovers he became a voice for the Church's position against the Copernican convictions of Galileo Galilei. (Cf. Bellarmine's letter to Galilei of May 26, 1616.)

Avoidance of such painful consequences by steering clear of mortal sin was to be taken seriously. Let there be no doubt in the current safe haven of doctrinal development that might have occurred even without Vatican II, the possibilities of mortal sin were at hand for six- and seven-year-olds. Try the answers to some of the "code" questions about deliberately eating meat on Friday or missing communion during the Easter Season. There was no comfort in waiting around till puberty set in and Sister's use of the words "impure" and willingly" began to take on a shadowy new magic.

Spiritual pain and suffering were available as well. There were reports of flames, however, even in the kiln called purgatory. So we were keen on the spiritual stock exchange known as indulgences.[15] They were all ranked by the number of "days" one could work off. Some were long ordeals, like the series of First Fridays. But others were easy, like short little prayers called ejaculations.[16]

By the time we came along, *The Baltimore Catechism* included limited illustrations. None of these drawings is as memorable as the quart milk bottle that stood for the human soul. A perfect soul, completely free of sin, even venial sin, was a bottle filled with white milk.[17] A soul compromised by a venial sin was depicted as filling with blackness, the level determined by the degree of the sin. One mortal sin rendered the milk bottle brim-full of blackness. Everything seemed detailed and practical, completely organized.

The first *Baltimore Catechism* was published before our school was founded, and by 1945 it had become solid rote for all American Catholics. It was a systems manual for understanding a creed and a code and a cultic panoply of sacraments and sacramentals physical enough to make even God seem tangible.

As we got older, school discipline became more definite and the only element of fear I have ever recalled was a probably unfounded anxiety over the prospect of having a certain Sister for fifth grade teacher. No problem. She was transferred and we got a brand new teacher, Sister Theodora, whom we all loved. During Lent, this fifty-something lady dramatically etched our memory of her through a detailed improvised recounting of Jesus' last days. So vivid was this daily performance, timed to climax before we were released for Easter vacation, that there was a universal student groan every time the bell rang for lunch and she had to stop. I have never experienced anything like such thorough and willing captivation in a classroom.

---

[15] Not solely spiritual. By Martin Luther's time, a lot of money was changing hands on the sale of indulgences. Happily, maybe, some of that money helped achieve the artistic wonders of Saint Peter's Basilica and fed Michelangelo Buonarotti's bank account.

[16] In high school my pals and I smirked at how convenient it was that an *ejaculation* could be an indulgence.

[17] Printed on white paper it *appeared* filled. It could have been empty.

Then Pabst began his own last days. He was diagnosed with terminal cancer, and the house changed. I sensed that he was in extreme pain, and I heard the word *morphine* for the first time. I almost never saw Pabst anymore since he and the medical attention he was given were deliberately concealed from me. I was even shielded from his funeral.

He was just gone. I don't remember having anyone help me understand how I should feel about the passing of this patriarch in our family who I had learned to respect, fear, and I suppose, love. But his death deeply affected me because it was then decided that I would spend the next year, my sixth grade, going to school five miles north of the ranch in Brownsville, California. I would be away from Doug and my friends of five and more years, but I would be with Mom and Dad and Susie again. It didn't take me long to figure out that my absence would accommodate the grief and mourning period at 618 Shasta Street, and allow Beth and Gramma to settle the estate. The beer distributorship had ended. The house's convent atmosphere was only penetrated by the incessant chattering glow of a new appliance, the television set.

Mom and Dad and Susie lived in one of the ranch's original caretaker houses close to the main road. By this time they had enlarged it with a spacious master bedroom and an extended living room. Susie had her own room and I had a whole cabin all to myself just to the rear of their house, only a few steps away. Besides, I was closer to the outhouse than the rest of my family. Till I was in seminary college, our family enjoyed indoor plumbing outdoors. Hard to imagine, but there it was: plumbing, porcelain and water, all installed in an outhouse. It was of course easy to ventilate with fresh air. Except once. Dad had shot a skunk under the outhouse floorboards. (Yep. Fired a pistol right through the planks.) The skunk contributed an acrid "bouquet" to its own demise. It was too much for Dad. He came in the house and ordered me to go out and remove the unconventional "Airwick" he had inadvertently installed.

My cabin had two rooms. I slept in the rear one and kept my projects up front: chemistry experiments, books on circuses, and, in jars, live snakes my friends and I had caught. It was perfect.

Once in awhile my new "ranch studio" got me into trouble. One sunny morning, Mom was up the hill behind our house hanging out washing on lines between two oak trees. My toddler sister was making her way up the hill and caught Mom's attention with "Lookie what I found in Nickie's cabin." She held up a squirming water snake. Mom dropped a wet towel and, when she caught her breath, ordered me to get rid of my specimen. To this day I don't know how Sue picked up that snake correctly: right behind the head. Water snakes aren't venomous, but they can have a hefty bite. My sister was a girl very comfortable with the countryside and to this day remains happiest when she has animals around her.

School was five miles north and east in Brownsville proper. Sharon Valley Elementary comprised six grades in two schoolrooms, three grades in each.

We sixth graders were the kings and queens and there were only two rows of us. I sat behind a girl who lived behind the Come Back Inn, a tavern not far from the ranch. More importantly, I sat across from a girl who lived even closer to us, Doreen. She was the best speller in the school (put me down with that damned second *i* in *ski-ing.*) and took me through the first hoops of a trick called "puppy love." Her kid brother, Chuck, was a year younger than I, and the three of us became very close friends. They were more experienced than the Catholic boy from Yuba City.

Besides a horse, the cattle, some ducks, and a few chickens, we still had about a dozen goats on the ranch. They became my responsibility, and I learned quickly that goats are very intuitive escape artists. Many were the days Mom greeted me as I got off the school bus with the tired news: "The goats are out." I did like the goats, except for Billy; he considered me competition and he had a vicious looking set of horns.

About ten miles northeast of Brownsville was another little town, Challenge. And one summer day Challenge got lucky: a circus came to town. What were the odds? This place was tiny and all mountain red dirt. But there they were, and they had chimps and a sideshow where I saw my first fire-eater. Well, sort of. When it became obvious where he was going to put those flames, I hid behind Mom. I can't remember what the name of the show was, but they didn't display horses because that truck had accidentally opened en route and the animals escaped. Honest. That's what the ringmaster said.

Our teacher was Mr. Ferris who taught me the importance of viewing a piece of art from a distance to adequately assess its perspective. He played the violin and once gave us a mini-concert in class. The only other music I remember from those days was the piano playing by "Lightnin' Fingered Mammy" in a minstrel show that played our Grange Hall. Best of all in that show was Mr. Bones telling Mr. Interlocutor that he had a nice roast of beef in his sack. When he held up a slice of lunchmeat and Mr. Interlocutor demanded an explanation, the saddened Mr. Bones said that the piano player must have sat on it. Terrible stuff, but we kids loved it.

Somehow biological timing and less organized factors had left the real discovery of sex till this open and well-aired year in the hill country. If Doug and I and our pals had wondered and joked about what we were beginning to feel, we hadn't personalized it very much. Such movements were puzzling, and boy-type references to them were two dimensional. Sadly they were also connected to words like *impure, immodest, indecent,* and the rest of the negative cadenza the *Baltimore Catechism* had developed for Catholic teachers and students alike. Such a context seemed destined to yield a tortuous reading and rendering of the facts of my life: maybe birds and bees should do nothing more romantic than molt and sting.

And Dad? The summer after my fifth grade, he blew it. I know he had lots of company in the group of dads that never got around to discussing sex with their sons. But my Dad? He could have had it easy. So easy.

It was dinnertime (okay, suppertime) and Mom sent me to the barn to get Dad. When I got down there I noticed he was standing at the edge of the corral. Our bull and a cow were in the center. I just stood to the side. I don't really know how I sensed that something special was happening. Suddenly there was the mount, precarious and so brief, and then the dismount revealing the startling change in the size of the bull's penis. I waited a moment or two, probably catching my breath, before I said, "Dad, dinner's—"

"*Je*-sus Christ. What are you doing here?" A bull's bellow of his own.

"Mom says supper's ready."

"Okay"—his final word till halfway through supper. He opened a gate so the animals could get to pasture, and we walked in heavy silence all the way up to the house. Needless to say when he regained his speech we weren't talking about the mechanics of bovine reproduction. And he lost the teachable moment of teachable moments. I know I was ready to be taught.

But those countryside days weren't completely lost to my sexual awareness. Pabst owned a chunk of property across the road that included a wide and rushing trout stream. The scenery along the edges of "Dry Creek" was truly calendar photo quality. Dad had tried to teach me to trout fish there. But one particular day my teacher was Chuck, Doreen's brother. The entire scene became our classroom as we stood at the edge of the noisy stream. He was about ten feet downstream from me. There in bright shafts of afternoon sunlight, while birds dipped for drinks and bees did honey in the hollow of an old oak, Chuck forthrightly guided me in the simple and ancient art of male masturbation. Anyone trout-fishing that day could have seen us; certainly all of animate nature did— and probably chuckled at this wide-eyed boyhood exploration of a commodity usually hidden.

* * *

In the fall of 1951 I moved back into Yuba City and resumed attendance at Notre Dame with my old friends, and the Sisters. Doug and I picked up on a friendship we never could have left off. I was debriefed about my adventure in mountain schooling, and our circle of friends fed itself with the gamut of mutual interests, hobbies, and new discoveries. It surprises me now that there was no boyish prurient prying about each other's sexual experiences, even though girls were on our minds and our phones.

With all the warnings that come with pubescence, it seems that there are no messages, even coded ones, preparing a guy for puppy love. It just happens, like so much of the real thing does in later life. And sure enough, that strain of attraction fired up again when I got back into Notre Dame. Doreen was history and someone took her place. Doug and I both had girlfriends in the seventh grade; everyone knew it, in school and at home. There was a difference for Doug, though: he never had any competition. I always had to compete.

Catholicism as we were taught it was exceedingly detailed in the mechanics of practice. Underneath that more tangible fabric of my adolescence, the ongoing fibers of my connections with the Bosses upstairs continued. They probably grew awkward. There was more attention prescribed for my loving on the ground floor. After all, a meager social life was developing.

We spent seventh grade doubled up with the eighth graders in a room presided over by a Sister who seemed nervous, too excitable, and prone to favoring certain students. She could be funny, was insightful, and knew her subject material, but we feared her outbursts. Somehow, under her guidance we made it to and through the sacrament of Confirmation, but it was perhaps too automatic and expected an event for seventh graders. I think First Communion suffered similarly from its seeming routine inclusion in the second grade syllabus. Anyway, whatever graces the Holy Spirit delivered through the sacrament of Confirmation, we certainly didn't seem relieved in our pursuit of junior high romances.

The summer of 1952 I was home on the ranch with Dad, Mom, and Susie, and there was a crisis as the months wore on. Cecil B. DeMille's epic film *The Greatest Show on Earth* was coming for a road show engagement at the State Theater in Marysville. Getting a thirty-five mile ride into town was not the largest dimension of the problem. The movie was rated "B" by the Catholic National Legion of Decency: "Morally Objectionable in Part for All." At issue were the women's costumes and an allusion to euthanasia on the part of the doctor-clown played by Jimmy Stewart. In the script, the clown was caught and sent to prison, and the costume issue suggested even to a grammar school kid that the Legion people needed to get out more. Everyone in my family, bless their hearts, knew instinctively that this film was an absolute must for me. So I got a ride into town with Clyde Bishop, our Brownsville grocer, on his weekly supply run. *The Greatest Show on Earth* will always be my favorite movie. It is not consistently artistic; it is, however, an important and elegant documentary of a period in the history of the American circus unlike anything else we have.

In the eighth grade, the whole school moved into a brand new modern building. There we had a sharp, short little teacher who had just arrived from teaching all boys in San Francisco: Sister Marie Robert. Someone we respected and loved a lot, she was on top of her game and on top of ours. It was she who would encourage Doug and me and our buddies to put on the sideshow for the school.

But before that all happened, Saint Joseph Parish brought a show of its own to town. I didn't know anything about it until Doug started behaving strangely.

He began swallowing metal sewing thimbles. Unlike me, Doug was a quiet kid, and if I got too excited about this behavior he would stop doing it. Then I would catch him separating linked safety pins without opening them. After two days I pressed him for an explanation.

Across the street from school, Saint Joseph's Parish was sponsoring a week-long "mission." In Catholic parlance this event is a series of inspirational talks designed as a spiritual uplift for the community. It is not altogether unlike the revivals sponsored in fundamentalist churches except that in those days Catholics couldn't sing.

Customarily a mission was preached by a visiting priest, and this one was by a member of a men's religious congregation, Father Bob. But for most of the week I had no idea what he preached about. Because I had met him.

*   *   *

On a rainy afternoon while we were waiting in the church vestibule for a ride home, Doug introduced me to Father Bob, and explained that he was a magician. Without any coaxing on my part, Father demonstrated a minor miracle right there, passing sponge balls through my lower arm into my closed hand. It was a shadowy day because of the clouds; we were in a church, and this was a priest. Just how was this done? And so it was that two boys who had never seen a magician in their lives began a captivating hobby. For me it was preparation for a professional mainstay.

Father Bob was a very skilled practitioner of sleight-of-hand, an art referred to as close-up magic. He could and did entertain for over an hour standing in our Shasta Street living room manipulating cards, coins, billiard balls, string, and rope, all simple objects he carried in his pockets. With these effects he routinely introduced himself to altar boys wherever he preached. Additionally, he would teach those interested in learning legerdemain. He carried extra sets of all the apparatus when he traveled. I would eventually learn that he had a collection of larger effects, stage magic he would loan to a kid who wanted to do a grander scale of the art.

But there was a catch. He was a recruiter for his community's high school seminary in the Midwest. And I was a sitting duck. He was the only priest I knew who belonged to a religious community. I had only heard of Franciscans and Dominicans. But from my earliest imaginings about priesthood, I knew I wanted to belong to a religious community.[18] The devoted diocesan clergy who brought us up impressed me as educated, caring, and generous, but through it all, alone. Theirs was a blessed life, to be sure, dedicated to making the divine

---

[18] Priests of the Roman Catholic church are either ordained as members of the religious community to which they belong (e.g., Dominican, Franciscan, Benedictine, Jesuit, Cistercian) or for work in their given diocese. Hence the distinction between religious clergy and diocesan or secular clergy.

power and love as tangible as possible. But I imagined the end of a diocesan priest's day as devoid of the most powerful and tangible power in all creation, other human beings. I wasn't at all thinking of sex; I was wondering how they managed without companionship. The religious clergy celebrated companionship and called it community. So I pumped Father Bob all I could for information about what it was like being a member of his group. I even got to visit his monastery. And of course I had the brochures.

But all this research had to compete for time with magic lessons. There was even a field trip to San Francisco's Golden Gate Magic Company. The store was above the Pig and Whistle Restaurant just west of Third Street on Market. A long wooden stairway led to the door. This time I walked the steps, politely. Many would be the times during high school that I would take them two at a time.

Golden Gate Magic Company was part museum, part store, part performance space. A very high ceiling afforded wall surfaces for a spectacular array of posters that took over where the open shelves of apparatus left off. Looking down on me were the likenesses of Kellar, Thurston, Blackstone Sr., and Harry Houdini himself. Where there were no posters, the walls were papered with signed, eight-by-ten glossies of contemporary performers, dozens and dozens. Waist-high glass showcases stood in front of the open shelves, and it was behind one of these that I first saw the proprietor, Mr. Tom Dethlefsen.

A professional magician and something of a legend, Mr. Dethlefsen was a thin, medium-height gentleman, straight of stance with white hair and a mustache. He might have been in his sixties at the time. He greeted Father Bob as an old friend. When he demonstrated his skill it was immediately clear that he was a finely tempered artist and the magic he performed had long ago yielded its focus on clever mechanisms to more important deception, the ceremonies of good routines. No mistake—part of him actually believed he was making magic happen. And in me, he was. I was hooked. It was the first professional entertainer I had ever met. Father Bob's seminary pitch and even our sharing of Mass were in the wings of a young kid's brightly lit fascination with show business.

Doug and I were constantly chatting about magic and experimenting with tricks on each other. It was a perfect arrangement because every magician needs a confidante to check him. We couldn't get into magic enough. And when Sister Marie Robert came up with the idea for the sideshow as a class fundraiser, the dream of a real performance venue came true. It was that event that further defined how my best friend and I differed. Each of us got a chance to define the other's artistic strengths in such a way that we came to understand how we complemented one another.

We both loved and admired circuses and magic and the ritual of our religion. But in the little sideshow we developed, Doug's place was quickly seen as organizer, advertiser, and marketer. Inside the actual show, staged in an abandoned concession shack on campus, if Doug announced an attraction it was just about as straight-laced an intro as anyone ever got from Ed Sullivan. "If I might have your attention" were the suave words with which he really did get attention. I didn't invite; I demanded. "Directing your attention" were such brassy words, no one hesitated to talk under them. He was always accurate, careful and on cue. Never hyped. If he was the performer, his commentary was unassertive; he deferred to what you were seeing. "If you notice…" again the conditional invitation. With me the words became "You will notice…" I was all over the audience with noise and distraction; he was alongside the audience with guidance. And we were both pretty good showmen. But he was always the better magician.

About the time I traveled to San Francisco and met Mr. Dethlefsen to begin my orientation in the world of magic, there was another, shorter trip to a large city.

Auntie Vern, Mom's younger sister, had told me about the Shrine Circus in Sacramento and offered to take me to it. She knew I was crazy for circus anyway, but I had laid down a challenge. I simply refused to believe a circus could happen in a building.

What the public referred to as the Shrine Circus in those days around northern California was the Western Unit of the Polack Brothers Circus. The Shriners sponsored it to raise money, and it was held in the Memorial Auditorium on J Street, animals, rigging, and all. For kids in those days the concept of an indoor circus was as rarified as that of a tented show for big city kids today. There it was, nevertheless. The old brick structure was surrounded by all manner of customized trucks and trailers, each connected to the auditorium by the maze of water hoses and electrical cables sustaining it. Inside, miraculously, it was all there: the three rings, a hippodrome track, and even more aerial apparatus than Clyde Beatty had. And, all praise, the smell was right.

It was during that performance that I saw the most exciting and dramatic circus act I have ever encountered: the Wallenda Seven-High Pyramid on the high wire. Now the image is fairly common in circus lore, since the famous stunt has been recreated and photographed so often.

The first pair of under-standers moved out onto the cable linked by a shoulder bar that carried the forward member of the second tier. There was no doubt anywhere in the building that something very serious and very dangerous was beginning. The vendors really did leave the arena as requested by the announcer, and the audience did offer only the respect of silence. By the time the second trio moved out and linked with the first with the second tier shoulder bar, pressure was tangible in the building.

Only organ music accompanied the buildup. Finally the top-mounter was in place sitting on her chair, whose rungs were balanced on a single pole between the shoulders of the two men on the second tier. It was a three-layer pyramid, thirty feet above the floor, balanced on a 5/8" cable. There was no net. Seven people, seven balancing poles, three shoulder bars, and a chair. And it moved— a slow procession, lockstepped with the disciplined barking of commands in German. I actually heard people near me praying.

At the center of the wire, midway between the two pedestals and safety, the entire structure halted. The organ yielded to terrifying silence as the girl rose from her chair and stood on the seat. No applause. Terror. Another barked command and the structure proceeded to the far pedestal. It would be twenty years before I saw them again, but I would hear about them sooner than that when a Jesuit classmate in Spokane informed me of their tragic fall.

Auntie Vern won. Not only was it a circus in a building, it was a damned fine one.

*   *   *

The last edition of *The Baltimore Catechism* any of us ever used was the one for the seventh and eighth grades. We would be in high school before some of us began to fault our old textbook. When one learned the text, the questions as well as the answers were captured cognitively as well. But of course the main attention was on the answers. Two questions never dawned on us. An alternative first one:

Who are *you*, the questioner?

And a final one:

Have you asked all the questions?

But in Yuba City and Marysville, California, between 1945 and 1953, we Catholic kids thought and felt we had a pretty firm and adequate grip on our world and our Church. We were satisfied about what we knew and why we knew it. And we persisted in such a stance, sometimes false or naïve, even though our emotional horizons were constantly changing as friends fell out or moved away, family members died or disappeared, and circuses came to one town or another every year.

But now there was something serious and unknown on our horizons: graduation and high school. I wanted to go to prep seminary in the Midwest but no one, least of all my family, seemed to be talking that way. Was I headed toward a move back to Brownsville and a commute into Marysville Union High School? Doug would be going to Yuba City Union High School.

That summer shook my world a bit. There was fresh-cut hay in the large pastures at the ranch. It had to be picked up and stored. So Dad and I found ourselves on either side of a tractor-drawn wagon pitching hay on board. Here was a teaching moment he did not miss. He spoke right out of the blue and he used his nickname for me, which was invariably a call for attention.

"Butch. I don't want you going to that seminary."

"You don't." I kept my voice flat. Just a repetition.

"No."

"Why?" By now I knew I was revealing my disappointment.

"You're too young. You need to have some experience before you do something like that. You have to grow up a little. You need to go to high school."

Done deal. Over. Settled. And I think I loved him like I hadn't. He was not just my Dad that day. He was my big brave Dad and he was trying to take care of me. It still took some years of maturing to look back on that hayfield conversation and admit that the Wallendas were not the only great balancers in the world.

Yet before graduation, there was still another shift: I would be going away to high school after all, a boarding school. And Monsignor had said that the Christian Brothers High School in Sacramento, forty miles away, was just a reform school. He thought the Jesuits in San Jose, a hundred and twenty-five miles away, ran a better operation. Just as importantly, Great Grandpa, Nick J. Weber I, was always quoted around our house: "If you want to know something, ask a Paulist or a Jesuit." It was decided that I would go to Bellarmine College Preparatory, the Jesuit high school in San Jose. And to this day I'm convinced that Uncle Art Bristow (and just maybe a few more of the Bristows) thought I was going to a seminary. I knew I wasn't. I did know I was leaving Douglas Mann behind in Yuba City. That was tough.

In those last days of the eighth grade, though, after all the hustle over the sideshow fundraising and the class picnic, Sister Marie Robert wrote me a very caring note, not without a risky prediction.

> Dear Nicholas,
> Congratulations. My prayers and best wishes go with you to Bellarmine College Preparatory. I know you will do well.
> Sister Marie Robert, SND
> P.S. Maybe someday I will address you as "Father Nicholas Weber."
> Sr. M.R.

5.
Stretches

"Men. That 'B' on your jackets doesn't stand for Bellarmine. It stands for Best."
—Father G. Flynn, SJ, Freshman Latin Instructor

We weren't exactly men, but we did hold our school to be damned fine. Maybe even the best.

In early August 1953, Beth and I traveled down to San Jose so that I could take the Bellarmine entrance exam. I remember how impressed she was with the Jesuit principal, Father William P. Corvi. For her the frayed sleeves of his cassock were evidence that the Jesuits were putting all their money right back into that school. By today's standards, there wasn't much money to put anywhere. Full tuition, plus room and board, came to $1,100 per year. There were eight hundred students in the school, and two hundred of them were resident students. Of course, the secret was that the Jesuits had a seemingly endless supply of free labor: themselves.

I was accepted and somehow arrived on what were advertised as seventeen wooded acres at Emory and Elm Streets. I was assigned a room in the southeast sector of Kostka Hall's first floor. I have no recollection of the trip down to San Jose or farewells to my family. Details of my new surroundings, however, are stark.

The wooded acres must have been logged sometime before, because there were no trees except on the city sidewalk bordering Elm Street. All the other open areas were either lawn or asphalt. Freshmen and most sophomores had class in Recitation Hall, a wooden building west of Kostka Hall on Elm Street. Directly north of our dorm was the picturesque older faculty building, a holdover from the property's earlier development as the College of the Pacific.

Our northeast corner was the north-south commuter train stop known as College Park Station. This station was very convenient for our commuting day students, who were commonly and nonchalantly referred to as "day-dogs."[19]

I had seven freshman roommates in our dorm. Eight two-high metal bunk beds were arranged on either side of an archway between two rooms. There was a sink in each room, and each student had his own closet space. One of my roommates was all the way from Honolulu; another was from nearby Watsonville, and one had come with me from Yuba City and Notre Dame Elementary School.

Jesuits were everywhere, especially scholastics in the teaching stage of their training known as regency. When they were monitoring us outside of their teaching function, we referred to them as *prefects* and always addressed them as "Mister." There was one priest who was the overall prefect of boarders, and he and several scholastics lived in the building. Jesuits, priests and scholastics, also lived in the other dorms. Very little resident student (boarder) activity was not under Jesuit scrutiny.

The daily schedule was punctuated with loud bells. Every school day was an unrelenting series of migrations beginning with a 6 am rise (6:30 am on Wednesdays), followed by a march-step through grooming inspection, Mass, meals, room cleanups, classes, and study halls, then lights out at 9:30 pm. Similar meticulous structuring of the day became my manner of living for the next eighteen years.

Kostka Hall was not used for leisure time. In another building, we had a recreation hall and TV lounge, as well as scheduled hours for pool and gym use. Juniors and seniors had some additional recreation and TV rooms in their dorm areas. Mercifully, on Wednesdays and Saturdays there was no Mass. We had a chance for a later rise unless we were serving a private Mass in the faculty residence. On Fridays and Saturdays, a chance to leave campus replaced study halls.

I immediately sensed that I was a small-town boy. The skyline of downtown San Jose was a fair distance from campus but looked immense, and the neighborhood areas stretched all the way to the edge of that skyline and in all other directions as well.

At the outset, the resident students bonded in their differentiation from the day students. Bellarmine and our peers necessarily became a second home and family. We saw each other constantly. Most of my fellow freshmen boarders, however, were not at all small-town boys. While they weren't exactly big city guys, they were at least big-*town* guys and a majority of them had sports on their minds and were eager to revel in the school's well-known athletic prowess. This was a source of tension for me because I knew nothing about

---

[19] Another dog, "Buck" in Jack London's *Call of the Wild*, starts out at that College Park Station.

sports, the cost of being so content with solitary hobbies. Much of the leisure conversation around me seemed uninteresting and unintelligible. Time would pass before I made very many close friends.

A few of those who were not so interested in sports betrayed a level of language and interests as unsavory as weapons (even the manufacture of pipe-guns); abusive, even violent sexual attitudes; and drugs. I sensed a kind of admiration for an upperclassman who was caught stealing a hypodermic syringe from the infirmary. I guessed these were the earmarks of big town, back alley pubescent life. Like that of the athletes, their conversation eluded me; moreover, it frightened me a bit.

It was the young Jesuits, both in our dorm and our classrooms, who sensed my difficulties adjusting. They made sure I found fellow students who were interested in the performance and service activities the school served up. Such alertness on their part so affected me that even today I cannot imagine working in an educational environment without like sensitivity.

Whether my performance on the exam was mediocre, or the top classes for the freshman class had already been filled, I was assigned to just an average class section, 1-E. By design, the alphabet didn't indicate the academic intensity of the level. The difficulty of the Latin class you had was the key, and 1-C and 1-D had Father "Best" Sullivan, who was all business. Those were the top freshman classes, and the rest of us shuddered at some of the stories about those strict, homework-laden Latin classes.

Being in 1-E held a qualified advantage for me. The classes, especially Latin, were not as intense and rapidly paced as in the higher sections. I was therefore able to acclimate myself academically, develop productive study habits, and achieve high grades. That would mean, however, landing myself in the top section for the rest of my high school career. Besides grouping me with very sharp peers, that section tracked me for three more years of Latin and two years of Greek. Other guys would get to take French or Spanish. Of course, everyone had to take physics, chemistry, math, history, and English. Religion alternated with speech.

The one freshman course in which I did not excel was physical education. A very unimaginative coach showed an utter lack of invention in a "syllabus" consisting of basketball and its attendant drills and exercises. If you couldn't dribble a ball, you hoped for good weather so you could be in the pool.

Wherever on campus I was at any time, I was in the midst of adolescent guys, an effervescent stew of self-doubt, bravado, competition, and horseplay. The commonplace rowdy settings of dorm rooms, gang showers and locker rooms mutually exposed all of us with a rawness we accepted only because we anticipated it. However, the exclusively male factor of our day-to-day surroundings and interpersonal relationships sometimes tortured our sensitivities about sexuality. Those of us who thought we were sure of our hormonal directionals got

fooled. "Regular" guys found themselves fascinated with male bodies besides
their own. Others, who without ever "naming the love" suspected they were
different, found themselves seeking companionship with girls. For me, the
desire for contact remained effectively shanghaied by my continuing interest in
priesthood, the rigid proscriptions of the church, and the lack of social interchange with girls. Even in the paltry satisfaction of my own body I endured the
tortuous scold of priest moralists and the bizarre ricochet of routine confession.

To be sure, the Jesuits caring for us resident students made efforts to provide
a balanced socialization. But these were awkward singles dances and mixers
that introduced us to kids who lived ordinary lives in the area: girls who didn't
spend most of their time in regimented single-gender dorms. Compared to us,
the day-dogs seemed much more normal.

Judged by today's conventional wisdom, I had already undergone a grammar
school experience that should have rendered me a sitting duck for confusion,
self-contempt, or even self-destruction.

Before I'd ever heard the word Jesuit or knew any priests very well, a priest
embraced me as we prepared for bed on an overnight. Young as I was, I seemed
to apprehend what was happening immediately. I was not frightened or disturbed,
though I knew it was a sexual act on his part. I have always been convinced that
he was as surprised by the event as I was. It was momentary and mutually embarrassing. And that was the end of it. Our lives went their separate ways. I never for
an instant then or thereafter worried that it would complicate my sexual development. Nor did I experience the least disenchantment with the priesthood. I was
pretty sure where I was headed for a career, and even then, I knew how I was sex-
ually wired and I knew nothing he had done could change the configuration of
my fuse box. In the context of the recent revelations of horrendously damaging
clerical abuse, I thankfully recognize how fortunate I was.

That is not to say that I was comfortable in an all-male environment during
high school. As I reflect now on that atmosphere, I am impressed that it was
charged with energy foreign to any I have experienced in ordinary life. I have
taught in same-sex high schools serving all boys and more recently all girls. I
am not convinced they serve as adequate preparations for a balanced life in
society. I know all the arguments. I have watched kids prosper and lag in both
environments, but I am not convinced the same kids wouldn't have prospered
or lagged in mixed-gender high schools. So often their guides were also the
products of same-sex high schools and not at all objective in assessing the
needs of students preparing for a life of sexual complementarity.

I am very thankful I went to Bellarmine because it introduced me to the
Jesuits and made possible some of the happiest and fullest years of my life. The
day-to-day practice of Jesuit life around me resonated with every facet of the
spirituality I had managed to make my own religious practice. And practice I

did, since the faith I had been taught remained such an important area of my life's self-control. Without so much as my thinking it, there was a sense in which God and I were tight. Practice made perfect, so the more I practiced the tighter I got with God. What I could only sense in those early high school days was that Jesuits themselves were practiced: detailed method in religious life was their specialty. Of course I was still using the two elevators, and the Jesuits were keen enough to recognize the benefits of both.

I came to realize that on the elevator where I pushed all the buttons, health, capacity for study, knowledge and practice of the Catholic faith, and an attraction to ministry were signs of a possible vocation. Simultaneously I discovered that in keeping with the meaning of the freshman Latin verb *vocare* ("to call"), the other elevator didn't even have to be called. Not unlike a theatrical agent, God would call me. It was complicated, though, and the Jesuits were tireless in explaining that the signs themselves were part of the call. That spoke to me.

Whether they were priests or scholastics my Jesuit friends discerned that I was attracted to their brand of religious chemistry and apostolic work. On my part there was open curiosity and on theirs a caring cultivation that truly met me where I was. They were interested in me, messy as that entity was.

Although my love for the circus was somehow relegated to a backburner by this time, my yen for magic remained keen. Not that my flame for circus was out; it was not as ready to hand as sleight-of-hand tricks. It took no time at all to find a magic store downtown on First Street where I spent $1.25 of my allowance for "The Siberian Chain Escape."[20]

Nor was it long before my freshman English instructor and his friend who would teach me sophomore English detected my interest in magic. During their years of philosophical studies at Mount Saint Michael's in Spokane, they had developed a mind-reading routine with cards. It involved very subtle signals between them to communicate a chosen card's identity. No matter how many times they did the routine, none of us students could discover the signals.

Somehow it became known that I was a fire-eater, and a classmate asked me to teach him the skill. I was confident in the technique, so most of my concern focused on safety. We were on the street side of Kostka Hall on a cement front porch that was never used. All the traffic was through the opposite side of the building.

Setting the place on fire wasn't the problem; the problem was my friend's mouth. When he tipped his head back ready to take the first torch, I fortunately

---

[20] Nineteen years later I performed that trick just a few blocks north on that same street in what is now called Fountain Alley. For that show I developed a rich routine for the simple escape I have performed close to a thousand times. My trusty shotgun from the Royal Lichtenstein Circus '87–'90 season, Kevin Curdt, now works in the San Jose area and informs me that Fountain Alley enjoys continual police surveillance. It is a notorious site for drug deals. Handcuffs have replaced the Siberian chain.

happened to notice he was wearing a retainer. Flaming and melting acrylic would have been added spectacle for sure. The lesson ended abruptly even though removal of the retainer would have been simple. He had felt the heat of the torch. Reality set in and I wondered if I wanted to accept responsibility for him, retainer or not. What neither of us had noticed was that our general science teacher, Mr. Jack Geiszel, had been watching us, attracted by the flaming torches. The Jesuits were everywhere.

I was even employed by the Jesuits. One day I was summoned to the treasurer's office to meet with Father James E. Morse, the school's chief bursar. He was looking for a freshman to train as a regular switchboard operator at the main faculty phone center. If it worked out, I would have the job throughout my stay at Bellarmine. I met my predecessor, the outgoing senior who would train me, and I took irregular shifts for practice. It worked out in spades.

Not that the job paid so well. I only made fifty cents an hour and worked twenty hours a week. But my relationship with Father Morse was the best benefit any employee could have. Not having the usual student contacts a teacher would have, he took an active interest in the student workers he hired, including the other phone operators and the table waiters working in the faculty dining room.

Twenty years older than I, he knew less about sports than I did[21] and discovering my interest in performing, soon shared his interest in theater and music and a dormant curiosity in the circus. He was not shy in bringing up key points in his own spirituality, and was proud to share the trademark aphorisms, traditions, and tales garnered from his personal trek through Jesuit lore.

Father James E. Morse, SJ

He became my spiritual advisor, my confessor, my boss, and my friend. Faculty and fellow students who knew me at all knew of this friendship. Graceful and fair as Father Morse was with everyone, however, our relationship must have made for awkward moments in his contacts with other Jesuits. For one thing, his best friend in the Jesuit community was our principal, Father Corvi. For another, Father Morse, as treasurer, was an official in the Jesuit community.

Like most Jesuits, he kept sensitive to the possibility a boy might be attracted to the order. He quickly spotted such an attraction in me. He and other Jesuits did not hesitate to make religious practice and devotion

---

[21] Over dinner, he once asked Father Robert Plushkell, an avid baseball fan and our dean of discipline, how many planes landed each day at Ebbets Field.

appealing to me. On one birthday, a holy picture of my patron[22] showed up on my pillow when I turned the covers back that night. On my birthday in 1954, Father Morse gave me a copy of my first daily missal, a big, fat *Saint Andrews* with ribbons and gold-leaf page edges. It included the liturgy for every day in the church year. We were still in the Tridentine era, so the Latin of the Mass and the English translation were side by side on alternate pages. On a flyleaf, Father had ended a brief message with "I continue to remember you at Mass daily. Please pray for me." That was his signature gift and request. Even on a phone call when he was in retirement and in ill health, those were his closing words. Moreover, that request for prayer was the last thing I would hear in every confession: "That's a good confession. Go in peace and pray for me."

I found the drama department easily because our first year speech teacher was the play director. He it was who taught us the delivery for the speeches of Shylock and Portia, as well as a six-step formula for composing a speech. However, I must have laid low. My voice hadn't changed, and there didn't seem to be a place for magic on campus.

For Halloween, the sophomore English teacher coaxed me into doing a magic routine in the boarders' dining hall. He designed everything: illusions, lighting (green), music (spooky), and even my costume (robe and turban, of course). The centerpiece was to be the Indian Rope Trick, complete with basket, rising rope, and a magic flute.[23] In spite of the sniggering in the audience and obvious lack of faith in my sorcery skills, the rope ascended out of the basket. Absolute silence replaced the jeering as about eight feet of the rope climbed the air, straight up toward the ceiling. Then it stopped. Dead. I panicked. The lights went out. When they came back on, the rope maintained its frozen mid-air position. I was clueless. Then the lights went out again. I could hear whispering backstage. Lights on. No rope. Vanish. Act over. I think I had the presence of mind to bow and run.

To get home at Thanksgiving meant riding the Greyhound. More importantly, it meant transferring between Greyhound routes in San Francisco with at least an hour layover. That was enough time to jog down Market Street and pick up a new magic routine at Mr. Dethlefsen's and jog back. The return transfer time wasn't as generous, so I didn't try it. However, besides learning new magic, I learned how to cope while traveling on Greyhound Lines and still use them for cross-country treks over fifty years later.

In the spring of 1954, I trouped with friends over to nearby Santa Clara University for a performance in their grand old theater, which we all knew by

---

[22] Even in the early Fifties, elegant soft-toned cards depicting one saint or another were popular among some Catholic kids. Often nuns used them as rewards and some kids traded them.
[23] Thankfully he hadn't heard the fabled climax of that trick, a little boy climbing the rope to the very top and disappearing into thin air.

its nickname, "The Ship." We watched "Bellrioties of '54," our school variety show for that year. It was on that occasion that a very elegant young magician demonstrated that a high school kid could make magic happen for his peers. He was a graduating senior. So I waited.

Somehow in this whirlwind of new images, friends, skills, and obligations I began to feel increasingly comfortable about the talents I had. Moreover, I was comfortable academically and earned good grades. No matter that it scared me, I was scheduled for 2-A, 3-A, and 4-D, the Greek and Latin track, for the rest of my high school career. Encouraged by the Jesuits, especially Father Morse, I paid attention to what I could do and to where my interests led me. I forgot to fret about what I couldn't do, and about my imagined need to "mainstream." I was beginning—slowly, tentatively—to follow the arrows. I just didn't know it yet.

*   *   *

Home for summer meant a return to the busy shuffle between Yuba City and Brownsville. Most importantly there was an exciting addition to my family: the month of June brought Sue and me a baby brother, John Thomas. There was a new kind of magic in knowing and saying that I had a brother *and* a sister. Happy as I was over the way he completed our lives, John and I would always have that fourteen-year difference between us, and the paths of our lives, especially mine, would make it very difficult for us to know each other closely.

By that summer, 618 Shasta Street had undergone an extensive remodeling of the two-story residence. The intent was to reduce housekeeping and pro-vide a self-contained apartment upstairs. But Beth and Gramma were intoler-able of the sounds of footsteps above them, so when the first tenants moved out, the last tenants moved out. Not only their apartment remained empty, so did their garage. Into that, I moved my magic and circus operations. Larger than the toolshed, it was a wooden building with a sloped tin roof and one light fixture controlled by a switch on Gramma's back porch.

There, where I had once taught myself to eat fire, I eventually practiced magic routines. And in the rear of that dusty space, I had built a fairly complete and involved scale-model circus. I spent hour upon hour of intense work there. Beth and Gramma watched afternoon and evening TV incessantly, and when-ever a circus or magic act appeared on the screen, my overhead light would blink as a signal. In I would hustle to learn from one of the masters.

After John's arrival, there was a second joyful newsbreak. Doug was going to transfer from Yuba City Union High School to Bellarmine. I couldn't have been happier. Now there would be another student around who knew where I came from and where I was coming from. The benefit for him was that he had someone to introduce him to that campus. He would also befriend Father Morse, who hired him for regular wait staff in the faculty dining room.

*   *   *

By the time we arrived back in San Jose for the 1954 fall semester, I had acquired an asset that attracted the drama director and the head speech coach. My voice had changed. It was considerably deeper, but I was unaware of how I sounded. As it turned out, however, I was not interested in being a regular orator or debater for the school's competitive teams. Although I won the sophomore oratorical contest, I was much more interested in the theater.

I should not have feared Greek. The excitement of a new alphabet, vocabulary and the kindness and patience of our instructor made it a pleasure. Reading and eventually understanding the prologue to the Gospel of John in its original was an unexpected thrill.

Our Greek teacher became one of my all-time favorite Jesuits in those days and he was moderator of the apostolic arm of the school's religious service activity. Under him, I developed the skills of a catechist, eventually was certified by the Archdiocese of San Francisco, and spent Saturday mornings teaching public grammar school kids the basics of the faith. As in the case of my friendship with Father Morse, the bond between me and this young Jesuit scholastic was also pretty well known around campus.

Home for Christmas during my sophomore year, I underwent a sudden schedule interruption no one could have seen coming. And I had trouble seeing much of anything for a month afterward. We were all in Gramma's living room at the ranch and I had baby John on my knee. In a flash of infant energy, his hand darted toward my right eye and the tiny fingernail sliced my cornea. Since it only felt like a speck of dust had gotten under the eyelid, I washed it out and went to bed. The next morning there was severe irritation and we decided to drive down to an ophthalmologist in Marysville. The diagnosis was ulcerated cornea; the eye was medicated and bandaged.

**My baby brother John Thomas,
1954**

However, I was virtually blind. Eyes move as one. Therefore, even though only one of my eyes was covered, I couldn't use the other one because when it moved so did its partner; and movement was painful. Everyone around me had trouble understanding that. Clearly, I could just open my left eye. Moreover, the irritation and pain were not subsiding. Daily examination only frustrated the doctor until he finally sent me to a specialist at Stanford Lane Hospital in San Francisco. My eye was a star. The ulceration was apparently a classic and they photographed it for teaching purposes. Fortunately, that doctor prescribed an effective treatment: daily medication with cortisone drops and a pressure bandage. Almost immediately, there was perceptible healing.

Nevertheless, that accident cost me a month of school and changed my life. Ironically, because my vision was temporarily impaired, I saw myself more clearly. While I missed my friends in San Jose and developed a modest anxiety over falling behind in lessons, I began to dream of the things I really loved, and they weren't academic.

In high school I had been teaching catechism to public elementary school students in Saturday programs and schoolday instruction referred to as "release time." I knew the *Baltimore Catechism* well, and it was easy to master any textbooks that had been developed for various grades of kids in public education. I was keen on the clarity of the Church's practices and beliefs and I loved to talk. Of course my students, wherever we met, comprised an audience. But that time off in Yuba City gave me an opportunity to evaluate my teaching. And for the first time I sought ways to infuse instruction with the gimmickry of magical apparatus. I invented a set of flip charts that would illustrate various doctrinal or dogmatic lessons. Diagrams would magically change to reveal, change, or complete an answer. I was able to prepare a number of these sets, and back at school other catechists learned how to use them. Even without the surprise element and downright curiosity about how a chart changed, the novelty of such a visual aid was itself compelling for little kids. The real magic, of course, did not depend on props. It was in our coming together as a little group to talk about areas of interest far more amazing than a novelty entertainment. That we could have fun doing it spoke to the place of ritual in whatever I would one day teach or preach. It also spoke to the style I would adopt.

Laid up at Gramma's, between daily trips for cortisone drops and bandage changes I also got to indulge my intense daydreams about the circus. And there too, without my articulating or even recognizing it, ritual captivated me. I wasn't sophisticated enough to understand circus as ritual, but I was familiar enough with these exotic ceremonies to sense that they held significant power. I didn't know the source of the power but I could recognize what educed a profound response from me. In the humblest of venues, a tent in an abandoned field, the circus, teased from its wagons by the confidence of brash trumpets, boldly danced forth a daring parade representing all of creation. And because of this boldness and willingness to risk, the parade seemed at once vulnerable and humble enough to include—even want—my heart as a fellow dancer. In that, I felt I could become as bold and risk-willing as the circus. I didn't parse this, of course. I felt it without language. It was obvious.

It was also obvious that I wasn't alone at the circus. I undertook this experience with friends, family, and people I had never seen before. We were all focused on a ceremony that represented us to ourselves and seemed to need us. Like my little circle of catechism students. Like the shows in my dark shed-studio. Like my someday celebration of the Eucharist and that one-day celebration of the Royal Lichtenstein Circus.

* * *

By February, I was back at school, wearing glasses for the first time, and gifted with extra help from teachers I hardly knew. Everyone wanted to make sure I regained my scholarly pace. Word had come to me in Yuba City that the physics teacher, Father Louis B. Franklin, had told Father Morse he would be more than willing to coach me in the math I had missed.[24] The scholastics teaching me Latin and Greek also came forward from very heavy teaching loads and prefecting schedules to help me out.

But I never really did recover my wind. I knew I wasn't a scholar. My grades dropped from A's to B's. Now that I was in the top academic section, teachers were proceeding more rapidly because my peers were so bright. Friends, magic, and the school's theater activities ran hefty competition with homework for my attention.

Though Doug and I were in different sophomore class sections, we still saw plenty of each other because of our exploits with magic. Since the faculty had moved their residence into new quarters, student activity offices moved into the old College of the Pacific building, and Father Morse pulled a string or two to secure us a second-floor room as a private rehearsal studio. This hang-out became free-time headquarters for our circle of friends. By then I had amassed a sizeable collection of magic apparatus. That hangout of ours was a secure storage site and a place for Doug and me and another guy a year ahead of us to eat lunch while we hashed over new ideas and better ways to present our routines. We were good audiences for each other. When we weren't doing magic, some other friends from the drama club joined us to rough out scenic designs for the variety show or the next play we were going to do.

Typically, it was Doug who held back in these pow-wows and then floor everybody with the best idea of the day. I don't think he ever performed in a Bellarmine play and I never saw him do magic before an audience. Although he was a far better magician than I, he became the assistant in my magic act and he was invaluable. As always he was a master at detail, and I couldn't imagine a better set of eyes.

"But I can see it." That meant, very calmly, that I had misplaced a gesture and revealed, for instance, the source I was using to produce a bowl of fire. Then he would be on his feet and gently move through the gesture, slowly,

[24] Louie taught the most dreaded course on campus, and we all had to take it. However, this generous offer from a priest I didn't know struck me as solid evidence that Jesuits were dedicated teachers. But in my junior year, I'm afraid "Dr. Weber" disappointed his physics instructor. I wasn't very good at science.

calmly, carefully whereby I could "steal" the object without the telltale moment. All of that while he purred "Maybe this way."

By this time, Saturday afternoons saw me doing my magic act between features at the Santa Clara Theater, the only movie house in the neighboring town. Working as a solo act in that theater was my first encounter with the lonesome dimensions attached to all theater performance: dark, dusty wings, often-dirty dressing rooms, and the terrifying moment before entering. For payment, management let me see the films free. Father Morse hauled more than my equipment back and forth; he also transported my ego, adjusting its goals, expectations and swings as my high school journey continued. I think we both probably knew that the movies I got to see were far better than my magic act.

*   *   *

Of course I was home for Christmas vacation in 1955. The week before the holiday itself, there was threatening news. Our Feather River was rising dangerously. Marysville was evacuated, since it has the Yuba River levee on two of its other sides. The evacuees swelled the population of our town and about a dozen of them, friends of ours, took over our vacant upstairs apartment. On Christmas Eve, the Feather River levee broke on our side, just south of town. No danger. Evacuation was not suggested in ours, a higher part of town. There was talk in Gramma's kitchen of our evacuating anyway, driving due west straight out of town. There was also enough gas left in the city lines to let Gramma light her oven to bake her Christmas turkey. And she was adamant.

"This is my home. I'm not leaving it. I am going to roast this turkey and we are going to have Christmas in this house."

Wrong. Well, sort of. We should have been evacuated but no one foresaw the back swirl of pressure that soon brought the muddy water rolling into our south driveway, then into the front east driveway. We were surrounded by two feet of water, and there was no way to tell how deep it would get. When the oven went out in the kitchen, Gramma and I went out the front door. I waded her through the water and steadied her up the long flight of stairs to the upper apartment.

On Christmas morning, boats moved along our streets transporting people out if they wished. Dad came into town to check on us and injured his leg on a submerged fire hydrant on Shasta Street. The waters were beginning to subside. The surge and threat of rise stopped and we moved back into our home thankful for its old-fashioned high foundation. We had that Christmas turkey in our home.

*   *   *

Back at school, I attempted a rigid academic schedule. Marginally, I rescued the curriculum of my scholarly lessons from my passions for performance of magic and drama.

I learned lessons about magic as well. There was a fellow ahead of me on campus, a day-dog, who was accomplished in routines that required true sleights as well as gimmicks, and he was a pretty fair ball juggler. Years before, Father Bob had tried to explain to me that there were two different approaches a kid could take to magic. One was to concentrate on apparatus and mechanics, which would leave the audience saying, "He can do tricks." The other route was to focus on the routine and the effect you were producing. This often had to be accomplished by hand movements (sleights) and misdirection, but gained you the superior reaction, "He does magic." My new partner at Bellarmine did magic.

But I could talk. I developed such lines of patter that by senior year, one of the scholastics said, "You don't need to worry about the magic; you'll just hypnotize them with the lingo." For me, that has been the most enjoyable aspect of my magic performances ever since. But I did worry about the magic.

Doug helped me with routines, and of course, Father Morse was our biggest fan. Both of them were much more modest than I, but we never hid our enthusiasm for variety performance. When magicians or circuses were coming to town, it was Father Morse who let us know.

On a San Jose morning reminiscent of one years before in Yuba City, Clyde Beatty's elephants again helped me to be late for school. Father Morse and I were both playing hooky to see the circus lot early. We didn't know where the site was exactly, but we knew it was east of downtown where Santa Clara Boulevard became Alum Rock Boulevard. So Father Morse just headed out of downtown on Santa Clara Boulevard. And then we found our directions: the elephants had left them for us, here and there, all over the street they had walked to get to that day's circus lot. We found the field where the show was setting up, parked and watched for about five minutes. I so wanted to get out and walk around. No way was that going to happen. Father Morse was in his cassock. Frustrating as it was for both of us, we returned to campus and a much less romantic set of images: his were decimals in the business office, and mine were the triangles of geometry class. This time I had a note for late admittance.—If I made it to the performance that night, I cannot remember. For sure, missing it after that morning's titillation would have been grueling. But I ran the school switchboard on school nights, and Father was the kind of friend who tried to make the best of an impending bad deal. So that he went out of his way to visit the lot in the morning may indicate I didn't make it to a performance. I suspect I didn't.

In the summer of 1955 I had a chance to observe firsthand what teaching, specifically catechesis, could be. As a catechist I was invited to attend the first Summer School of Catholic Action to visit California, specifically, Fresno. Originating in Saint Louis, this traveling "college of Jesuit workshops" would typically headquarter in a larger city for a week, offering courses in social justice and apostolic works.

Working the magic act in the ballroom of the Fresno Hotel—SSCA talent show, 1955

That year their faculty included a stellar pedagogue, Father Aloysius Heeg. At the time, Heeg was arguably most famous for his little catechism, *Jesus and I*. While the approach of *Jesus and I* has been reevaluated repeatedly, doctrinal substance was not what I took away from Father Heeg. It was the place of dialectic, honesty, and imagination in the exchange that teaching really is.

Heeg taught little kids with the aid of a picture roll, a flip chart collection of huge, warmly colored realistic depictions of the bible stories. The lesson in point for one morning was family, specifically familial love. The model was the Holy Family, Jesus, Mary, and Joseph. (Currently, those folks arrive in many imaginations as an exclamation somewhere near an invective about glory to Saint Patrick.) At some point in the demonstration, a student in this teenage class asked how Joseph died. And then the pedagogical genius of a master took over.

"Well, we don't really know just how Saint Joseph died." (Honesty, truth.) "But would you like me to guess?" (Dialectic, engagement.)

None of us was over sixteen or seventeen years of age, but not one of us was too cool to pipe up with an eager collective "Yes."

And then he fed our imaginations from his.

*   *   *

That fall, circus dreams for me suddenly transcended the Clyde Beatty show. Father Morse took me to San Francisco to see the Ringling Brothers and Barnum and Bailey Circus for my very first time. This was the Big One, as it is known in the trade, and it lived up to its reputation even in 1955. In San Francisco, the show had a history of playing indoors at the Cow Palace in Brisbane. Because of the building's height, this changed the scale of the show and what it looked like compared to the impression it could make in the tent. After all, it was designed for the tent where everyone was closer to the action and even the spectators in the highest seats really did look up to the aerial acts. Nonetheless, the Cow Palace that night held more people than I had ever seen at one time. There was movement everywhere in the accessing of seats. Voices blurred, always excited, always sounding wonder and readiness for surprise. The building's warm air compounded with at least the scents of so many bodies so near one another. And I caught myself, I confess it, almost tilting my head in the air to try the residual smells of the afternoon performance. While Father Morse and my audience neighbors waited for the performance to start, I was already in thrall to elephants and horses. In that cavernous room, I could smell that I was home. Father knew I'd never been to the Cow Palace before, and he had.

"Are you sure this is the Cow Palace? That doesn't smell like cows."

"Well, you know female elephants are cows." Naturally I was wearing a "Gotcha" smirk.

"You got me there."

"But they aren't called cows."

"What are they called?"

"Bulls."

And he had another quip. "You're sure that's not *bull?*"

"It's true. They're all called bulls, the handlers are called bull-handlers, the sticks they guide them with are called bull hooks and the entire department is called the bull department.—But I'll bet we're smelling more than elephants. See what's in those cages right there? Meat eaters."

The shifting cages for the cat acts had been rolled into place. One set was exclusively for lions and the other held Trevor Bale's famous Bengal tigers. There were two arenas setup side by side for these acts to work simultaneously, something I had never seen before. I mentioned that the big cats were carnivores and had their own contribution to make to the rich aromatic cocktail. But Father Morse had noticed some other movement. Next to a third arena around the first ring, there were more shifting cages.

"Those aren't cats over there."

He was right. They were bears. Just as in my favorite movie, De Mille's "The Greatest Show on Earth," this performance was going to open with a simultaneous display of three cage acts all working at once. Of course that was in keeping with the Ringling motif of "overload." They were known for abundance and they were masters at it.

Even in the building, the sheer weight of the spectacle overwhelmed me. City traffic congestion had long ago forced the traditional circus street parade indoors, and that characteristic of any large show had conflated with the performance proper. As a forty-piece band intricately pointed the way with fanfares, marches, waltzes and galops, horse-drawn wagons and motorized floats merged with dancers, marchers, and prancing animals at various intervals in a program calculated to effect nothing other than spectacle. There were four of these ceremonious "interruptions" of the less elaborate displays of featured acts. Such production numbers were deliberately intended to stifle one's ability to focus on only one section or component of the outlay. Each one featured an original vocal number written by the show owner John Ringling North and his lyricist Irving Caesar. It was pageantry for the sake of pageantry and brought off as only the circus could. There was more of everything—in the air, on the oval track around the rings, and in the rings. There were more performing people and animals interplaying with each other than anywhere else in the world. It was a precise and dangerous outlay of decoration and grace that meant nothing in itself but spoke directly to the heart: this is what is possible. Not only was that true, but the beauty of it all closed the bargain. It was also good.

There were four of these elaborate production numbers including a Honolulu themed display, a celebration of the holidays and the closing patriotic spectacle. The most elaborate traditionally took place before intermission and was described as "Celestial Calendar Cavalcade." Beginning as a parade around the rings, somehow units from the parade would leave the procession and find themselves dancing in the rings. The entire floor space became filled with the whirl and dash of sequins, brocade and gilded floats.

Then I spotted him. At the edge of the track near the ring to our left was what today's euphemism would label a "homeless person." In those days he was a tramp or hobo. Ragged, battered, decidedly overweight, his tatters jarred against the sequins, velvets and gold braid passing by. His age and bulk became a bas relief set off from the trim physiques of performers who didn't notice him. He was shy, needing to flirt, needing to communicate, and yes, needing a drink. Because he was a masterful mime, he conveyed such a web of emotional hunger without a sound. What the hell. From under his jacket he pulled three grubby pie tins, which he juggled with all the muted bravado he could muster. It was Otto Griebling, a German immigrant who had become a legendary American clown after a career in horseback riding. It would be some time before I realized his power. He was a place-marker, a reference point so that no one missed the fact that what was passing by us—and him—was exceptional, rarefied, unusual. It was real but didn't exhaust reality.

It was no accident that the Ringling operation pulled their productions off with the care and precision of a Broadway musical. For years artists trained for the New York theater were advising the show's designers. This rich and meticulous glamour didn't percolate in some Florida pasture. There was long a connection with professional theater, music, and New York expertise. Thirteen years before I saw that performance, Igor Stravinsky had written "The Elephant Polka" for the show only to be choreographed by George Balanchine, complete with a *corps des elephants*. Years later, I would have the conceptual tools to recognize in such theatrical pageantry a continuity with the ceremony I so emotionally embraced in the sanctuary: a ritual embodiment, a moving set of signs and sounds that pointed to goodness, human and divine. It was a jump, and it required intellectual bravado, but I would eventually see Otto as serving the same function as an altar server. A place keeper. An assurance that even a lowly mortal had a place at the grand table. Sadly, Ringling management would cut the following season short and eventually redesign the show for arena exhibition only. I would never see the tented version.

*   *   *

In the spring of 1957, there was another important trip to San Francisco with Father Morse. We went to the Curran Theater to see my first professional stage production: Mary Martin in *South Pacific*. There I succumbed to as intense an experience as at any circus; but this intensity was subtle, sneaky, and almost gentle. The underlying continuity with the circus? Very skilled and magnetic people worked terribly hard to take me beyond my unskilled, ordinary, and lazy life. They, like the Jesuits, cared enough about me to dedicate their lives to the rescue of mine. I was a goner from those first thin overture strains of "Bali Hai."

In those days, our high school did a play in the fall and another in the spring. The fall shows weren't major productions, but the spring ones were usually done in "the Ship" at Santa Clara University. A stage area of that size called for full sets and detailed production values. I recall doing minor murder mysteries or comedies in the fall and only one extravaganza.

Our drama director at Bellarmine knew how to block a scene. He knew how actors should sound and move. He also knew all the mechanical details producing a show requires. However, he didn't know very much about motivating an actor; we learned by imitating him. And if he was off, we didn't feel a fit in our character. Unless a student got lucky with intuition, there weren't many moments of truth. Once, in spite of myself, and only in retrospect, my own real-life character got lucky.

In my senior year, we did *Golgotha*, a passion play written by a Jesuit for the Santa Clara University Players years before. It was to be almost literal. Every worn holy picture rendition illustrating moments of that part of Jesus' life would be exploded to fill the stage. Jesus was represented by a rolling arc lamp hidden with scenery or behind actors in mob scenes. I won the role of Judas' father. Who ever heard anything about Mr. Iscariot, right? I took the character's single appearance for a tag scene because it was short. So I went to the director.

My argument was that it was my senior year and maybe I deserved a larger part.[25] The director made a couple of adjustments and I got a very large role, one of the Pharisees. (I was too full of myself to recognize the irony.) So there I was at the first dress rehearsal, parading around in all my golden robes bellowing lots of pompous hateful lines. It was glorious. I had arrived.

Then there was a break after the first act. Most of the cast had watched the act's closing scene from seats in the house. And most of us were sobbing. The

---

[25] Now the vanity in such a posture makes me cringe. But in a valuable and backhanded way, such experiences become useful in teaching. I have told this story to many an acting class.

student playing the heartbroken father of Judas had just disowned his infamous son and exited. In what is arguably the best and most original part of the show, my classmate had come up from inside his character and found even *our* truth. The director himself had to recover and when he realized what had just happened to all of us, he brayed into the darkness, "And Weber turned that role down!" That might have been the most important lesson I learned at Bellarmine.

However the most significant passion playing itself out in my life by that time was a major decision. Should I apply for entrance into the Society of Jesus, and meaningfully join the family of those who cared for me and tried to teach me at Bellarmine? Four of us were seriously considering such a vocation during our senior year. I think we firmed up our decisions during the senior retreat that year.

Retreats are central to all Jesuit work, privileged and protected times enabling an individual to reflect, pray and discern without the distraction of his usual routines. This program, based on the *Spiritual Exercises of Saint Ignatius* had found its way in an abbreviated form into each of our years at Bellarmine. For several days, regular classes would be interrupted by chapel talks, silent reflection and increased time for the sacraments and prayer. Visiting Jesuit priests would preach the various talks and in the first three years, they were given right on campus.

Seniors, however, made their retreat away from campus, usually at the Jesuit retreat center in Los Altos, El Retiro. For this very special occasion in 1957, the guest preacher was Jesuit Father Peter Newport, something of a legend as a retreat master. I had met him very early in my stay at Bellarmine, since he was one of Father Morse's closest friends. As he had pursued his career in training for the Jesuits, Father Newport had succeeded handily in theater himself, and we shared stories of our triumphs and failures, mostly his triumphs and my failures. I first encountered his readiness to trump after I waxed enthusiastic about an impressive mature actor. Father Morse and I had just seen *A Witness For the Prosecution* onstage starring Francis L. Sullivan. Newport's sparkling eyes rolled up to catch Father Morse's, the lips pursed as his head went to a characteristic slight swagger. (He was an avid bridge player and in moments like those you realized that *trump* is really a corruption of *triumph*.)

"Tell Brother Weber he should have seen me as Cardinal Wolsey." It was even worse if Father Morse bragged about some performance I had given. When Newport heard I had won the sophomore oratorical contest with an emotional speech, he was right on cue, *avec* swagger, about his effect on a retreat group. "When I reached the section on the last words of Jesus, the handkerchiefs came out." He got away with such pomp, because he really did have the presence of a star. He was head of the Western Branch of the United States League of the Sacred Heart. His guidance of that particularly Jesuit devotion with its radio, television and print outlets, and his popularity as a preacher established Peter Newport as one of the celebrities of the California Province of the Jesuits.

But it was in his retreat work that he most memorably came into contact with us high school kids. His style and well-honed dramatic timing still lends sharp definition to my memories of that retreat. I will never shake the cadence and scale of just one line, the clincher to a story about a couple of Catholic high school kids coming home from a date. Of course they sinned; of course the sin was sexual, so of course it was a mortal sin. They were in a bloody accident and the girl was killed. By the time the boy got to his priest all he could do was scream "I hurled her into hell." No one, no matter what they had done, could have achieved the angst Father Newport got out of that line. By that time, moreover, we had little doubt about how hot hell was. We not only believed in it, we could feel it. That's because Newport had already given us the story of Sister Josefa Menendez. She reportedly scared hell out of her superiors as they watched Satan literally burn her clothes off her body.—It takes star power to get such material by a group of senior high school boys.

Sadly, however, he was best known for his frankness in discussing sexual issues both in formal talks and in question-and-answer sessions with students. I suspect he was convinced such candor was sorely needed, and his reflexes as both an inveterate teacher and spiritual director shaped his approach. However, it was an approach too easily exploited. Because his reputation preceded him, a certain type of male student would be waiting with ever-new castings for the old questions about "how far you could go." There was a jaundiced curiosity about hearing an adult speak on these issues, and such Newport metaphors as "Guys, you've got a stick of dynamite hanging between your legs," became prurient legend.

Later I would discover that "I hurled her into hell," was a stock line from a stock story used by Jesuit retreat masters for over a century. Moreover, Peter's tradition shared an artistic one. In *Portrait of the Artist as a Young Man*, James Joyce recounts his own adolescent experience of the *Spiritual Exercises*, detailing the same types of talks, dramatic frightful tales and identical schedules from half a century earlier. After nearly forty years of Jesuit life, and the guaranteed privilege of an annual retreat over so many years, I am left with a startling question. Had we petrified this brilliant set of reflections distilled from the conversion of Ignatius himself?

We would eventually be taught to view *The Spiritual Exercises* as an ingenious method for freeing every pursuit, no matter how holy, from the systematic paralysis contracted when we blindly embrace means as ends, wrong means, and outright evil. Had the rigid and formulaic use of the *Exercises* rendered them just another system, inert and unable to enlighten a discerning judgment? In the way they were applied, had they become too static to even *address* the spirit, let alone *exercise* it? By the time I reached theological studies, a decidedly positive and corrective trend emerged with a dramatic decrease in "preached retreats." And the correction derived from a reevaluation of the little book itself. It began to be seen as a radically open method, very distinct from a closed, automatic system.

Even at Bellarmine in the spring of 1957, though, Jesuits were keen in prodding my capacity to discern. I had so long fixed on a vision of myself as a Jesuit, that other avenues in life, including preparation through college, eluded me. I had very little notion of what was "out there" beyond high school. Except for the Jesuits, I had little familiarity with anything like a college education. So when a Jesuit counselor would ask me what I was thinking about pursuing, I would randomly offer careers truly foreign to my interests. To most of those suggestions, the reply was a variation on "You can achieve more than that." There it was: the call to discern what was for the *greater*. Nothing is more characteristically Jesuit.

In those last months of high school, my attraction to the Jesuits was foremost in my heart and spirit. The Jesuits responded to my own need to serve, to make my personal experiences of God's goodness and strength visible and available to everyone. Their own approach to this need was practical, human, step by step. In the classroom and in the counseling session, they knew what they were doing, had a plan. Four of us opted to enter the Society of Jesus. Fear? Hesitation? Not really. Much of the process fell into place. Even my penchant for performance, and the literal baggage of stage magic and circus, did not seem an obstacle. The Jesuits were human, Renaissance, incarnational. They had accepted my worldly skills and they knew what they were getting. I sensed all that. Without knowing the contours my priesthood would assume, I had a hunch that somehow it would include my artistic drives.

My fixation on becoming a Jesuit was tantamount to an obsession. Everything I did seemed to take its bearing and its worth in relationship to that project. The emotional weight I gave it seems to have overpowered my attention to everything else: studies, relationships, my performances and even graduation. Memories of everything else are now overlaid with the processes of application, interviewing and testing. Sadly, I have lost even the recollection of my last times with Doug. I remember that by the end of the retreat he had resolved to apply to the diocesan seminary. Surprisingly, our two, long-awaited and cherished dreams would separate us completely for eight years.

Making that decision to join the Jesuits was the culmination of a process that began in my heart's vague rumblings long before. They had been far ahead of the onset of the other rumblings, not so vague, of pubescence. Neither type of movement really ever achieved much clarity. But at least in the matter of a vocation to the Roman Catholic priesthood and the Jesuit order, there was a treasury of language and a careful culture that might help define what a guy was getting himself into. Not so for the other jarring developments everybody has to deal with. As late as my senior year in high school I was craving more light about what my sexuality meant. On the one hand, it was a very strong and assertive component of my physical and emotional life. On the other, Catholic teaching just about denied its existence. There was to be no positive response to it that did not risk eternal punishment. Sexual responsibility at our age meant no response. No wonder so many guys reveled in getting Newport to hedge around the subject of "how far can you go?" Hindsight gives the entire scenario a contour of humor: we were all stumbling onto life's freeway playing "chastity chicken" with transmissions that were more automatic by the day.

Even in the California of the late Fifties, the development of sexual culture and language to express it were lacking. Our less stereotypically macho companions found themselves mocked, and frequently caricatures of masculinity were championed as desirable goals. While *homo* had not yet found its milder counterpart *gay*, *manly* had already been charged with the endorphins of *stud*. In short, none of us was very secure in our identities as men. Of course, the more cognitive impulses toward self-discovery and self-acceptance were very often surprised and distracted by hormonal promptings. And through it all, guided by the hallmark humanity so long characteristic of Jesuit pastoral care, we tried to remain guided by a religious code that nevertheless was often remote, mechanical, and repressive. Consequently, crassness, guilt and even fear too often clouded our perception of who we were and planned on becoming.

And it was decidedly a cloud that accompanied the sexual side of me through high school graduation and into the Jesuits. I am now brave enough to see that life as a Jesuit at least seemed to promise a ray of sunlight, a way of controlling sexual weather at least by making sure it didn't control one's enjoyment of the day that is life. Dangerous? Damned right. If it weren't funny I would tremble remembering that I was finishing up four years of Latin and still thinking of "genitive" only as what came after the nominative case and before the dative; "conjugating" as something done with verbs, some of which were "copulative"; and associating *vagina* chiefly with a sheath for a weapon used by Caesar's army. Besides that, our religion instructors had preempted such words as "venereal" and "cupidity" as warnings. Given such negativity, it's hard to understand our sexual development in those years as anything but delayed, perhaps stinted.

Applying to enter the Jesuit novitiate entailed a long process of interviews, and a battery of psychological examinations, a new instrument the year we applied. One of the forms we had to secure was a recommendation from our individual pastor. For me that meant a trip to see Father Bernard McElwee, pastor of Saint Isidore's Parish in Yuba City. Very soon after he greeted me he got a few things straight between us.

"Well, now. The Jesuits. Sure, and it's fine to become a priest, but you don't have to leave the church, Lad."

He wasn't so keen to straighten things out when I indicated there was an error on my baptismal certificate. Dad's middle name was given as my own, *James.* When I said that it was properly *John,* there wasn't a moment's hesitation.

"Well, sure, and we can't be changing things whenever somebody comes along and says it's wrong."

He recommended me.

I soon found out that various Jesuits on the Bellarmine campus knew of my decision and one of the first to hint that he knew was Brother Thomas Marshall, the school librarian. I had told him what a pain it was to take notes and to keep track of them and he said, "Shoot. By the time you leave the Mount, you'll need a special trunk just for your notes."[26]

*   *   *

Home for Easter break, I stayed with my family in Brownsville and one day Dad and I had gone up to shop for groceries at Clyde Bishop's market. I had been wrestling with how I was going to break the news to him. I knew that I wouldn't be as gentle as he had been when long ago he *asked* me how I'd like to have Gracie for a mom. Here I was about to *tell* him he was going to have a son who was a priest So as we pulled into the driveway, I "popped the statement."

"Shit, Butch. Your mother and I have known that since you were in the second grade."

I was teaching catechism in Willow Glen one weekday afternoon when Father Morse showed up at my classroom door. Dad had called to say that Beth was hospitalized and probably breathing her last. I was to fly home. I made it in time to see her and she recognized me in what I could tell was an almost sacred moment for her. It was my first time to see how death can steal a person's face before it steals everything. And this was occurring in the building where, seventeen years before, I had first drawn breath. She died just short of a goal she had anticipated more than I had: my graduation from high school.

Now Gramma was alone. Even after the savage pain that no amount of sobbing and howling ever really relieves, I could sense the loss she experienced. But there was to be more loss. On the day of Beth's funeral, the mail brought my letter of acceptance to the California Province of the Society of Jesus—another palpable burden in Gramma's lonesomeness.

*   *   *

---

[26] Actually, because of all the magic apparatus that traveled with me, I had three trunks. Early on, I had checked out the library's sole biographical work on Harry Houdini so often, Brother once joked that I said my prayers to Houdini.

When talk of growing up turned the least bit philosophical in the Weber households, I would hear, "Do anything you want, honey. You can be anything you want. Just be sure you're happy doing whatever you choose."

Consequently, when I came into Gramma's living room somewhere between my sophomore and junior years of high school and said, seriously, "I would really like to find training somewhere to become a circus clown," I wasn't ready for her reaction.

"Oh, honey. Now why would you want to go and do a thing like that? Don't you know nice people don't do things like that?"

There was another commonly espoused philosophy in our family. "Be sure you get a good education, whatever you do. No one will ever be able to take that away from you." At least for Gramma that was another axiom easier to believe than facilitate.

My folks were to take me down to Bellarmine on the morning of August 14. A Jesuit faculty member would then take us to Los Gatos and up the hill to the "house of bread," as the novitiate was called. That would have us onsite for the next day's vow celebration and the Feast of the Assumption, a very big day on all Jesuit calendars.[27]

Gramma couldn't or wouldn't make the trip. I think her emotions were physically debilitating at that point. This meant our farewell would occur in her Yuba City home, where she had spent so much time raising me. Leaving Gramma, even to go on a trip to the store or post office, was a ritual in that home, for Pabst, Beth, or Dad. Minimally it was a kiss; if she was standing, a hug was expected. "Hey, Mister" was all she needed to say before I realized I'd forgot, turned around, and *properly* took my leave.

But that departure was abrupt and cruel for both of us. As soon as she saw me come into the room, her face collapsed into tears and audible sobs. When I started toward her chair to hug her and kiss her, she waved me away.

"Well go on. Go on! Get out of here!"

Silently, with the awkwardness of an embarrassed teenager, I did just that. I got out of there and moved on down the road to seek one of the finest educations around, become a priest, and find my life as a clown in the circus. I would become a Jesuit.

---

[27] August 15th was the day Ignatius and his original companions pronounced their vows.

6.

Hallowed Hillside

"Suscipe Domine"[28]

—Ignatius Loyola, *The Spiritual Exercises*

You don't get many chances at a replay in life, but if I had the chance, I would want to take the last stroll to the car across that backyard a lot more slowly than I did on August 14, 1957. The very space had worked important tracery into me over the best parts of twelve years. Such space served up the opportunity for seclusion, even for selective sharing. It really was a kingdom I had controlled, early on, to play priest, then to learn and perfect circus skills, and finally to secret the equipment and practice of a magician. For all three of these interests, that rambling backyard enabled a sinewy eccentrism. Happily, *center* comprises a wide social stretch, but as personal pursuits go, priesthood, circus, and magic unmistakably place a guy toward an extreme. And there on the less traveled gamut, a pattern becomes visible. All three of my pursuits entailed my directing a ritual. Such direction and the rituals I imagined demanded an esoteric training and interest most of society did not have. In both these aspects, directing and training, I was rehearsing a need to control. I am convinced it was a benevolent need. After all, it had begun in the sharing context of kids' playing, dreaming. But one day my disparate interests would find a gentle and altruistic common ground, performance as priestly. No one could see that coming on that heady summer day—not even I.

But the leave-takings would continue as a fact of life. The only constant was a road leading out of wherever I had been. My father's second family and his

---

[28] "Take, oh Lord," from a prayer included by Ignatius aligned with his "Contemplation for Obtaining Love" in *The Spiritual Exercises*, #234.

father's family had nurtured me, protected me, raised me, but in a helter-skelter kind of *here today, there tomorrow* pattern. Yuba City, Brownsville, and back. Then to Bellarmine in San Jose and back to Yuba City—or Brownsville. But that last trip from Yuba City to Bellarmine brought me into the more extensive itinerary I would follow for my Jesuit training: Los Gatos, Spokane, San Francisco, Phoenix, Los Gatos again, Berkeley, San Francisco, Berkeley, and back to San Jose. Never anywhere more than three years, a guy long whacko over the circus was being conditioned for his life as a professional wanderer.

It was a life of constant distraction. Even my goodbyes to a loving family as they dropped me off for the ride to the novitiate were distracted. Already my focus was on whatever it was I would find in this new adoptive family, the Jesuits. Of course I had early on memorized the general course of studies, and even knew some of the spicier novel aspects of ascetical training such as penitential practices and horror stories still dredged up in "spiritual reading" classics. Legendary Jesuit lore. And Bellarmine had already given me four years of a life answering bells.

But the daily rhythms of meditation, instruction, reading and work, the quiet, and the straining for whatever spirituality and prayer were supposed to feel like—those were new and challenging adventures, each capable of pulling one's attention from the other.

Everything was designed to captivate us in our first twenty-four hours at the novitiate, but probably nothing more than the ceremony of first vows the morning of the Feast of the Assumption. We had not yet seen the main chapel of the house in full light. That morning the sanctuary was literally ablaze with the altar's lighting and ranks of huge candles embedded among masses of skillfully arranged flowers and foliage. Every detail, everywhere you looked, bespoke care.

In the context of the Mass, the rector of the community would hold the host and face each "graduating" second year novice as he pronounced his perpetual vows. This was the cherished and preserved manner in which Ignatius of Loyola and his original companions had pronounced their vows. Historical continuity alone guaranteed focus, precision, and pride in the performance of such ritual. The composition of visual details and sacred gesture were nothing less than artistic.

Accordingly, there could have been no more appropriate accent to the music of the ceremony than a solo performance of the renowned "Suscipe" by the house's best tenor. This was another Ignatian tradition keyed from the founder's use of the famous prayer in his *Spiritual Exercises*.

Western theater traces its rebirth to the sanctuaries of England, and that morning there was ample proof of why such a rebirth was possible. Everything was designed to make you pay attention and surrender to the opportunity for growth. Theater at its best. Only later would I discover that the house's best tenor had been accompanied by the house's best organist: a lay brother, Thomas Carmichael, who in his pre-Jesuit days had been a silent film accompanist at the Loew's on Market Street in San Francisco. I hadn't left show business completely behind. Nor had my senses, emotions, or heart caught up to a key realization. There in chapel some of the same powerful forces were at work as those that moved Brother Carmichael's audiences many years ago in that movie palace. More important for me, those dynamics had moved me more recently in the Cow Palace. The ritual of the sanctuary, the theater, the circus, the common appeals to the human spirit. I should have got it, for God's sake: Brother Carmichael even looked like Otto Griebling.

Immediately the minute-by-minute discipline and attention to new habits, new mini-goals in the spirit of the twice-daily examination of conscience, and the work of gleaning from history the "Jesuit way of proceeding" were the appropriate tasks at hand. Methods of prayer, the very nature of distraction and its control, sensitivity to the practice of virtues—all were nonstop concerns. I was continually occupied and preoccupied. When I first became a novice I was praying for perseverance over the thirteen years till ordination. In short order I adjusted my prayerful horizons to the less ambitious two-year goal of the vow ceremony we had just seen, and then readjusted them again—to the next day. (In the film *The Greatest Show on Earth*, C. B. DeMille himself had reminded me that "in the circus, only two days count: today and tomorrow.")

That is not to say that I didn't romantically fantasize on vows and ordination. But in such reverie there was distraction in imagining the life that such ceremonies made possible.

From childhood, solitude had been an agreeable playmate of mine. And in that relationship my imagination became the most formidable component of my personality. I could dream, invent, reinvent. Making things, and making things happen, were easy corollaries to what went on in my head. I never competed nor felt the need to compete. I invented other games: not games that players fought each other to win, but games that won the players. And from the onset of Jesuit life, I was imagining the shape my life as a vowed religious would take and the creative way I would then fashion a priestly ministry. But the only creativity that seemed possible was restricted to the overarching chief apostolate of the American Jesuits, institutional education. At that time even parish ministry seemed only an offshoot of the major work. So my daydreams about my future were obsessed with how to teach well. For years, my imagined audiences were students, in rows of desks in rows of rooms, combing texts.

Utterly incredible as it seems even to me, those enticing images about my future—as a vowed Jesuit scholastic and then as a Jesuit priest—were never of a life in art, entertainment, or (heavens) the circus. To be sure I remembered and talked about the circus, to the boredom of the more mature brethren, and I was even asked to provide a magic act for entertainment on special occasions.

With superiors' approval my equipment was finding its way to Los Gatos. By the time I headed north for my studies in philosophy, most of my key magician's apparatus had found me, via the routine visits from my folks. But never once did I remotely conceive of a ministry in and through such skills. I was going to be a teacher. I didn't dare let the old hobbies tempt me.

*   *   *

Still, I jumped at every chance I had to perform in theater or to direct. And here there were conflations with the history and teaching apostolate of the Jesuits. I knew the Jesuits had developed flourishing theater in the past, but until my success as a director in the first year of teaching, I hadn't any idea of working as a priest in theater. Eventually I would own up to where most of my real energies had been directed and ask for advanced training in theater. But that was seven years in the future. And even after that training, my working concept of theater would be re-imagined.

To be sure, by the time I arrived for courses in philosophy, my interests in performance were full-bodied distractions. But at the outset, in Los Gatos, I don't recall such a problem. So if there were distractions during my early formative years and they were not from my fascination with circus or theater, what were they?

A guy training to be a Jesuit in 1957 had a lot on his desk. For one thing, he had to hurry up with his household Latin so he could ask for the pancakes at breakfast and take instructions on how to operate the restaurant-grade dishwashing machine. He even had to learn how to walk again, or at least get used to his ankle-length black cassock. Then he had to learn the customs and rules of the novice community, the general rules of the order, and the rules of modesty, including that control of wrinkles on the nose when he laughed. Okay, so we didn't get out much. And that was the point. Here we had time to pay attention to detail, physicality, gait, what we looked like, how we moved, and how we reacted. Who ever knew their nose wrinkled when they laughed? Who ever paid attention to all those muscles they now tell us are involved in a smile? Well, we did. Then my motivation was to somehow be a good religious; years later, directing actors and developing my own character as a clown, I would be seeking to reveal motivation. In either pursuit, we had to focus on the physicality we had so long taken for granted.

We had to get used to minute interior self-examination, and the careful mapping required to avoid scruple and find balanced virtue. Everything was organized and time-tested; logistics, schedules, monitoring, and skill review were evident everywhere.

And history beckoned. Not just a novice's own, but the huge collection of remarkable Jesuit chapters in history from the founding in 1534 to the present. Every centuries-old international organization has amassed a collective memory to be repeatedly revisited in the interest of the present. So a seventeen-year-old meeting up with sixteenth-century idealists led by a Basque mystic once bent on rescuing the Holy Land would be distracted. When that same seventeen-year-old watched that same band establish a renowned intellectual mission to aid a papacy in defense against the Reformation—only to be suppressed and then reconstituted by later papacies—he might even be overwhelmed.

The program itself seemed beautiful, the mechanics themselves engaging. It became obsessive to wait through the present activity in anticipation of what was to come. Anxious waiting often supplanted calm presence in the moment. I bought into every bit of the superficial mechanics and succumbed to that anxiety. I wasn't just fervent. I was a red-hot, bent on becoming a model religious to the point of contracting a fine case of religious scruples. Fortunately the master and my confessors helped me steer a manageable course.

We were systematically rotated through recreation "companies" so that we constantly interacted with everyone in a novice community of fifty. Not quite a lab, the organized leisure time allotted was ample exercise in the practice of charity, even in the lowly modicum of tolerance. There was no missing that fraternal charity was to be a hallmark of our communal existence. So were self-control, modesty and the application to assigned tasks. We had before us in assigned private reading and lectures from our novice director, the examples and admonitions of the saints, all of them—not just the Jesuit ones. Fortunately we were allowed a sense of humor about some of the bizarre extremes zealous hagiography had depicted through the centuries.

We didn't have much time to be bored. If the activities of common order in the house weren't changing our objectives, special times of the year were. When the harvest was ready in the fall, we picked grapes to support the Novitiate Winery which, in turn, was helping support our training. I hated it. I loved being outside and talking when it was permitted. But I didn't take to the physical labor of the field at all. And once I got into some trouble.

In our 1957 class there was an older man who had studied at the University of Paris and was trained in music. When one of my classmates discovered that this man knew opera, he begged him to sing "Un Bel Di" from Puccini's *Madama Butterfly*. I had never heard it before, and I hadn't heard any serious music for months. So our brother obliged. Right there in a dusty California field, he rendered Cio Cio San's celebrated song of hope. I was paralyzed with every bit of awe Puccini could have intended.

"This company will pick in silence for the rest of the afternoon."

It was the voice of the master of novices who had approached from behind us. Chastened, we stuck our heads back into the grapevines. And that evening I was summoned. The topic sentence of the reprimand was that I should either apply myself to picking grapes or I would be assigned to stay home and study. Today that strikes me as a strange penance to use while training men for life in an academic religious order. Even then I didn't respond humbly. I remember that later that night I happened to meet the friend who had requested the aria. We were supposed to observe silence, especially after evening recreation, and when we had to speak we were to use "necessary Latin." Well, I spoke first. At night. In English. Angrily.

"I got called in. Did you?"

"Of course. It used to be 'pick or pack.' Now it's changed to 'pick or study.'"

"He doesn't know how good 'study' sounds."

Making up my mind to take advantage of the elevator I operated myself, and then getting on the one that was calling me was a major moment in my seventeenth year. So was the running of that maze of interviews, written applications and tests to apply. Getting into the Jesuits, even as a novice, was a big deal. Huge. The most major step I had ever taken. So from the moment I set foot on the Los Gatos property, I was determined to excel. I was back on my first elevator, determined to get myself to the floors "above." The supernatural was made to sound as natural as every day. Notions such as *sanctity* and *holiness* were paraded before us as though they were not only accessible but right there for the taking. No "second besting" seemed appropriate especially given the Jesuit penchant for the *magis* ("more") in our service and love, and that ever-insistent *majorem* ("greater") about the glory we were to give the Creator. Bottom line: we were to imitate the saints and strive incessantly to attain their degree of perfection.

I had made the start. I was committed. I bought the promise and the packaging. But the packaging, like the buttons in my elevator, were deceptive. They were manageable; I liked to manage. It was a form of control. It would be years before I was mature enough to attain interior stillness, engage even my own internal presence, or sense my own magnetic resonances, my personal history and my place in the universe. Nevertheless I set about adopting a list of behaviors and attitudes easily identifiable as ascetic. I was actually packaging my self-image as a saint. Given the down-to-earth practicality of the Jesuits, it was easy. I ticked off prayers, mortifications and uses of silent private times that would make me holy. I took stock of my progress or failure twice daily in the characteristic Jesuit "examen." I'm not sure who else was convinced, but I was. Worst of all, I had let a misguided pursuit of spirituality distract me from whatever the real thing might have been.

I was so obsessed with timetables and goals for my growth, I tried to bail out when I didn't live up to my mistaken objectives. Once during my first year as a novice I bit a fairly dire bullet. In the course of my regular weekly colloquy with him, I surprised my novice master, Father James Healy, with "I don't think I have a vocation."

Healy's directness and social discomfort could seem cold. "I think you do." He was my superior. I was taught to accept the least sign of the superior's will as God's will. So I had a vocation.

But there was a cynical caution around. I first heard it during one of Father Healy's very own "exhortations," the daily half hour talks he would give us. He habitually referred to warnings about the dangers of losing one's vocation. The ghastly implication was always that if, after your vows, you found yourself on the outside of the Society, you had been careless. It was your fault. Other organizations had temporary vows and could admit the possibility of "temporary vocations." Jesuit vows, the first ones pronounced after two years novitiate, were perpetual. The notion of "temporary" didn't fit the equation. That problematic distinction was even the subject of a series of talks. But at the end of the last one, he uncharacteristically repeated the joke of a Jesuit wag: "Just remember, you're never really sure you have a vocation until you're six feet under in the Jesuit cemetery."

I went on with my formation. Sadly I got away with my delusional manic pursuit of asceticism for four years, until I was jarred into getting on with a Jesuit life in the real world. But for then, I carried my saintly self-packaging back into the dust of our vineyards. I picked grapes. And would pick them again the next season.

*   *   *

The chief event in the calendar for first-year novices was the making of the Long Retreat, the full thirty-day course in the *Spiritual Exercises*, which were in essence the mapping of an interior workout that changed the lives of Ignatius and his sixteenth-century companions. Perhaps more than any other characteristic of this program, the sheer variety of meditations, ascetical techniques, contemplations, and mental and imaginative experiments is evidence of its practicality. The little handbook has continued throughout more than four and a half centuries to guide Jesuits laboring to bring themselves and those they serve to God. Only now do I realize that I had been given a glimpse into the circuitry of my two elevators. Of course they both got you where you wanted to be. The "push your own buttons" one obsessing me was only one option, offering a tempo and process my life would sometimes demand. The other, "express" or "automatic" service provided an option suitable for other times, easier times when prayer and the experience of God's presence were well-nigh automatic. Ignatius even referred to "movements" in the soul. A key ascetical skill was discerning the movements of my soul and what it needed in a given situation. But who knew? I sure didn't.

For us, the first full course in *The Spiritual Exercises* entailed a talk-ridden, heavily scheduled series of invitations to meditate and pray. The program Ignatius

prescribed was as practical as it was rich. Even the times for given meditation top-
ics were specified. For years to come, like every Jesuit, I would make a shortened,
eight-day version of the program annually. I would retrace the thirty-day journey
of the full course after ordination and before solemnizing my vows. But even in
that first exposure, there were several moments when Ignatius, the novice
director, and the Spirit seemed to get my attention big time. And those were
the cardinal areas of concentration for me every time I made the *Exercises*. In
fact, they were the lenses through which I was able to see my life in ministry as
a Jesuit priest.

At the outset of the program, Ignatius proposes a "First Principle and Foundation." After stating that we are created to praise, reverence, and serve God,
he describes the other things of creation as given to us to help achieve those
goals. The third sentence in this "First Principle" struck home. The words at
once advance the Ignatian argument and explain the trademark practicality
expected of every Jesuit. "From this it follows that I should use these things to
the extent that they help me toward my end, and rid myself of them to the
extent that they hinder me."

If underground Jesuits ever needed a password to identify themselves to
each other (and so many did in times of persecution), the terse mnemonic all
of us learned from the Latin version of that sentence would suffice. It is known
throughout the order as *"tantum quantum."* Basically, insofar as something
helps, that's how much you should use it; insofar as it doesn't help, that's how
much you shouldn't use it. The first part hooked me: there was a chunk of the
world I was supposed to use, even to serve God.

One of the creatures Ignatius himself did not hesitate to use was his own
imagination. For the first day of the second week of the course, he proposes a
contemplation on the Incarnation. The word is a cold substitute for something
hot: assuming flesh. In fact, the steps outlaid for this exercise are more than
warm because they are bold. The Divine Trinity are depicted as watching
human activity on Earth from their throne on high. Perceiving the convolu-
tions of wrong choices endangering all populations, they develop a remedy.
That plan, of course, is the divine entry into human form. Only after such a
scenario is the exercitant directed to the humble interchange with Mary and
the birth of Jesus who will be the Christ. Takeaway for a wide-eyed eighteen-
year-old? Flesh must be okay. God not only made it, he wore it.

Two weeks later, before he'll let you go, Ignatius makes sure you've got the
big picture with something he called the "Contemplation to Attain Love." The
second set of considerations he proposes in this exercise truly fired everything
I had experienced before.

"I will consider how God dwells in creatures; in the elements, giving them
existence; in the plants, giving them life; in the animals, giving them sensation;

in human beings, giving them intelligence; and finally, how in this way he dwells also in myself."[29]

The principle of *tantum quantum*, the Incarnation, and finding God in all things managed to capture my religious imagination. It would be years before I realized how much those three moments of my first and subsequent treks through *The Spiritual Exercises* propelled the strange way I pursued my life as Jesuit.

When we were second-year novices I taught myself to type while transposing my notes on *The Spiritual Exercises* of Ignatius. And it was during that time that I recall imagining how I would "give" a retreat. Similarly, I went to Latin class and imagined how I would teach Latin if assigned to. Such earnest daydreams were driven by the same images that had led me to this wonderful family: the examples of the Jesuits who had taught and guided me in high school. What would I do in such a setting? How does this particular problem I am having with prayer or kindness or pride bear on what I will be like as a formed Jesuit? These occasional musings were definitely distractions about things Jesuit. But they were not yet able to be about art, clown, magic, or theater.

*   *   *

There were myriad household job assignments that became part of the novitiate life fabric. Some jobs were just for part of a day. Others were for months, positions heading up various operations such as the kitchen and dining room, the gardens, the chapel sacristy, hallway sweeping, and even the bathrooms. Either I was judged overly fastidious or too proud, because during my second year I was given the bathrooms, showers, and toilets as my responsibility. That was the highest appointment I was ever given in the novitiate.

John and Sue on a visiting Sunday, 1958

Ever so faithfully during those years at Los Gatos, my whole family, including Gramma, would visit one Sunday a month for two hours. This demanded a long trip that made the eventual completion of the new freeway down through Martinez and Walnut Creek most welcome. In the first months the Webers would even stop by Bellarmine and pick up Father Morse, so I got to see him, and they relished his putting all my newfound fervor into perspective. But I was eventually informed that Jesuit visitors were not allowed, so we no longer enjoyed his company on visiting Sundays.

[29] Ganss, SJ *Saint Ignatius of Loyola*, Paulist, 1991, p. 177.

Of course our own vow ceremony was a major event in our lives, but not nearly the earth-stopper many lay people would expect. In all such ceremonies, including weddings, the extreme anticipation itself can shrink their reality into a mainstream of context. The event itself simply accompanies individuals as they enter another phase of their lives. We had been schooled in the spirituality and practice of the vows for two years. In the sacred setting we had already witnessed twice, we said "yes."

And then got on with it. We moved to the other side of the house and began our studies in classical Greek and Latin, English literature, and history. We were now designated as "junior scholastics" or "juniors," and our side of the house was called the juniorate. But in the mental and emotional suitcase I carried to this new environment there was a stowaway souvenir: that Ignatian concept of "finding God in all things." The brave Incarnational impetus would accompany me through years of classical and philosophical studies, my teaching stint and then be reinforced in theology.

As a Jesuit, I spent years sitting in desks watching teachers' behaviors as they brought the unique favors and foibles of their personalities to bear on student management. As important as course material, these daily, year-in-and-year-out demonstrations supplied me with examples of social interchange that my childhood solitude did not. I learned from these teachers how to be with people as an adult who had passions and wanted to share them. Besides the technical apparatus I would need as a teacher myself, I learned that students even unwittingly tease joyful wisdom out of the person instructing them. The grand Jesuit commitment to liberal arts exposed me to social arts and skills I would indeed find liberating. Lecture rooms and texts provided some rich exchanges and some feisty ones. Both resonances continue to hold place in my own teaching.

My favorite professor was Father Walter Kropp who taught us Latin and Greek. Well, that's what was in the textbooks we used. What he really taught us was a teaching method which would one day ghost my own efforts in a classroom full of high school kids.

I'd guess Kropp was in his sixties when he uncovered Horace and Xenophon for us young Jesuit scholars. At first he seemed distant and grumpy. We joked that his advertised office hours were from 5:55 pm till 6 pm. (They were.) He looked a bit like Alfred Hitchcock and he knew it. I always suspected he worked at a stern image deliberately. It was pretty severe. But the first time you saw him smile, you instinctively knew why he assumed such a grave mien. Within was a huge, happy and intellectually joyful spirit. And it was a bit timid.

He only had seven of us in class. There was ample time for interaction with every student through many exchanges each session, enabling me to fantasize on how he prepared class. The texts of Horace's *Odes* and Xenophon's *Anabasis* were part of his skin; he probably didn't even glance at them. What he did figure out was a plot. If Brother X replied he didn't know the answer to a given question, what related question could he ask Brother X that he *would* know? Then he could work Brother X through the connection back to the first question's answer. And *that* Kropp learned from a contemporary of Xenophon.

I have never experienced a clearer application of the Socratic method and we were privileged to benefit from this process daily. It was Kropp's ingrained pedagogy. It was a reflex. Of course he didn't have to sit in his room and plot anything out. It was easy for him. He played at it like a jazz musician working a theme. And that reminds me: Father Walter Kropp was an accomplished pianist.

We also inherited a professor too modest to really explicate the Nurse and Mercutio's lines in *Romeo and Juliet*. His successor arrived freshly armed with his Ph.D. from the University of London and explained everything in *Othello* with such fervor and comprehension that Shakespeare began to live for me. One afternoon, this professor had a little fun at the slight expense of one of my classmates.

"Father, I thought Cassio and Bianca were meeting for dinner in the late afternoon."

"They were."

"Then why are they on their way home in the early hours of the next morning?"

If you didn't know the questioner, it was obviously a setup, but all of us knew that wasn't a trait of this young man. Judging that the rest of the class saw the delightful naiveté in the question, the professor responded in deadpan scholarly fashion.

"Most certainly they had a lot to talk over."

That faculty had a lot of fun breaking us in to what would be a long academic trek. Once we read an *Ode* in which Horace revels in the pleasures of conversing with his girlfriend Lalage in a vineyard. Later in the day I passed Father Kropp on a stairwell.

"Uh, Brother Weber. Did you suspect me of suggesting that Horace is some kind of libertine?"

"No, Father."

For all his studied sternness and reactionary politics, I think Walter Kropp had the most fun of anybody in those two years. One of the members of the class ahead of us was the bright and soon-to-be famous politician Jerry Brown. Jerry's father was then the Democratic governor of California, and everyone knew Walter was a staunch Republican. House rumor spread a story certainly not from either ancient Athens or Rome. It might have been apocryphal. It certainly had the stuff of legend.

"Uh, Brother Brown."

"Yes, Father?"

"Brother Brown, do you know the difference between the Panama Canal and Eleanor Roosevelt?"

So characteristically, Jerry thought.

"No, Father."

"Well, Brother Brown, the Panama Canal is a busy ditch."

Hold. Freeze. Then explosive wall-to-wall laughter enjoyed in the glimmer of Walter's warm smile. On visiting Sunday, the governor would show up in his limo with security in attendance and, if it really happened, Jerry would get some mileage out of such a remark. But then Pat would have probably already heard it.

Joining us for those years of classical studies were some fellows our age who belonged to the Jesuit Province of Wisconsin. They seemed to be more scholarly than we were, certainly more scholarly than I was. I always felt that they had set for us an example of how important academic matters were for Jesuits. Under the leadership of one of the "Wisconsinites," about five of us decided that we should use part of our holiday each week to practice our speaking skills. The plan was to alternate between short, impromptu speeches and interpretive recitations. Thursdays were break days from our study schedules, and all the juniors would walk four miles up into the Jesuit-owned redwood groves south of Los Gatos. The site was called Villa Joseph, and afternoons would find the five of us fledgling orators assembled under a tree.

Whether such exercises affected my later life as a performer or teacher, I don't know. Thanks to one of those men, though, I discovered a literary jewel in those redwoods, a soaring poet I would come to love. To ascribe to him the last words of one of his most famous works, Gerard Manley Hopkins was for me an "Immortal Diamond." Years after that discovery, I would escape the freezing back end of my camper at circus winter quarters and travel the U.S. singing an hour and a half of the Hopkins poems wherever I could get an audience. But back on that warm California afternoon, just the opening line of one sonnet became a powder charge. The Incarnation, and the quest to find God in all things, exploded with meaning:

"The world is charged with the grandeur of God."

There, in four stressed syllables, was all the muscularity and daring and love that has become synonymous with the Jesuit way of doing things. Of course. Hopkins had made the meditations on the Incarnation and finding God in all things all his Jesuit life. That line and those meditations became the hinges of my own youthful spirituality. But one day an even more daring Jesuit imagination and my own risks with the Spirit would engage these hinges and render them forceful springs. During theology, I would take from the writings of Jesuit Teilhard de Chardin a poetic and passionate expression of the world's own calling to be holy. Especially in his *Phenomenon of Man* and *The Divine Milieu*, he took "finding God in all things" to the limit. His development of that theme would one day help me redeem even the secular raunch of theater and public performance. I wouldn't have to run away to the circus. It would just about come to me.

During the two years of classical studies I got to perform some Shakespeare (Marullus in the opening scene of *Julius Caesar* and my dreadfully hammy "simpatico" take on Shylock, who might as well have bled when you tickled him). Lots and lots of Greek and Latin texts were spread before us, but sadly, we didn't get to roll around in Ovid's *Metamorphosis* as the schoolboy Shakespeare had. Ours was, to be sure, a chaste exposure to literature even with Bianca and Cassio. Significantly, the library of more recent and ribald English fiction was housed in a closet referred to as "the hole." You had to gain permission to use it.

                                                   *   *   *

In late July 1961 we prepared to depart for Spokane and our three years of philosophical studies. Our infirmarian, Brother "Mack" McNamara, (aka "Jack Mack" in vaudeville) set us up with the new clothes we would take with us. He was also the guy who collected the jewelry and watches with which we had entered four years previously. No surprise, then, that he found a pair of rabbit–in–top hat cuff links and steered them back to me. But he also found a pair of links with the letter *N* on them, and I was the only one who had that initial for either name. Of course they had been my cuff links. But this occasion served up a lovely little history lesson right out of Times Square about one of the "boys on Forty-second Street," another "N" in Brother's memory.

"So I want you to have these too. But let me ask you something. Did you ever hear of a guy, a straight man, named Ned 'Clothes' Norton?"

"No, Brother."

"Well, they called him 'Clothes' because he dressed impeccably. Two or three different outfits a day. And you never saw him without a carnation in his lapel. Quite a character. Friend of mine. You should dress impeccably as a professional man, Brother. But that's not my point. Someday, you'll be wearing these cuff links. If you're saying Mass, when you go over for the *Lavabo* to wash your hands I want you to shoot out your cuffs and say a prayer for Ned 'Clothes' Norton."

My showbiz yen seemed to follow me. Shortly after that reverie about the old days of variety entertainment, I discovered that my former novice master was beginning his retirement teaching folks weight control and abstention from tobacco with self-hypnosis. He had told friends he first became intrigued with hypnosis watching a sideshow demonstration.

Through my self-imposed distractions of mechanical asceticism and the wrappings of religious decorum, there were echoes, sonar soundings even in classrooms, of an entire world of my boyhood fascinations: sideshow, vaudeville, the theater and its actors. I didn't realize that in the long run, these images might have been less foreign to who I was than my obsession with sanctity. But though I wasn't absolutely sure what would become of it, a trunk load of my magic apparatus was approved for delivery to the next stage of my education.

When Dad and Mom picked me up for a home visit on the way to Spokane, the rector bragged about my recent performance as Shylock. Dad was flattered but I was startled by his imagery.

"Oh, yeah. He's quite a machine."

I never knew what he meant or what part of that he believed. I don't know why I never asked him. Most likely, such conversation seemed unimportant. I really was gloating over my Shakespeare performance, and my head was jammed with expectations of another move, the first big one as a Jesuit. Besides, the order's scheme of educating younger students in the emotional territory of literature had worked too well. My imagination and memory were brimming with an array of characters, plots, language, and downright beauty that no one in my family had dreamed. I didn't have the words for it then, but I felt removed from them.

Home we went to Yuba City where even Gramma's house seemed very small after my institutional environs of four years. Back in the kitchen I remembered so well, good stories, good food, and better goodbyes were not up to displacing the distinct effect that Los Gatos made on me. That had been the first place I ever lived continuously for four years with the same group of people challenging me and caring for me. Even though I saw my family nearly every month during that first four-year stage of my training, it had become progressively clear we were losing the contact of common interests. Jesuit community had taken the place of family. I saw my family as being closer to each other than I was to any of them. I felt that, and there was nothing I could do about it.

Then there was the promise of a new horizon, even as a Jesuit: more studies, but in a discipline I could only feebly imagine. Out of state for the first time, I would be traveling to eastern Washington for a three-year residency in Spokane. There would be the chance to meet other young Jesuits who came from different provinces and different regimens.

Gramma and I handled this farewell warmly and gracefully, but it was expected and therefore less dramatic than when we had last tried to say goodbye in that kitchen. Then Dad and the family drove me fifty miles down to Davis to catch the train my Bay Area classmates were already riding.

We rode north into Oregon where I truly felt haunted, if not pursued. In Portland we had to transfer to an eastbound train. There were odd sections of Pullman and flatcars on side spurs in the yards. Long silver cars bore the lettering *Ringling Brothers and Barnum and Bailey Combined Shows.* They were playing their annual Portland date. It was just a parked train. And how I wanted to park. Guilt, longing, even confusion all fused to lessen my enjoyment of a fresh salmon dinner as our train wound through the Columbia River Gorge.

We went right through Cascade Locks, where one day I would have to rush a trapeze artist to the village hospital for oxygen. By then, I was a Jesuit priest running a circus. Perhaps only now, from the vantage of a quieter time, can I appreciate the real journey that train ride began.

The Royal Lichtenstein Circus characterized itself as a circus that talked to you. How it talked. What the audiences heard from us could be vaudeville humor, magician's patter, conventional announcement, dramatic narrative, poetry, and sometimes, from me, outright social commentary. It wouldn't be too much of a stretch to say that a university student seated at our show, say at Purdue, Yale or the University of Utah, might think of the show as the most colorful lecture on campus that day. I remember overhearing students talking in the student union at the University of Utah once. "Hey man. You going to that circus outside at noon?"

"Yeah. What's that all about anyway?"

"It's pretty cool, man. This dude's really funny—talks about everything. Even teases the Mormons."

We did talk about everything. And it was hard, risky work. Most people can learn the physical conditioning it takes to effectively produce enough voice to be heard by hundreds of people even outdoors. They can learn the repertoire of postures effective oral interpretation calls for. But before they undertake such physical projects they have to muster the courage public address demands. The desire to be heard is not enough; the initial power to dare such exposure is required. In a circus ring at high noon, wearing clown make-up and tights, a guy reciting poetry is exposed. As an adolescent actor and magician, I had achieved only a feeble approximation of such power. I was always afraid of exposure, never free or calm enough to really perform.

With that train ride through scenic northern Oregon, I unwittingly began a six-year stint of conditioning for strenuous public performance. In my early twenties, I found in the course of Jesuit philosophical studies a new transparency about the nature of thought and learning. There was an establishment of self possible because I learned about learning, understood my own understanding and took my first steps as a stage director. More than revelatory, these moments of growth were a call to ownership of talent and responsibility for gifts. My talent and my gifts. Then, during my mid-twenties, I was given several years of exercises in which I was expected to reveal who I was to varied audiences, and helpfully respond to their responses. At base, that's what teaching demands, no matter the subject matter. There is probably no more demanding a teaching environ than five classes of senior high school boys a day. Knowing who you are and understanding what you know, get ample room to dare transparency. The goal? To encourage similar light and daring in your students.

Usually the three years of philosophical studies and the three years of teaching, the so-called regency period, are considered separate stages in Jesuit training. Those six years, however, were an integrated training period during which I discovered and rehearsed the skills enabling most of my professional life.

7.

Discoveries

"There are more things in heaven and earth, Horatio,
Than are dreamt of in your philosophy."
—Shakespeare, *Hamlet*, I. v. 166-7

Mount Saint Michael's, the Jesuit seminary for philosophical studies in suburban Spokane, was an academic adjunct of Gonzaga University downtown. Our class arrived simultaneously with Father Tim Fallon, a young professor who had just completed his postgraduate work in Canada. He had been a protégé of the distinguished Jesuit philosopher B. J. F. Lonergan, whose comprehensive analysis of human knowing, *Insight*, was to become our textbook. That work lent Tim his twin battle quests: "self-appropriation" and "the pure desire to know." Tim made sense for us out of Lonergan—and just about all else.

How readily we yielded to Tim. Everything about him commanded attention. With height, good looks, wavy salt-and-pepper hair, and a carriage and posture that masked his ample girth, his sheer physical presence dared you not to encounter him. It helped, too, that he was younger than our other professors. Late thirties. But more than any of that, he was confidence itself. He was a preeminent metaphysician in his and Lonergan's sense—he really did "know what he knew."

He could express himself elegantly, clearly, and, if need be, bluntly. Besides, he was so much of what I was not that I'm sure I held him at a shy arm's distance. Some of that distance was still operative years later when I was stationed in the Jesuit Community at Santa Clara University, where Tim was a professor of philosophy.

At the Mount, the project of our curriculum was simple. We came at centuries of philosophy both historically and through each distinct discipline. Simultaneously with our march forward from the Pre-Socratics, we were working our way through the developed disciplines of metaphysics, cosmology, philosophical psychology, natural theology, and epistemology. Of course the long-held goal of the Church was to equip us with skills needed for an intelligent interpretation of the myriad and disparate data we confronted in the universe of thought.

At least that was the plan. All these systems of "making sense," however, were camps of thinking very content with their own insightful campfires. They seemed incapable of communicating with each other even to share recipes for the most important menu item, the earthy stew of ethics. They weren't talking to each other: materialists, formalists, idealists, existentialists, nihilists, phenomenologists all laying claim to whatever realism might be. Lonergan focused on the mechanism underlying all of the systems: *how we know.*

History is replete with philosophers who sensed that the problem was in the area of perception, how the raw data underlying theories are known. Lonergan seemed most seminal, however, in setting forth the findings of contemporary science bearing on how we perceive. With his guidance, the study of knowing, epistemology, became the key to how we evaluated most of our courses at the Mount.

There was a course we were subjected to early on which we relegated to the category of "lightweight" among its graver neighbors on our transcripts: logic. The classical training in careful argumentative mechanics was meant to discipline rhetoric. We hated its aridity. However, from this vantage in my life, it is hard to imagine either the reputation of the Jesuits or their trademark approaches without the rigor of logical dialectic. The scalpel of the syllogism uncovered "undistributed middles" and "false givens" and the protection demanded for legitimate "majors" and "minors." The Latinisms *ad hoc, ad hominem, reductio ad absurdum,* and the possibilities for double effect, equivocation, and mental reservation, were all the terrain of our elemental logic course. But it was a cold, spare landscape, so I'm glad we explored it in the more verdant and populated countryside of the chief philosophical disciplines.

As any real student of philosophy reading those last few paragraphs can tell, I did not become a whiz at this stuff. But Tim led us through the entire complicated haze of those syllabi, and passionately gave us the key takeaways: the factors interfering with objective knowledge; the distinctions between system and method; between myth, mystery and metaphysics; and respect for the noblest drive of the precisely human endeavor, the desire to know. Those themes became so reflexive that even I could hang onto them.

Of course my predilection for performance art continued to compete with any impetus I might have had to study formal philosophical disciplines.

Happily, there was a tradition of theatricals at the Mount, and a real, if spare, auditorium to house them: Bellarmine Hall.

We were always doing plays, sometimes fresh ones, published but still running on Broadway (think Allen Drury's *Advise and Consent*, and Paddy Chayefsky's *Gideon*). Sometimes I directed and sometimes I was an actor. I even got to out-strut Father Newport when I played Cardinal Cajetan in John Osborn's *Luther*. As a change one year, I decided to pull together a variety show. I grew to love that format in the days of Ed Sullivan and our similar productions during high school in San Jose. Such a program ensured a large cast, a potpourri of acts, and plenty of entertainment. Because our formal title for each other had by this time shifted from "Brother" to "Mister," our show was titled *Call Me Mister*, with an obvious nod to the Ethel Merman blockbuster *Call Me Madam*.

We had a glorious array of talent. Everyone knows that Jesuits are at least a bit hammy, but many of them are also very skilled in performance art. So there were pianists, vocalists, comics, two magicians (a classmate from Oregon joined me), and dramatic monologists. Three of the Italian guys revived a wacky musical bottles act they had framed years back in Los Gatos called "The Stringbini Brothers." They used old wine bottles filled to different levels with colored water. When they had unveiled the routine in California, our *Aeneid* teacher, Ray Kelly, opined, "Well, at least we found a use for Mogen David wine."[30]

The show came off without a misstep. The pacing was right, the performances on their marks. The rector asked me how I managed to produce the largest man in the community from a shoebox house we had visibly built onstage. So I told him.

"Every magician has a favorite girlfriend, Father." Believe me, that got his attention. "Mine is Miss Direction." It was the truth.

The first full-scale drama I ever directed was Chayefsky's take on the biblical legend of Gideon. It demanded elaborate period costuming and even singing. The form was partly that of pageant and we had an extensive cast, including fellow Jesuits who were years my senior. Those weeks of rehearsal honed my abilities to coach actors and block scenes. But probably the key reflex I began developing with *Gideon* was a penchant for organization and schedule. Ever since, I have never undertaken a rehearsal period without a detailed timetable in hand.

Whether performing or directing, my efforts in the productions of Bellarmine Hall were key to what was emerging in my soul. There was a confidence curve developing and a readiness to imagine a possible ministry in the performing arts. The idea of asking for a specialized training in theater began in that bare and sparsely appointed theater.

---

[30] In his pre-Jesuit life, Ray was one of the Disney illustrators who worked on *Fantasia*.

I had a happy brush with commercial show business during my stay in Spokane. This occasion refreshed my confidence and curiosity in an area largely neglected during my early studies as a Jesuit. The circus came to town. Not just any circus, but "the Big One," Ringling Brothers and Barnum and Bailey Combined Shows. For some reason I had decided that this might be a chance to meet one of my favorite performers, the brilliant German clown, Lou Jacobs. So I approached the rector. That I had such forward determination amazes me now. It must indicate how weighty such a contact had to have been. Though I had only seen Lou in person once, he had been in my heart for years. He would always be there.

"Well, I can permit you to meet the gentleman, but I'm afraid the "Rules for Scholastics" stipulate that I cannot give you permission to see the show."

I found out subsequently that the wording is something like "*Scholastici spectacula non adsunt.*" If there ever was a *spectacle* it would have to be the Greatest Show on Earth. But I had permission to meet Lou.

It wasn't easy. I left word for him at the box office, and he kindly extended the possibility of a meeting during the show's intermission on a given date. But the Ringling management was not into handing out complimentary tickets to fans. So I had two problems: discovering the intermission time and gaining access to the building. The first solution was easy. I would just show up during the performance and wait (the end of course justifying the forbidden means). The second solution required bravery: to merely walk in the backdoor looking like I knew what I was doing. Since I wore a Roman collar, someone might have misjudged that I *did* have a reason to be there. And so it was that I and a companion from the class behind me walked along a line of elephants, all trunk-to-tail awaiting their cue, and found our way into the arena.

Directions to the men's dressing room were forthcoming, but it was clear that we were about to see "spec" (short for "spectacle"), the traditional major parade and display before intermission. There we were, poor scholastics trapped into witnessing the most spectacular component of the spectacle at which we were not supposed to be present.

Then we resumed our mission and purposefully walked into a large concrete-walled changing room chaotically jammed with guys manhandling the expensive and demanding details of their wardrobe. At one end of the enclosure the clowns stacked their prop crates to demarcate the traditional inner sanctum of clown alley.

And there was Lou, sitting in front of a trunk. He had taken off his cone-head prosthetic, a signature component of his famous makeup. He looked like he was waiting for us. There was an immediate interlocking of eyes, mine probably hungry and uncertain, his hesitating, puzzled. I wasn't ready for the husky hint of his German accent.

"Mister Veber?"

"Right, Mr. Jacobs. Nick Weber. This is my friend, Bill. Thank you for taking the time. I'm a great fan of yours."

In retrospect, I'm convinced he did not anticipate the clerical garb. But there is a sense in which I'm glad we were dressed the way we were. How readily this legendary performer could span culture, idiosyncrasy, age, and profession just to greet another human being. He had to come through his own Judaic ethnicity and greasepaint and around our celluloid collars. That seemed as indicative of skill as his contortionist's ability to fit into the smallest of the midget clown cars. Since that first meeting, I have felt that Lou's power to reach huge audiences as a silent comic was in part a function of his gracious outgoing warmth as a person.

Sometimes beginning is more important than wondering where to begin, so I began. "What is circus life like now that it's all buildings?"

"When we verk, it's fine. You know. No verk, little paycheck." Again, the hint of German playing with the w's. There was also just a hint of a naughty boy's smirk. He was implying a complaint about routing such a big show only to towns that had large indoor arenas. More time was spent traveling, less performing. It was only six years since they had played their last tented dates. "But it's a good life. Yah. Still. Ve used to say, when der sun shines, and der flags are flying and dere is green grass—no better life.—Hah. Now never any flags, and no grass. Hah."

"How long have you worked on this show?"

"Almost forty years. Some better, some vorse. All pretty good. Now my own train compartment. Could be bigger. I came from Germany as a contortionist kid, yah? But don't want to be contortionist in der house. Dat's for little car in act."

We talked about "the business" of circus a little and I gushed, very much the fan, over two of his most celebrated routines. There wasn't much time. Only to connect. There would be several more meetings "down the road." A dwarf clown was sitting on his trunk adjacent to our huddle with Lou. He couldn't take his eyes off us. To this day I imagine the panic that could very well have telegraphed through clown alley when we left: *Oh, God, Lou's getting religion.*

In 1962 Lou Jacobs was in his late fifties. A few years later he would be featured on the circus commemorative postage stamp. Years later he would be among the first inductees into the Clown Hall of Fame. He had left Germany in his late teens and joined out with Ringling in 1924. After that meeting in Spokane, he would spend nearly thirty more years on the Ringling show before retiring without a pension. He was eighty-nine at his death.

So the circus continued to distract me. And it was not unknown what an attachment I had to a world most of my brothers knew nothing about. I cannot remember where I was when I heard that John F. Kennedy was assassinated. But I can remember returning to my room at the Mount the morning of January 31, 1962, when a classmate asked me if I knew of some performers who went by the name of Wallenda. He brought sad news: the day before in Detroit the troupe had fallen during their signature high wire feat, that marvelous pyramid I had seen as a kid. Two were killed and one was paralyzed for life. They had left Germany to join Ringling four years after Lou did.

Spokane and our three-year stint in philosophy were expansive in many dimensions. For most of us it was the first time we lived out-of-state and we were introduced to the traditions of Jesuits from other provinces. It was the beginning of our access to a large open library, even though many of the volumes we needed in our work (like Kant, Nietzsche and Schopenhauer) had a prominent "H" above the call number. Such works were on the Vatican's Index of Forbidden Books. Reportedly the "H" stood (I'm not making this up) for Hell, and you had to have permission from the rector to read them.

Spokane meant our first private rooms as Jesuits. The building was huge and the rooms were spacious. Quiet and concentration were possible in a new way. But so were private conversations and a degree of honest interpersonal exchange we had not known with each other.

Probably the brightest man in our class was from the Midwest. Significantly, his own relationship with Tim Fallon brought me closer not only to our professor, but to a better understanding of what he professed. Gene became a treasured friend of mine who probably saved my life in the most important of manners.

He laughed. Even when I knew he was down, his loud guffaw when I least expected it would jump into whatever break there was in a conversation. Anybody can be down and angry. Gene was so bright he could find humor everywhere. He respected Tim as much as any of us but he had long ago owned his own smarts, so he didn't share our fear of a professor who really did cherish us and the religious order we were growing up in. And through Gene, I managed to climb farther up Tim's pedestal so I could at least hear better.

There was a goofy mode Gene would allow himself, almost as our class jester. He was tall, and except for his demeanor, he might have been imposing. His eyes often told a different story than the smile or smirk on his face; wheels weren't turning so much as frequencies humming. Even the bulbous shape of his head's backside gave off a cerebral vibe because he wore his hair very short except on top. Today he would seem like a military recruit or a football player. And he had the slightest overbite that showed off a prominent set of teeth whenever that guffaw opened him up.

Everybody loved Gene. He was bright, jovial, generous, and gregarious. Open. And as far as most of us knew he loved everybody. But by the time our own paths crossed in our first year, depression had tried to straitjacket a charming free spirit.

Once Gene came to my room to borrow a playscript and when our predictable revisit of his own drama waned, there was a silence. Such moments were never awkward with Gene, because you knew his brain was just shifting gears.

"What do you really think of Tim?"

"I'm not sure what *really* implies."

"You told me you respect him. But you never say anything in class. And when you and I talk you never volunteer his name or anything that has come up in class." And then he managed about as much self-assertion as he could only to have his humility transpose it to a question: "Don't you think he's the best professor we have?"

I hadn't rated the faculty exactly. "Well, he might be the brightest, even the most articulate, but the—" I thought I was caught. What more relevant characteristics can a professor possess?

"You're so cold. He's also very human you know."

"As in?"

"You respect him too much. As in *whole* and, I guess *honest*. Nothing real is off the table."

"You're sure? How do you know?"

Uncharacteristically, he broke eye contact with me and then almost visibly forced out what he really wanted to say. "In class he just said the right amount about subconscious motivation so I made an appointment and went in and unloaded this depression mess of mine on him."

Gene had sought out Tim for healing. He had learned, and would teach me, that Tim was much more than a philosopher or professor; he was a wise, caring man with a generous and disciplined spirit as large as his body. Our professor knew more than we realized outside his professional field of philosophy. He knew some clinical psychology, and he was honest. You could ask him anything, even in class, and he would be frank. If you were off the subject, you knew it immediately. But if you sought honest insight, he was your man. And he strenuously and patiently helped Gene pull himself through. My sense was that Tim could love Gene in a way that rescued him. They were both intellectuals. I don't think I have ever known another friendship that was so balanced and restorative.

Gene was already an academic, a very acute young historian. So he was in a position to locate and contextualize just about everything, including the philosophical developments we confronted in Tim's classes and my feeble probing in the world of theater and dramatic literature. Because he knew so much about where ideas came from and how they related, he could be fearless, and I owe him a good measure of my own intellectual confidence. Without his input I would never have risked letting Freud or the existentialists into my thinking. And I certainly would never have understood such stuff.

But more important than the heady content and catty chatter of our times together, Gene turned my head around in a way that only he could. And that's how he saved my life.

"Why are you doing this?"

"Doing what?"

"Talking necessary Latin. Keeping silence. Ignoring people who really like and respect you. Cutting yourself off from what's human around here. That 'good Jesuit' stuff. Why?"

Silence. I had no answer. I didn't know I had made myself a caricature. Almost instantly, though, I realized I had transported all the mechanical baggage of ascetic discipline that virtually haunted Los Gatos to a much more open house of studies. Moreover, I was justifying this self-imposed and restrictive template with my conviction that I was "keeping the rules." He didn't let up.

"You have a keen, challenging, and creative mind. You must keep it engaged. You must. That's why you have it. And that's what is really Jesuit. You are depriving yourself of the oxygen of an intellectual life. Stop it."

In high school, I had found enough Jesuits who truly cared for me to recognize in their number a stable and coherent family. That's a large part of why I entered the order. However, inside the family, it took five years to find in Gene a peer who objectively loved me enough to chew me out.

My family visits me in Spokane, 1962

Eventually Dad gave me a chewing out as well. By the end of our second year at the Mount we had completed four years of undergraduate course work and were to graduate with our bachelor degrees from Gonzaga University. It was a non-event for me and many other Jesuits. We were very aware of the years of study ahead and somehow ordination seemed the important milestone. So my casual mention of the upcoming ceremony in a phone conversation provoked some paternal ire. "Jesus Christ, Butch! Why didn't you tell somebody? You're the first one in the family to graduate from college!"

*   *   *

Because the Oregon Province geography included Washington, Idaho, and Montana, summers found us traveling to help with the Jesuit-sponsored religious education programs on Indian Reservations. We served the Coeur d'Alene, Blackfoot, Flathead, and Northern Cheyenne Reservations. Not just everyone has had the privilege of working and playing and eating with Native Americans in what of their homelands are left to them. My suspicion is that the Indians helped sensitize me as a servant of society.

One evening before sunset in Heart Butte, Montana, my little band of Blackfoot kids took me on a journey up a hill to show me some discoveries they had made. Roughhouse and chatter subsided at the side of a three-foot-high boulder. Granite, I guessed, and nondescript—except for the splattering of blood at the bottom, close to the ground. Wide eyes turned on me with an unstated command: *Ask us what it is.*

Days before, a young officer in the meager village police force had been dragged to death behind a horse up this hillside. The next morning those kids had found his blood where they thought his head struck this rock. And five yards farther uphill, his wallet, then a shoe, his watch, and finally, him. All I saw, after the blood, were the carefully memorized places, respectfully walked around, each bearing the tell-tale marks of hooves and disturbed grass. There was nervous kid-chatter and the tension of large-scale wonder. I was halfway down the hill before I realized I had just walked the most moving Stations of the Cross in my life.

But by the time that hit me, I was surrounded by kids racing in all directions, hiding behind rocks, aiming bows and arrows and rifles at each other with a ran-dom enabling perfectly credible pantomime, only to fall and scream accordingly.

"What are you guys doing?" I am really dense.

"Playing Cowboys and Indians. Whaddaya wanna be, Mister?"

I laughed myself into a hysterical soupcon of memory and re-warmed acad-emics. How readily these little guys would have welcomed the drunken jokes the Gravedigger brought to Ophelia's grave in *Hamlet*.

Of course the long-ago tutoring of Father Bob went with me anywhere there were kids: sponges changing hands, thumbs coming off, safety pins separating illogically. But there was a problem. I needed more tutoring, this time in cultural differences. Unexplained effects demonstrated in the context of even an artistic ritual could be magic in a far less innocent sense than in a theater. Moreover, these kids knew that the guy doing the "minor miracle" was a religious of some degree. Of course every good professional stage magician is an actor. In mainstream U.S. culture there is no such thing as a magician. There are only actors playing the roles of magicians. But there, in that situation, I had to be careful.

The simple old sleight-of-hand ploy effecting the removal of the top part of one's thumb was my first clue that there could be a problem. Usually if a kid seeing the trick has seen it before they give it away as soon as you call attention to your thumb. If they've never seen it before, most kids immediately recog-nize it as a trick and file it with "magic," laugh and get set for something more. Not these kids. The "wow" expression on their faces was serious. Even con-cerned. Even after the thumb was revealed intact. The trick was on me. I had to help them recover. There had to be merriment. Without realizing it I drew on a device from logic class, the *reductio ad absurdum*. I began a mock crying fit, jumping up and down in fake pain, and screaming every time I brought my perfectly healthy thumb up to a stupid expression on my face.

Then they got it and began laughing at me instead of worrying about my powers. There had to be a signal that these little slips into the fantastic were indeed light. The key was my ability, sans makeup and costume, as a comic of the circus, to invoke the clown. Somehow he was harmless in his guileless statement that he, too, was just an actor. Only now can I appreciate what a fortunate mix I had trucked with in my childhood: magic, circus and theater.

And religion. Here, too, the work on the reservations served as vital education. Heart Butte had long enjoyed the rough-edged ministry of a Jesuit pastor. He gave out gruff love, and he was cherished. He didn't know it, but he taught me the radical dimension of Jesuit ministry and the two-way resonance of faith and fidelity, faithfulness to the faithful.

It was all in a story from his past. Because of economic hardships and lack of staff, some fellow Jesuits manning similar missions farther east in Montana had received the provincial superior's approval to close their missions. They delivered the news to their brother priest in Heart Butte. He remained silent.

"Well, you're coming with us, aren't you?"

"Like hell I am. Who you think's gonna take care of these Indians you've been baptizing out here?"

Actually, I never completely left the Indians either. Of course they would always be in the affection-laden areas of my memory. But I got back to them years later. Dave Myers was an Oregon Province Jesuit in my class who became a lawyer. He has given his life to fight for Indian rights all over the country. He was one of those friends who came forth in 1971 when I put out a call for help finding places to take a very special circus. A year later found us playing our way through Idaho and Montana on seven different reservations and I got to see my old pals again. Of course they were older then and some of them had little ones—and a real live circus to take them to. It was so easy to let them continue teaching me over the years. I will never forget pulling out of Saint Ignatius, Montana one night. I had been so very proud that the evening show displayed our tutu-sporting bear. But the kids running alongside the van were shouting, "Will you bring the monkey again next year?" After all, monkeys really are *exotic*; they come from a different place. Those children could see a bear around the corner—maybe not wearing a tutu.

*   *   *

During those three years, we philosophy students developed new muscles and immune systems in all manner of ways. Mentally, emotionally, and even physically[31] we surpassed our earlier self-imaginings. We grew up.

---

[31] It was during this time that my fellow Jesuits began teasing me about hair loss. I honestly didn't take them seriously. I had always had a full head of blondish hair and it was even a bit curly. Then one wintry day I leaned against a drainpipe. When my scalp almost stuck to the metal I was jolted into the realization that there was no insulation on the top rear area of my head. That was the part I couldn't see in the mirror.

I knew that much of my own psychological and intellectual growth had really been germinated by Gene. It wouldn't have happened otherwise. I left the Mount convinced he had given me a large part of my life. Years later, when the circus came through the city where he was teaching, he would always take time off to drive me out into the countryside or to a scenic park. On the way back, we would stop at some tavern where he would have a beer and a shot and I would have something lame like a bourbon and seven.

"I have to be careful with this stuff."

"Don't we all?"

"Since all that depression at the Mount, I now have something serious. Found out I'm a diabetic."

I didn't know enough to ask what type, but he knew enough about his condition to be wary of "spells" that would send him into a seizure and a hospital room. There had been several such events. Emotionally, however, his teaching work filled him and bouts of depression no longer crippled him.

But as years passed, Gene seems to have begun medicating himself with alcohol. I was as shocked at his nonchalance about denying drunkenness as I was disappointed over his carelessness. "Maybe I'm just a harmless drunk after all." Not to me. Not to himself, either. But among his fellow Jesuits, including his superiors he was considered an alcoholic and a severe threat to himself, especially because of his diabetes. Eventually he was admitted to his province's infirmary as a diabetic with serious alcohol problems.

Continuing examinations eventually revealed a longstanding brain tumor. But it was too late for successful surgery and the world lost a magnificent person.

*   *   *

There were lessons even I was able to hang on to from our studies. In most cases they are almost an automatic readiness to make a distinction in just about any context. I would not discover until many years of conversations and books later how characteristically Jesuit making distinctions is.

One distinction I have found invaluable in its application to very different areas of life is that between *method* and *system*. They are no longer vague words I can use interchangeably and they apply to programs affecting most dimensions of my life. All of us use and are used by some kinds of systems. In some instances, they often seem absolute, unchangeable—until they don't work or they set up conflict with other systems. There was a fine example of such a systemic clash that appeared at Mount Saint Michael's the year we arrived.

In the winter of our first year at the Mount, someone unwilling to read the decidedly non-Latin writing on the wall got Pope John XXIII to sign an apostolic constitution named *Veterum Sapientia*. It required all seminary philosophy and theology lectures to be given in Latin. That should have been no surprise to anyone observing an institution that had been using Latin *system*atically as its official language for centuries. Some of us had been studying Latin for eight years and speaking a piggish "code Latin" (as distinct from proper idiomatic use of the language) for four years. The *system* seemed logical: all over the world, the same language was used in worship, in study, and in official communication.

The problem was that the life of such a huge institution had managed to embrace far more than the life of early Rome. Nationalism and native language ensured clearer understanding and judgment on weighty matters. Most churchgoers didn't know a word of Latin and so it was an apt and predictable joke that first shed light on the dysfunction of the Latin liturgy.

"Isn't it beautiful. No matter where you go in the world, the Mass sounds the same."

"Isn't it horrendous. No matter where you go in the world, no one understands what's being said at Mass."

A growing number of clergymen didn't understand Latin and they certainly couldn't speak it. Many bishops could not read official Latin documents typical in the workings of church government. Nor could they speak or write in Latin. And of our six professors, only one persisted in lecturing in Latin. One compromised by beginning each lecture in Latin and then continuing in English. He finally judged that was unsuitable and gave up the Latin. It was the tail end of the Latin crisis in the Roman church. The system no longer worked. How to find one that did. Or was it too late?

When the search for a new system is pursued honestly, one enters the realm of *method.* The question has to be asked: What was the old system attempting? That question is almost analogous to the common Microsoft choice "Up One Level." Simpler, more focused mechanics must yield to the wider, more abstract examination of goals.

Our professors in philosophy had come frustratingly face-to-face with the difference between system and method. The revered use of Latin was historically recognized as an attempt to efficiently communicate on vital matters. For a host of social, scientific and political reasons, communication in Latin no longer worked as well as native languages. *Systematic* enforcement of its use was crippling. *Methodical* examination of the historical choices and objectives for which the Church had embraced Latin revealed criteria and goals: effective arteries of communication. These became guides to the discovery of a different *system.* Eventually, given an abundance of adequate translators, indigenous languages proved superior in seminaries, offices and especially worship.

This view of method as a needed governor in the pursuit of alternative systems has enlightened and facilitated parts of my own administrative journey repeatedly. Contemporary pop-psychology adapted for hectic officials coined "thinking outside the box" as an effort to discover resolutions. I never did convince a principal

I worked for that the slogan is only clever and not automatically effective. Folks trying to think "outside the box" are nevertheless thinking "in reference to the box." A safe investigation must rise to a level where the box does not exist. Perhaps then, for the first time, how the box was even made will become fresh valuable data. My admittedly accidental choice of the circus as a working performance method might be illustrative: if anything, circus is an embracing dynamic that can include most performance art. In its light, what I was doing with theater and religion became almost tangible.

Another takeaway from my studies in philosophy, illuminated by Tim Fallon, was a triad I have found very helpful in distinguishing levels of perception that govern behavior: myth, mystery, and metaphysics. In this context, each word has a definition precisely framed in the light of human knowing. So this application is not completely aligned with the way we usually understand and use the words.

Myth is understood to be the unknown unknown; one doesn't know that one doesn't know what one is talking about. I usually draw a simple example from my childhood home. My family was convinced that you should put a silver half dollar in a sauté pan with fungi because if the coin did not turn black they could be judged safe to eat. Given the amount of mushrooms we ate, it's a wonder I'm writing this. There is nothing scientific behind such a belief, but we thought it was absolute. We had no idea we didn't know what we were talking about.

The Greco-Roman myths so frequent in classical literature are not so clear an example. What is clear is the definition of *myth* in this context. Insofar as the Greeks believed there was a Zeus with various bedroom adventures that explained the universe, a Zeus legend would be a myth: the believers did not realize they didn't know what they were talking about. If they knew clearly they were making up stories to explain what they didn't understand, a Zeus legend could be seen as signifying a *mystery*. The key is what the knower knows or doesn't know. Shakespeare's audience in his own time and ours lets him throw all sorts of gods and goddesses around knowing full well they didn't make his plots happen. They are rather like "secondhand mysteries."

What is indeed the *mystery* in Shakespeare, and the theater in general, is a powerful force driving the human need for such rituals. In the drama, I allow characters and a plot, with or without classical allusions, to stand for important human interchanges that I recognize but know I do not fully understand. That puts the theater and all fiction squarely in the realm of *mystery*. I consider myself fortunate to have struggled with the charged psychological stew such mystery-making demands of individual actors and ensembles. In that I don't really understand what makes for "finding the truth" in a line or scene, rehearsal and performance itself are truly dances of mystery. For me, this is no more clearly expressed than in a tiny scene Marc Norman and Tom Stoppard penned for the film *Shakespeare in Love*. Joseph Fiennes as Shakespeare is in panic mode because the chorus for the opening of *Romeo and Juliet* is stammering with fright. Even as the "two households" are being described onstage, Shakespeare reveals his own terror to another actor.

"We're doomed."

"No. It will turn out."

"How will it?"

"I don't know. It's a mystery." Cue theme and the prologue begins and, sure enough, works itself out.

Finally, my ability to write such stuff about "such stuff as dreams are made on" leads me into full-bore recognition of what I know, or the known known, and that is *metaphysics*. I don't spend enough time at this level.

* * *

At the Mount I had almost no reason to reflect on such matters. I was inexperienced and unfocused. But somehow the importance of our drive to know, the difference between method and system, and the distinctions between myth, mystery, and metaphysics stuck. That I owe to Father Tim; that I paid attention to Tim, I owe to Gene. Both of them prepared me for a central discovery in the next stage of my journey, the power of knowledge not just communicated, but so passionately seated in the history of a young person's consciousness that it can be celebrated. With such dreams I hopped a train to Saint Ignatius College Preparatory in San Francisco.

* * *

Fool: Dost thou know the difference, my boy, between a bitter fool and a sweet one?
Lear: No, lad; teach me.

—Shakespeare, *King Lear*, I.iv.130-32

The problem was that when I started teaching in 1964, I didn't have passion. The fire in my childhood belly, show biz and performance, had been doused with inactivity and the antacid of scholastic priorities. And in the array of academic helpings served up to all young Jesuits over the first seven years of their training, there was hardly anything ever on my plate that would even heat up a passion; forget fire. I was no philosopher. I was mediocre in Latin, and more mediocre in Greek. And though Ben Jonson would have considered those paltry linguistic skills as qualifiers for a kinship with Shakespeare,[32] I was certainly not equipped to take senior high school boys through four of the Bard's most famous tragedies.

---

[32] Jonson, an early rival and contemporary critic of Shakespeare, famously remarked that the Bard was equipped with "little Latin and less Greek."

All young Jesuits knew the moves. Many of us had been in the order's classrooms for eleven years, including high school, college and graduate programs. That was a substantial parade of teachers initiating us into dozens and dozens of disciplines. Admittedly, some teachers were duds. But most of them we loved, and early on some of us wanted to join them. In most of those disciplines so many of us remained only initiates. Fortunately I brought to my apprenticeship teaching deep affection and respect for some very inspiring Jesuit teachers who instructed me along my way.

Teaching is above all an act of love. Of course that's where the passion comes from. Once you fall in love with your material, you really have to find the way to risk loving your students enough to do the work of sharing what you love with them. That's exhausting. And it's scary as hell when you're starting out.

Thanks to my department head's enormous amount of organization there was minimal time required for syllabus planning. Teacher and the kids already knew from the assignment schedules what stuff we would be covering. Education took place when the voiced drama of question-and-answer, repetition, and coaxing care *un*covered the veins of value in those schedules. And you didn't have to have a graduate degree in theater to know that "voiced drama" includes heated argument, jokes, one-upmanship, cajoling, apologizing, laughs—and sometimes, tears.

The kids and I sat at Shakespeare's feet together, they for the first time, their teacher for his third and fourth. Together we read *Macbeth*, and *Hamlet* and *Romeo and Juliet* and *Othello*. Sometimes moments of discovery were nearly mutual. We also did *Beowulf* and Chaucer and Wordsworth and Keats and Graham Greene—the gamut of British literary monuments. Lightly. Cursorily. It was high school. And we joked and fought and argued and—as when our popular varsity shortstop had to have a leg amputated—cried. A few skills were learned, a modicum of content gleaned and retained, and a lot of truth uncovered in spite of all of us.

The hearty and stern aphorism "practice makes perfect" couldn't find handier testing grounds than the classrooms of a young Jesuit's first year of teaching. I had for a principal a guy who knew his way around Jesuit high school classrooms. In a response to the oft repeated request for new video and audio teaching aids, often the provenance of today's I.T. person, he famously replied, "Mister, pick up your textbook, grab a piece of chalk, and by damn, get in there and pitch."

So we went through the motions, practiced, and practiced some more—"repetition is the mother of learning" (and what a *mutha* she can be with up to five classes a day of the same course). And, by damn, we pitched.

For me, my "pitching" even took on the varsity mound. I had a lot of skilled athletes from a range of sports because of an unimaginative scheduling ploy known as "double English": the same class first and last periods of every day. (In other words, the administration didn't know what to do with these kids. So we made the best of it.) The pitcher was a star, had personality ample for about five guys his age, and kept his classroom neighborhood entertained. He was not a scholar and I wasn't much of a teacher, so we got along. One day when I came into the classroom, he was exceedingly animated and had his quarter of the room in chaos. Without hesitation, I grabbed the teacher's wooden chair by the back, aimed the legs at the kid, and virtually charged him. "O'Reilly, back! Back, O'Reilly! Seat now. Seat O'Reilly! That's it." And as he quieted down and righted himself back in his desk, "Good boy!"

They were all clueless of course. But they were in their desks and quiet except for the very loud expressions on their faces, which screamed, *Where in the hell did that come from?* We all froze for about thirty seconds until the teacher couldn't hold it any longer. And when a smile began to relax my mouth, we all dissolved into a great laugh. Horrors. There was a famous dictum preached to young Jesuits beginning their teaching careers: Don't smile till Christmas. As a standard for classroom management it was bunkum. First, it was unhealthy for all involved; second, it deprived the students of a sizeable chunk of their instructor's personality. Besides, is reading say, Chaucer, with a sourpuss really reading Chaucer?

Surprisingly, students are human after all, and they are most curious about other humans. So block a kid's access to the riches of what your life has given you, render yourself just the guide to a library or a search engine, and you've lost a student. Irrelevant as it was, I had just let O'Reilly and his pals into one of the happiest settings in my memory: the Clyde Beatty Circus. And just maybe I had begun to admit to my pedagogical arsenal one of my most compelling weapons: my devotion to show business, especially the circus.

Those kids only saw a guy imitating a lion trainer. It was totally out of place but somehow relevant, and it worked. They probably didn't know of the famous lion trainer who made his fierce students recite in a dusty tent twice daily. But *I* knew of him and his circus and all that was then much more alive in my makeup than Chaucer or Wordsworth or, well, Shakespeare. Once I allowed that piece of me into who I was as a teacher, life was easier. It was all right to view the classroom sessions as performances, mine and the students'. Perform we did.

And we laughed. Oh, how. Especially in that "double English" arena. And the best jokes were on me, generated from my (honestly) inadvertent setups.

Because San Francisco is topographically circumscribed, it is really a small town. So the kids knew all the various districts by heart: the Richmond, Nob Hill, the Sunset, the Fillmore and Cow Hollow (including the Webster Street neighborhood's red lights), the Mission, Twin Peaks, and on and on. So one day, in discussing a British poem, we encountered an unusual compound noun

describing a field's wintry white cover: *hoarfrost*. I had defined the word before
and I was banking on their remembrance that it just meant a very white frost.
Whether they remembered or not, when I asked what *hoarfrost* meant, one of
my jokers volunteered with a fiend's straight face: "A cold morning on Webster
Street?" We didn't laugh; we screamed our amusement. It was deft, and it was
keenly performed. Most importantly it had a lot to do with what we were
doing: honing language skills, rehearsing the verbal acrobatics that are, for better or worse, historically associated with Jesuit education.

But at least once, all of us got into some rather sweet trouble over laughing
at a joke. Same bunch, but it was that last boring period on one of those muggy
fall days only San Franciscans know and dread. Their fog has turned on them.
So we were all down, dragging our wits behind our attention spans, and my
star pupils were cross, restless, and beyond climbing the walls. They were
papering them. I made a hesitant move to start and achieved not a dent in the
overall din. Finally I shouted, completely innocent of malice aforethought a
line such as playwrights prize. Into a classroom of rowdy seventeen-year-old
haphazardly horny males, I bellowed, "Keep it down, I know it's hard."

Stunned paralyzing silence for about a count of three. Then the finest explo-
sion of laughter I have ever experienced, first from them, then from a humbled
me as I walked to the chalkboard and drew a huge checkmark for them. Or me.
Who knows? We laughed and laughed some more and then we settled down.
But just as we started to focus on a bit from Shelley, the windows on our north
side rattled with a hearty male chorus loudly intoning, "Mr. Weber! Be quiet!"
We had been checkmated in humor. American History students one floor
down, all positioned at their windows, had been allowed to echo our enthusiasm. Of course my students wanted to retaliate once we had all figured out
what happened, but we did get down to business of a more bookish sort.

*   *   *

My Jesuit world had been even more exciting than I had ever anticipated it
would be. It enveloped me with an identity and strenuous work that left little
time or energy for awareness of other worlds, other work. For eight years,
while I was Jesuit-ing, Doug had been just as energetically pursuing his dream
of ordination as a diocesan priest. During that time we had no contact with
each other. Surprisingly, our respective preparations for the priesthood had
separated us. More surprisingly, we both welcomed the possibility that I could
be the subdeacon at his first solemn Mass. Since the diocesan seminarians
didn't have novitiate or teaching stints in their training they were regularly
ordained sooner than Jesuits. I still had five years to go. But by the end of that
first year of teaching I had minor orders and was allowed to "anticipate" the
order of subdeacon. Neither of us were prepared for how we found each other.

I had just completed the repetitive, if exciting, work-a-day drill all teaching entails. Doug had not only finished up his course work in theology, he had just undergone the heavy ordeal of preparations and ceremonies for the subdeaconate and deaconate orders. We were both tired. He looked the same to me but my baldness amused him. We joked about tonsure, one of the minor orders involving the clipping of hair. Although he was concerned with the sung parts of the next day's liturgy, I was startled at how unprepared he was liturgically. In a sense, we were both victims of the ecclesiastical time. The new constitution on the liturgy developed by Vatican II had been out only a year and besides rumors, not a lot of official adjustment had come our way. Whether it was fatigue or history or both, Doug knew we both had to depend heavily on the seasoned priest who would be his deacon the next day.

"Maybe we should do a sideshow in Gramma's backyard," I joked.

He was his cautious self. "I guess we knew what we were doing then. Do you still eat fire?"

"Not if I can help it. My students sometimes think I *breathe* fire."

"Of course you're in touch with Father Morse."

"Sure. Your ordination is a big deal to him, you know. We'll see him tomorrow, I hope."

We made it through the solemn Mass and then he rode off to his first parish assignment and I returned to complete my years of Jesuit teaching. It would be over thirty years before we saw each other again.

*   *   *

In the late fall of 1965, I was accosted by a wolf. Actually she was a wonderful creature. Jean Wolf was the first in a long list of wonderful women, agents of mercy every one, who would come forth wherever I was doing theater. They would help me pull together the mass of practical personnel and materiel resources invariably needed whenever a production was on the horizon.

So it was, amid the discussions about a possible musical for spring 1966, that dear Jean suggested *Oklahoma!* Even though I had only seen the Gordon McRae/Shirley Jones film and needed lots of study on the show, we launched it, along with audition schedules, rehearsal schedules, Jean's costume designs and the selection of support staff. Phil Kelsey, a senior who had composed the previous year's musical, came on board as our vocal director; the school's pep band conductor would be our musical director; a young dancer I had never met before answered our call for a choreographer. Joe Specht, another Jesuit scholastic a year ahead of me was our technical director. A sharp business-minded scholastic in the class behind me, Dave Klein, handled the show's publicity and fiscal matters. One of the English IV students I was trying to lead through Shakespeare's own plays, Mike Figoni, very capably constructed the sets.

Luckiest of all of us was the stage director because I got to spend three solid months with a rich milestone in the history of the American theater and one of the most unabashedly lyrical scores ever. There can't be a more agreeable environment in which to develop the skills you need to direct a musical. It's all there, and so artlessly logical from beginning to end, you are surprised to discover the parts for the success of the whole. It's as organic as that opening haze and that morning's busy breeze.

I had to learn plenty about music in the theater, and Phil was such a fine teacher. I learned the conventions that pull it all together. I learned how to ask for an edit or a vamp. I learned how to refer to numbered measures and the so important detail of a dialogue cue above a vocal staff telling the orchestra when to start an intro. But those were just the mechanics that make a show work. What it's all for? The objective? Learning that was one of the most magnificent experiences of my life and it took five minutes.

Phil knew he had a teaching moment. (All developing teachers must learn to recognize them.) One night I was rehearsing some of the leads in the first floor auditorium while he worked with the chorus upstairs in the band room. At one moment I noticed Phil at the rear of the auditorium, politely waiting for a pause to get my attention and when he did, he whispered, "When you take a break, could you come upstairs? There's something I want you to hear." Fearing a decision might have to be made that I was unqualified to undertake, I nevertheless agreed to come up. Upstairs he welcomed me and placed me in the center of his forty or so singers garnered from among our own students and four of the Catholic girls' schools in the city. They were all on their feet as he sat down to his piano.

I don't think I had ever heard harmony of more than four parts in my life. And I had certainly never paid attention to it if I had. But that seven-part arrangement—developed on a train ride from New York to Boston in March 1943 for a worrisome show being called *Away We Go*—demolished me. The full chorus arrangement for *Oklahoma!* is so grand it solved the problem of that long ago wimpy title and gave its name forever to the show itself. Little old Mr. Weber was sobbing in the very center of the room surrounded by the sweet smell of that " wavin' wheat" carried by wind coming "right behind the rain." I think that Richard Rodgers knew as well as his sidekick and first-time partner, Oscar Hammerstein II, that eventually in the number not even the singers were going to be able to hold it together. So when they set "Yeow! Ayipi-oeeay!" to a full-out melodic yell, everyone would get an excuse for a full-body push, physical enough to buy a tiny comic break for everyone's emotions. And after that, through my own tears, I was convinced our *Oklahoma!* was "doing fine" and everything would indeed be "O-K!"

Not that we didn't have our share of struggles. After a very clumsy first run-thru I gave the cast customary director's notes, including some that didn't disguise my passions about what I knew we should be achieving onstage and were not. There was an emotional silence afterwards as tired performers and crew members pulled themselves together and prepared themselves for a few "fix it" reruns. Sitting next to me was our tireless and faithful set captain, Mike Figoni. In the quiet darkness he put his rugged Italian face right in front of mine and described my feelings exactly: "S-l-o-w-b-u-r-n." I wouldn't know for some while after his graduation how well he'd figured out *Hamlet,* but he had me down.

The show opened strong and played gloriously. On cue, my supportive family came clear into San Francisco for a performance, and Peter Devine, our Curly, surprised all of us by having the house manager pin a corsage on Mom when she arrived in the lobby. Afterward, at a late dinner, there was another surprise. When I asked him if he'd had a good time at the show, Dad made a confession. "Hell, no! I cried through damn near half the thing!" We were at San Francisco's classic and classy Fior d'Italia restaurant, a long way from Oklahoma. And what I'd just heard was far removed from the Dad I knew best.

Carefully, I pried a little. "Why?"

"Well, what did you have, maybe sixty young kids up there?"

"Seventy-five counting orchestra and crew."

"So you turn damn near a hundred good looking young kids loose on us, singing and dancing over music like that—and you don't think older people are going to get a little emotional?"

I was too immature to get it. Now I know. Forty years later I directed the show and at a dress rehearsal, a very talented Curly didn't get through his first eight bars before I was a wreck.

*   *   *

Oklahoma! was locked in our hearts as a grand musical land we had belonged to for three months of talented labor. Not for nothing did Phil our vocal director go on to Harvard to become the accompanist to their famed touring glee club during his freshman year. The Aunt Eller, Jean's artistic daughter Kate, was perky and graceful and pretty, and would return one day to teach on the faculty at Saint Ignatius. Our wonderful "Curly" also joined that faculty where he would teach a future luminary on the horizons of Broadway theater and international opera, Bartlett Sher.

And me? I finished my second year as a Jesuit scholastic teaching at Saint Ignatius. I had found my footing in the classroom, on the rehearsal stage, and on an outside first-floor kitchen windowsill where I had to sneak in after late-night rehearsals downtown. Father Minister didn't give out house keys to scholastics.

And I had raised some administrative temperatures. Once, when ordered by a presider at the altar to throttle two kids who were talking during Mass, I resigned from moderating student liturgies. Then there was the matter of some seniors whom I had failed in their last semester. That would automatically require them to come back to summer school in order to receive diplomas. (At graduation they would get empty covers.) The principal was not happy. Oh, my. I yielded to the principal's assertion that he could and would change the grades. But I told him if he did change the grades he would never get another grade from me again.

I don't know if he changed the grades, but I never submitted another grade to him. I was transferred to Brophy College Preparatory in Phoenix, Arizona for my third and final year of teaching as a scholastic. This was very unusual and very serious. Trembling, I made an appointment with the rector-president of the school. I told him I needed to get an answer from a knowledgeable superior: "Was this a disciplinary move?"

He assured me it wasn't. "You haven't heard about this because we've been fighting it with the provincial ever since it came up."

All my fellow California Province scholastics knew I was being transferred, and among my Jesuit classmates, I had good friends at Brophy. I felt comfortable about the reception I would get in Phoenix—until summer vacation. I shared that I really wanted to do the hit musical *Oliver!* at the school. There was a mighty balk and a very scary round of "You'll never get our kids to sing and dance!" They persisted even though they knew how popular *Oklahoma!* had been. Brophy had never done a musical. Ever.

I continued to prepare not only the script and score for the musical, but material for a couple of classes of English II and (surprise!) Latin IV. The literature for the sophomores was a potpourri of selections and, par for the course of Jesuit secondary education in the sophomore year, Shakespeare's *Julius Caesar*. The Latin students were expected to work their way through Virgil's masterpiece *The Aeneid*.

I met Phoenix in August and welded myself to the air conditioners in my room, my classroom—everywhere. For a long while if there wasn't A/C I didn't go. But I gradually adjusted. And the kids adjusted to me. They were so different from the Saint Ignatius kids. They seemed more approachable. (Probably the Saint Ignatius kids had rendered *me* more approachable.) And they were every bit as friendly, truthful and eager as the San Franciscans.

There were laughs. Again. As we finished discussing a Jack London short story in a very bright sophomore class, this little wiry red-faced kid in the back raised his hand and asked, "Mister, do you know if London ever read any Nietzsche? He sounds like he has been influenced by Nietzschean philosophy."

A loaded silence gave way to my own laugh. "Kid, I can't even spell *Nietzsche*!" Then the kids laughed with me and so did my questioner. That student,

Tom "Chip" Sheridan, was naturally academic and went on to become an oft-published research anthropologist. His family and I became very close friends.

Again, I recognized that unless a teacher is vulnerable and somehow lets students get to him in the best of ways, that teacher foregoes the benefit of a very strong teaching dimension: relationship. Teaching is nothing without that.

My new principal and I tussled over a change of syllabus I had arranged with my sophomores. They came in one day early in the first semester and announced disparagingly that their speech teacher was going to take them through the famous soliloquies of Shakespeare's *Julius Caesar*. This was pretty standard procedure in Jesuit high schools. Study a play in English; do the soliloquies in speech class. But I knew that Father Speech Teacher wasn't really up to doing Shakespeare justice, and worse, he was really jumping the gun on us since we would not be starting the play for months. Like hell I was going to take them through that tragedy after he'd assassinated the great speeches. So I told them we would take *Hamlet* instead and assured them they would be able to handle it. Because they were going to be "special" their spirits lifted. Then, one day in the hallway crush of class changes, someone grabbed my arm. The principal's face was in mine. "I really have to insist you take *Julius Caesar* with your sophomore classes."

I held his eye and quickly replied, "Give me seven reasons." I have no idea where those words came from. But I knew no such reasons would ever come forth, and he released my arm and walked on into the crowd. We did *Hamlet* and had a ball.

The fall play was Archibald Macleish's Pulitzer winner, *J.B.*, a modern retelling of the Job story. The work is in verse, and I have long wondered whether Shakespeare would have written it had he been an agnostic of the twentieth century. It would be risky trying to surmise how much of it our audiences comprehended. (Hamlet might have said it was "caviary to the general,"[33]). The kids in the show learned a lot and I gained plenty of new friends to lay the groundwork for *Oliver!*

But there was still resistance to the idea of a musical. One night, I found myself sequestered in a heavy conversation with two close student friends of mine, Peter Martori and Vic Prosak. Respectively, they had been the Mr. Zuss and Mr. Nickles in the Macleish play.

They led with, "Are you sure you want to spend time on this?" and off I went.

I had already spent months researching and designing the show. My defense, provoked by constant objections from them, must have gone on for half an hour. Suddenly everything changed, even their bodies. They seemed to relax, and then for the first time, they looked at each other and smiled the smile of

---

[33] II.ii.425-26.

conspirators. I didn't relax until one of them said, "We just wanted to make sure you were absolutely determined to do it. We didn't want to have you back out on us!"

All the bills were paid in advance and we opened to terrific reception. It was a complete sellout. But most important of all, Brophy College Preparatory now knew it could do musicals. And my great pals among the scholastics readily understood why one night I returned to the dinner table shaken and tearful after taking an urgent long distance call.

It was Phil in San Francisco. "Mr. Weber, there's something I want you to hear!" Home on spring break, he had mustered all the cast of *Oklahoma!* to sing *that* number on *that day*, the first anniversary of their opening. Try forgetting something like that.

The stuff that a typical college prep was helping kids process and appropriate into their lives, was summarily described as "the humanities." And the too often unspoken objective was to cultivate better persons through contact with the peaks of human endeavor that had been achieved in the past. That was the trail education had pursued for centuries and at least around so-called college preps, still is. In the English syllabus, from Chaucer's Prioress through Shakespeare's drunken gravediggers, knights, and sober-but-ridiculous clowns, to Dickens's Mr. Macawber, and Evelyn Waugh's Mr. Joyboy, laughs have earned their keep as sublime humanizers.

So have tears.

It was not easy to come to the end of my formal teaching stint without remembering how it started. Phil's phone call, jarring the memories of my start in San Francisco evoked earlier images from a time when students showed me the way. And the rugged directness of an Italian football player—with his diagnosis of my "s-l-o-w-b-u-r-n"—holds the foreground, Michael Figoni. After graduation he seemed to sympathize with the very visible culture of the hippie movement for awhile and then broke my war-resister's heart by enlisting in boot camp for the military. But one of my treasures is a handwritten letter postmarked from a U.S. training base. It closes with "But don't worry boss. I have a copy of *Hamlet* under my mattress!"

Very simple, easy words about a play he knew was complicated about the hard stuff.

My three years of teaching had not been simple or easy. They were supposed to be something of a trial, a test, a way to demonstrate to yourself and your order that you had what it took. Before you were approved for theological studies, the aptitude for intelligent work, emotional stability, and religious dedication had to be apparent. My teaching stint was unusual because it was completed in two very different cities and student cultures. And I was unusual with my penchant for performance and the theater and some forms of show business my students would never experience. Where it counted I guess I was usual enough. In the fall of 1967 I began my three years of theology at Alma College, four miles southwest of where I had begun my Jesuit training ten years before in Los Gatos. But I returned to the area with two convictions: I had a right to stand up and say who I was; and that was my professional responsibility, as a Jesuit and artist. Without knowing exactly where those coordinates would take me, I had finally developed a grounding for my life in and around performance.

8.
Studying God

"You are a priest forever"[34]
—Psalm 110, 4

Nestled between two lakes and surrounded by redwoods and vineyards, Alma College, like Sacred Heart Novitiate, was an academic adjunct of Santa Clara University. It also was the last academic stand for most California Jesuits prior to priesthood. That was where the Jesuit priests I knew, including Father Morse, had made their theological studies. I spent ten years getting there, and my graduation gift after this three-year course in the science of God would be priesthood in the Jesuit order of the Roman Catholic Church. That would be in June 1970. I knew the date. I knew the details of the preparation. I knew how long I had anticipated this goal.

And I spent the entire three years in theology distracted.

Nothing new there. What was different was the source of the distractions. In the past, the mere mechanics of the training process so fascinated me that I had often missed the substance of my formation. Too much of the time I was lost in externals, focused on what a Jesuit as religious teacher would look like, and forgot to concentrate on what a Jesuit could *be*. Fortunately, Gene picked up on that at the Mount and set me on a healthier path. But by then I had long been wired to seek out what was easily controlled, and the external mechanics of any program are ready clay for a controlling hand. But at Alma College in 1967–1968, and then in Berkeley after the province moved the theologate to the north side of the University of California campus, my distractions were not about even the trappings of theology. They were from a hangover.

---

[34] Spoken in the Rite of Ordination.

Okay. I didn't go directly from Phoenix and my third year of teaching to Alma College and my first year of theology. With my superior's approval I "cashed in" one week of my mandatory vacation on an artistic orgy in San Francisco. In seven days, I saw nine different plays at the American Conservatory Theater. It wasn't easy: I *had* to go twice on matinee days and I *had* to choose among the twenty-seven different plays they were offering. It was the end of their first season in residence in San Francisco and what a season it was.

But part of the blame goes to Phoenix. After directing two shows at the Mount, and the success of two musicals at Saint Ignatius, the Brophy College Preparatory community, Jesuits, students and parents, allowed me to gain the emotional footing I needed. Otherwise I wouldn't have dreamed of asking for that A.C.T. binge in San Francisco. For the first time, I seriously entertained conflating my life as a Jesuit priest with my love of performance art. With the success of *J.B.* and *Oliver!* and an impromptu student Shakespeare festival, I had finally admitted to myself that somehow theater was to shape whatever my ministry as a priest was meant to be. Here was an arena in which my hankerings as a performer met the academic and social configurations that circus could not. Moreover, I knew there were Jesuits working in this art as there had been throughout history. I had asked and received permission to pursue graduate work. There seemed to be buzz about my artistic passion among the provincial's consultors and I would soon receive official encouragement to seek an apprenticeship with a New York director. So during this stage of my training I had contracted a very different strain of distraction.

Nevertheless, with my classmates, I tried to dive into a curriculum that self-consciously and carefully laid out for us the current issues and accepted commentary involving sacred scripture. There were also dogma classes in which we reviewed the doctrinal positions of the Catholic Church including the bases for its own authority. And we were guided thoroughly in the applications of both scripture and dogma as they pertained to the celebration of the sacraments and pastoral care. But it was a struggle for both professors and seminarians. What had been troubling murmurs about doctrine and practice had by now become strident calls to revisit every room in the comfortable mansion of the Church that had been our home. In the late Sixties, the Church was still finding—even *fighting*— its way to a faithful embrace of the *aggiornimento* John XXIII had in mind in calling for Vatican II. Paul VI had just published his startling encyclical "Humanae Vitae" and almost every member of our faculty was outspoken in his surprise and alarm. At the Mount we had found ourselves in something of a running battle between traditional scholasticism and the more modern approach of Lonergan. Now in theology we recognized the need once again for methods of discernment as distinct from rote systems. But Lonergan wasn't quite available to us yet with his *Method in Theology*, to be published in 1972.

This course of studies met us in the late Sixties. It met us in California. It met us just an hour south of the Haight-Ashbury in San Francisco. Beyond our lakes, our redwoods and the few miles of country road that separated us from what would become Silicon Valley, society itself was in a maelstrom of discernment about the most vital reflexes it championed: community, sexuality, religious belief, social production, government. Probably more than any other catalyst maintaining the fire under this social stew was the Vietnam War.

So I wasn't the only one distracted. Talk about theater. The Free Speech Movement flexed its muscles in Sproul Plaza at the University of California, Berkeley, while the Students for a Democratic Society championed a younger rethinking of civic political icons.

Our class arrived on the peaceful campus of Alma College to find that we were, precisely as classmates, political units. The traditional appointment of a senior scholastic representative by the superior had been abandoned. The three years of students were now viewed as a democratic entity that elected not only a president but class representatives. I became representative of my class for 1967–68.

Sorry about that, guys. We were college graduates, Jesuits preparing for master's degrees in sacred theology. Some of us were working simultaneously on graduate degrees in our fields of specialty. We were preparing to be priests, Jesuit priests—and you elect me? I am no academic. Never have been, never could be. Yes, I can talk and I can persuade. But I can also be persuaded for the wrong reasons. Yes, I can argue, but I have a usually silent temper (that "s-l-o-w-b-u-r-n") and my argument can suddenly deteriorate into blind and vain stubbornness.

That's what I should have said, but instead I agreed to represent my class and set out to do the best I could. I only remember that I didn't do very much very well in the arena of petty politics. Thankfully, there were more fruitful endeavors at hand. They were distractions, but they were positive and creative.

Somehow I discovered a public appeal from the Santa Clara County Council of Churches for theatrical presentations to be part of the January Week of Unity, an ecumenical celebration. By the end of January 1968, I had created for the Council of Churches a unique theater company, the Council Players. The concept was that of a traveling group of actors presenting plays in various sponsoring churches. These plays were to be chosen with the intent of provoking reflection and discussion in "talk-backs" after the performances. The very kind, brave and imaginative County Council director, Reverend Ken Bell, had put me in touch with John Rose, an Equity actor and director who had relocated from Manhattan. As our first project, John directed three other local actors and me in Christopher Fry's magnificent *A Sleep of Prisoners*. The staunch and creative verse drama, set in a church being used as a wartime prison was more than timely. Our moving and convincing production almost perfectly fit the sanctuaries we played. Discussions were as animated about the issues underlying the text as they were about the concept of our company. What we heard was encouraging enough to convince the Council and the artistic staff to continue with other productions through the spring and summer at least.

I became the executive producer and would also help direct. My superiors were most supportive. I'm not sure the theologate staff had any advance notice of my success in theater work during my teaching years, but I was surprised at how readily administrators helped accommodate my needs. I needed a car to get back and forth for rehearsals in San Jose. The company needed a truck to haul scenery once a show began playing its weekend dates around the county. I needed an account in the treasurer's office because I was banking stipends for our work and paying expenses. To the credit of my courageous superiors, the project took off and continued throughout my theology studies, even after we moved up to Berkeley in the summer of 1969. Eventually, the company, still connected with the Santa Clara County Council of Churches, would become "Council Players, Inc. d.b.a. The Royal Lichtenstein Circus." All of that was launched because our rector, Father Richard Hill, a distinguished canon lawyer, was willing to risk a guy's setting out on a creative ministry.

Joe Specht, from the 1966 Saint Ignatius College Preparatory production of *Oklahoma!* was in the Alma College community a year ahead of me. Joe generously spent hours constructing a heavy duty electrical board with power feeds, dimmers, and a patch area. He also helped me fabricate dozens of spotlights from humble seal-beam lamps whose sockets we mounted onto #10 cans with gel clips. We built heavy standards out of galvanized pipe for mounting the spots. It was all homemade, but it functioned well and it moved. Now there could be blackouts, cross fades, and general area lighting anywhere we needed such effects.

There was an open meeting to call for production help. Thae Murdock came to us with the generous offer of her skills as a seamstress but we soon discovered she was also a very capable business woman and personnel manager. Before long, as is the case with most of us who ever worked in community theater, she was doing something of everything. Importantly, she would introduce me and our unusual apostolate to her husband, the Reverend Bart Murdock, rector of Trinity Episcopal Church. Between Trinity and the First Unitarian half a block away in San Jose's Saint James Park area, we always had rehearsal, work and storage spaces.

Fellow scholastics pitched in as both performers and needed crewmen. Making use of what equipment and personnel we could attract, we pursued a repertoire that included an original take on *Everyman*, Edward Albee's *The Zoo Story*, *The Fantasticks!* and the original west coast production of a pair of one-acts by William Hanley, *Mrs. Dally*. It was our production of the William Hanley piece that became my master's thesis for the San Francisco State graduate program in drama.

Besides my work in that master's program, I had also been studying a less formal dramaturgy developed by a brave band of performers in city parks: the San Francisco Mime Troupe. Out of California's heady festival and political soupcon of the Sixties, came audiences and artists ready to support a theater directly addressing popular cries in the most accessible spaces. *Commedia dell arte* characters infused the texts of Moliere with topicality, and original compositions ignited conversations of the day, even of the hour. As a ritual, it was a medium bent on replacing itself with immediacy, even in its deployment of theatrical trappings. It was as low-tech as the street theater Shakespeare may have seen as a boy. The Mime Troupe could arrive, play, and relocate to another venue with considerable facility. I took careful notice of the lightweight pipe-framing holding simple backdrops, and the posh seating a lawn could afford an audience. Inspired by this model, the Council Players mounted summer revues to present in San Jose's city parks.

David Robb with the Council Players in front of the State Capitol, Sacramento, California. 1970

There were two of these, programs of variety sketches, some with outrageously blatant political satire, innocuous vaudeville, musical numbers and my circus tricks of balancing and fire eating. The first of these was "The Menthol Mousetrap," with an obvious nod to *Hamlet*. The second was "Slower Traffic Keep Tight," which our friend Father James Straukamp booked and presented on the capitol lawn in Sacramento in the summer of 1970. This production and the fact that it was able to travel that distance suggested the more ambitious touring that would be realized in the Royal Lichtenstein Circus. And in Jim's generosity and encouragement, cast after cast of the circus would find an unforgettable host, friend, and guide.

Nevertheless, I was in seminary, specifically a Jesuit scholastic pursuing his theology studies just prior to becoming a priest. There were mountains of material I had only heard about. The Old Testament was largely a blur; revisionist interpretations of the New Testament origins were compelling but technical. Some of our faculty were brilliant lecturers. But I could sense there were professors who had almost been frightened from lecturing by more scholarly students who wanted a reading and seminar format. I wasn't scholarly enough for the seminar approach. I needed lecture. I

couldn't be trusted to read and analyze on my own. I needed a teacher to entertain me with what he knew. I think that need had been there since sophomore
year in high school when the eye injury effectively removed me from regular
honor roll performance. The smarts were still there but I was distracted from
the careful work of a real scholar. There was more to do and it was all asking
me for my time. Daydreaming about teaching in my early years as a Jesuit, theater directing and acting at the Mount, and now my supercharged memories of
high school teaching and current directing and producing details—there was
always something more active and romantic to siphon my attention from the
books.

I did okay, but I never felt secure. I knew I wasn't on top of the issues. I
could articulate problems; I knew I could not lay out the history of the church's
answers to those problems. My strength was in "people stuff," the pastoral
areas. I could talk to people. History had always eluded me so the time differences between the oral traditions and the subsequent transcriptions that gave
us our scriptures? In both testaments I was one confused puppy. No surprise
then that I aced my "ad audiendas confessiones" exam (nicknamed "ad auds")
for hearing confessions. No surprise either that Angela Lansbury cost me a
"retake" for my scripture finals.

Father Morse had gotten tickets for *Mame* with Angela in the role she created for Broadway. We were to see it in San Francisco at the Curran Theater
where we had seen Mary Martin in *South Pacific* years before. I was ecstatic.
Too ecstatic because the ecstasy was misplaced. First of all I should have studied better. More conscientious guys were huddling together in groups to prepare. It was no secret what the material would be. It didn't help that the exam
was the afternoon of the very day of the performance.

Secondly, *Mame* never was and never would be *South Pacific* or even great
musical theater, no matter who was in it. It's what one comes to recognize as
derivative music. And in a theatrical driven by music, if the music is derivative to
the extent that the listener can always guess the next phrase, then everything in
the show that depends on the music is predictable. The show seemed mechanical. I remember leaving the show convinced that, given those dancers, I could
have choreographed the show in an eight-hour day—and I am not a dancer.

I am also not a scripture scholar and came home to find a note in my mailbox
that I had to retake my final. So I settled down, prepared, and did fairly well.

The *"ad auds"* consisted in an oral role-playing exam in which four of my
professors would take turns "going to confession" to me. I was sweating canon
law, pastoral technique and case studies for weeks. Except for the myriad loop-
holes and legal technicalities, I felt reasonably prepared.

And after all that, what nearly finished me? A saint, a child, and a deaf guy.
It was very clever and I'm sure there were people in the house who had been
given the same "problem cases," probably by the same professors.

I was expecting deficiencies in the area of the Commandments. In came a saint who was disturbed that she was distracted at prayer. A child felt guilty because she had angry feelings toward her brother. And the deaf guy screamed out the formula "Bless me Father..." and then screamed out his sins. I was all set to counsel—every neophyte pastor is all set to counsel. Forget it. I couldn't touch the material he had confessed loudly enough without breaking the Seal of Confession.

I was by no means the type about to be upset by distraction at prayer. The saint's problem was a call for me to enter into her experience. There it was, and it was very Jesuit—right from the *Exercises*: always take your strength from God's presence; through every possible distraction he never leaves you. Return to that presence. And let yourself feel loved.

The kid? Assure her of her goodness just because she wants to be better. It wouldn't hurt her to remember what she feels like when she thinks her brother is angry at her.

So I got through those. Then the deaf guy. I was absolutely stumped. I mentally raced through the scenario over and over, imaginatively switched roles with the guy, and could just about feel the second-hand sweep on my watch.

The examiner knew his game. He shouted, "What's that, Father? I can't hear you. Can you talk louder?"

I don't think he sent me the cue deliberately, but there it was. I had to talk, and I had to talk loudly. Kiss off the counseling. God does it all anyway. So I screamed back, "That's a good confession, now. For your penance say one Our Father and one Hail Mary, and now make a good Act of Contrition." As soon as I began shouting the formula, all the heads of the examiners generously nodded their approval.

The most creative was a "kid from Santa Clara University." The professor was a very bright and imaginative man, well-liked by everyone, but I didn't know anything about him except his reputation as an inveterate counselor and a character. I did know enough to sense that he would appreciate a creative "penance" for his confession, so I was laying for him in a way.

The confession started with the usual formula and the mention of some fault or sin and then got to the "heavy material."

"Father, I am really troubled about whether to receive communion tomorrow. It's Pentecost, I know. But I'm not sure I have a right to receive."

"Why?"

"I'm confused, Father, about what that sacrament is. Ever since Father X brought up the distinction between the historical Jesus and the Jesus as Christ in the Church or whatever, I don't know what it is I receive."

"Do you respect or trust Father X?"

"I think he's full of shit."

I'm sure the professor was especially playing to the conservative moralist on the board. I was stunned, so there was a pause.

"Do you *want* to receive communion tomorrow?"

Immediately the other board members began enthusiastically nodding, very much like jazz musicians encouraging a soloist to "work with it, work with it."

"Very much, Father."

"Well, that's what you must run with. The sacraments are given to us to be used, and if you think you will be nourished by receiving, go for it. Don't worry about understanding everything clearly. Okay?"

"Sure, Father."

"Good. And for your penance—do you read the *Chronicle?*"

"Yes, Father." I had the professor's full attention.

"For your penance, I'd like you to look at today's "B.C." comic strip and spend one or two minutes just thinking about it."

My professor was so amused he forgot he was a tentative student in confession. His reply was hardly that of a penitent; it was the acceptance of a challenge.

"All right, I *will*."

Smiles all round. Home free.

I did well. And I enjoyed the process. Of course it was overkill preparation for the day I would walk circus performers around the oval track bordering the rings, hearing their confessions before the celebration of Mass in the center ring.

Then there was the distraction of the move to Berkeley.

This had been a long-planned and forever discerned shift. The Graduate Theological Union on the University of California at Berkeley's north side had wanted the Jesuit seminary in its ranks for years. The library and faculty were of course plums for any such consortium, but it meant a significant contribution to the ecumenical student body of the school. For Jesuits, it meant serious adjustment in Jesuit formation attitudes, and a more than modest expenditure in real estate. For conservative Jesuits throughout the province, the project was suspect as symptomatic of a caving to the forces of evil evident throughout the Bay Area. For some of them, it was almost a harbinger of moral apocalypse.

On our first night after the move, we were having dinner when Father Hagemann came over to my table. He was our longtime advisor who would in a powerful way all but launch the Royal Lichtenstein Circus.

"Nick, there is a lecture on the other side of campus tonight, at the Newman Center. It is on Buddhism and prayer. Would you be interested in attending such an event?"

It would be a bit of a "dive" into real campus life for me, so I was interested. But I also knew that Haggy needed a companion to walk with him over to the center, and so we went.

Hagemann House, one of the student residences at JSTB was named for Haggy after his death. He had indeed been part of the spirit of our theologate throughout his life. How mistaken were some of his peers in judging they had in him a voice against the shift to Berkeley. After we were in place awhile, one of these frightened older men asked Haggy what he thought of the move. The answer was a short course in Jesuit history and spirituality.

"Well, Father, when I used to take walks around Alma College, I'd look up around me and I saw those trees. Now when I take walks I look around me and I see people. And, frankly Father, I think that's what we're all about."

There was an immediacy in our studies now that we hadn't experienced before: we were going to be ordained in less than a year. The course work at hand had much more to do with our sacramental profession than anything in the previous years of study. We had informed, conscientious, and scholarly professionals instructing us. Some of these folks were also bent on caring for us as human beings who needed to remain humble as we approached priest-hood. Our new rector seemed to me a prime example of how apt the Jesuit method could be in discerning appropriate leadership when a successful system needed radical adjustment.

Father Michael J. Buckley had known me since he was a scholastic teaching at Bellarmine in 1956. He never taught me in high school but he was moder-ator of my group of catechists during my senior year. I knew him as a scholar through his reputation as the school's new Greek teacher. But he was also pos-sessed of the human "smarts" it takes to see what makes guys like me tick. I am almost certain he recognized my fatal temper before I did. After all, my "slow burn" was quiet most of the time, so quiet even I was unaware of it until I real-ized I hadn't spoken to someone for a long time, or that I had made a very important and surprising negative decision about something.

Mike was known as an exceptional academic, read very widely, but was keenly insightful about applying what he had gleaned from history to "every-thing the (Berkeley) traffic would allow," to reference Irving Berlin again. Once I was behind him in the lunch line after an embarrassing seminar meet-ing with him for which I had not prepared.

"I'm not so concerned about your not having read the Plato for today's meeting, Nick. But if you haven't read the Augustine passage for Friday, I'll rip your ass off."

I needed it all: the threat, the humor, the care, and, for then, the Augustine. Mike would go far out of his way to care for me on at least two occasions in the future. It was him I sought in the blinding surprise termination of my first year of teaching as a priest; and he would seek me out in another bewildered moment of my Jesuit life.

Mike didn't seem to be afraid of much. He certainly wasn't afraid of Berke-ley. One day there was an important rally being held on Sproul Plaza and we had heard that Mike, among others, was going down to attend. When it was noticed that Mike came home early someone asked him the reason.

"Oh. Simple. I realized very early on in the main speech that you can only decline 'motherfucker' through a limited number of cases!"

And he surely wasn't afraid of me. I had decided to let my hair and beard grow out, even before the move to Berkeley. (I can no longer recall the reasons, but I'm sure they did not exclude vanity.) I really did have what was then referred to as the "hippie look," and I played a "hippie" (whatever that was) in a sketch in our summertime park revues. It was neither more nor less than the look I would have as the lead performer in the Royal Lichtenstein Circus. The network of province worrywarts, already shaken by what they perceived as Bay Area social disintegration, took their concerns to the provincial. Mike was asked to explain why he tolerated such hirsute at the theologate.

"I really don't care if they have hair down to their butts, as long as they pray."

My hair wasn't that long, of course. Nor was I to be characterized as prayerful. I worked at prayer. I always had to. I sincerely trusted the advice of Ignatius that one should pray to want what one is supposed to want. And I trusted Mike. Mostly. I'm sure my last decision as a Jesuit let him down. But I have always carried him in my heart.

There were new distractions. There were streets with traffic and shops and—Haggy was so right—people. There were the sprawling hills of Tilden Park with a magnificent carousel, and even more people. There were the people in other seminaries, the Dominicans and Franciscans, and Unitarians and Episcopalians and the Pacific School of Religion. And there was the University of California campus itself, hordes of people, both an audience potential and a temptation for any performer.

One of those performers, Holy Hubert, was trying to protect us from temptation. He was a fundamentalist preacher and a cartoon of a cartoon: it was easy to imagine that he had tasted the brimstone, survived, and wanted to be sure we were rescued. Most of his audience, including me, periodically sought him out for at least a few minutes of entertainment. He knew his audience and was calloused against any threat that would easily have diluted the message of a less tested, less stalwart colleague. Nothing fazed his zeal.

"Fuck you, Hubert."

"What do you know about love, you miserable devil?"

Not a moment was lost for turning everything in his purview back into the thrust of his message. We laughed and groaned, never guessing the power his ilk would one day command even among the governing elite of American society. But one day when the Royal Lichtenstein Circus finally managed a performance at the Berkeley campus, Holy Hubert not only attended, he stayed to watch teardown and insisted on making a contribution.

Another Sproul Plaza performer was a little tramp of a man who could recognize ready-made bleachers in a set of steps, and an inchoate audience in the few students eating lunch there. He always arrived with at least two shopping bags, the treasury of props he needed for his show about peace, hope, love. He was a vagabond and the best example of a troubadour I have ever encountered. He spoke original monologues and sometimes sang his poetry, often badly. But if the medium and his message were not congruent, there was no mistaking the intensity of purpose. Tommy's heart was bigger than the ragged hand-puppets who spoke and sang his lines. His body, also ragged, was way past the youth or beauty he obviously espoused. His was the pathos of the heartsick ridiculous circus clown pining for the lovely aerialist. Tommy, too, would typically single out a pretty young female student for one of his recitations. And when he handed her a fresh rose, both of them won your heart. No brimstone, here. No fear. Only promise, even in spite of our pasts.

I would later have the opportunity to tell Tommy that our own pasts had intersected. By the time our circus played the Santa Barbara campus of the same University of California system, Tommy had also relocated to that area.

By the time our theological seminary moved out of those redwood forests to be remade in the urban bustle of Berkeley, some of my own most basic presuppositions were being remade. Just as I no longer conceived of theater as the proprietary domain of theaters, I had razed some sturdy sanctuary walls built during my carefully Catholic upbringing. Ritual could no longer exclude what was happening in any theater, including circus. Indeed, I had stopped thinking of ecclesial veracity as hinging on Catholic or even Christian identities. For me, religion itself, and the practice of faith, were human enterprises too precious to be entrusted unquestionably to authority and institutions. I hadn't lost the faith; I was beginning to find it in what I thought might be the early rubble of faltering systemic structures.

The discovery did not enjoy the benefit of much light. It required confidence in one's basic orientation to truth and a relentless quest for method. When the lights came up, they revealed the bare stage of my creative life. I was made in the image of a Creator; when I created I perfected that image by imitation. It was God-like to make art. Therein was sacred power. And in its celebration, I was called to create a communication of that energy so beautiful that it would be shared with others unable to resist the attraction of the power's truth. I began to see myself not just as an artist, but as a ritual maker. My imaginings about priesthood assumed inchoate form. I was to fashion ceremony beyond sacred walls. The ceremony would be sacred because it was true. It would be true insofar as I strove to be fully human. As a priest, I trusted I would be granted the grace for such striving. Without meaning to, I had almost stumbled on a theology of performing art. But it was tenuous. It wouldn't congeal. I was learning all this through the incremental lessons of happenstance, deliberate reading, memory, and conversation.

It is conversation that undergirds the traditional form of education we were given. Of course there is the conversation students have with professors and advisors. But there seems to be an urgency and immediacy about the casual exchanges over food, drink, work, and play that very often yield fertile insights, plans, and even decisions. As Jesuits, we pursued studies in classics, philosophy, and theology as members of communities, actually living in the same buildings that housed our faculties and lecture halls. That meant there was no clock or corner on when or where learning could occur. And during my years in the theologate, these exchanges with my brothers drew me into revisits of Jesuit spirituality. We explored new thought, and wondered about what parts our individual and collective charisms would play in the world we were to serve.

Conventional lectures and seminars unfolded the doctrinal and dogmatic tenets of the Church, sacramental theology, Church history, and sacred scripture. But there was a far richer cauldron of bull sessions about charism, ecclesiology, creation spirituality, transcendental causality, ecumenism, the Spirit, holistic health, social justice, and science. Much of it was beyond me, some of it stuck, and all of it made me aware that theology could touch real nerves. It seemed only scattered data. It took a poet to convince me that integrating the data was possible and necessary.

During the Fifties, friends of another Jesuit, Teilhard de Chardin, posthumously published his *The Phenomenon of Man* and *The Divine Milieu* in English translation. Teilhard's poetic muse shared his mind with the discipline of a trained paleontologist, his deep Christian faith, and his Jesuit imagination. In the chapter on "The Birth of Thought," in the *Phenomenon*, his prose catches flame. "A glow ripples outward from the first spark of conscious reflection. The point of ignition grows larger. The fire spreads in ever widening circles till finally the whole planet is covered with incandescence."[35] That is Earth's thinking layer. "The earth 'gets a new skin.' Better still, it finds its soul."[36] With the case made for divinizing the secular in *Milieu*, I was finally completely embracing my annual meditation on the Incarnation and what it meant that God could not only make flesh but become it. "Now how does the human world itself appear within the structure of the universe?...Around the earth, the centre of our field of vision, the souls of men form, in some manner, the incandescent surface of matter plunged in God."[37] My long ago poetic hunch about the glowing rightness of Hopkins' vision that God's grandeur charged the world had caught up with my own effort to find God in all things. I knew Teilhard and I shared the poetry of Hopkins and with him the wisdom of the *Exercises*. So for me there was Jesuit soundness in pursuing a life given to discovering what I called the dream of God in Christ. Significantly, I wasn't dismayed that the Church hierarchy and other Jesuits, Teilhard's superiors, were not so convinced. After all, the founder of our order had once been dragged before the Inquisition for what he wrote and taught.

* * *

[35] Teilhard de Chardin, *The Phenomenon of Man*, Harper, N.Y. 1959, p. 182
[36] *Ibid*. p. 183
[37] Teilhard de Chardin, *The Divine Milieu*, Harper, N.Y. 1960, p. 125

Somehow we made it to ordination, the first class "graduating" from the new Jesuit campus in Berkeley. There was something in me that resisted making it the social event that I could sense it was supposed to be. For some there was a virtual fever over announcements, invitations, and home parish arrangements for the first Mass and receptions. I had never been to a wedding in my life. Except for Gramma, my family members were not practicing Catholics, much less parishioners anywhere. Making a social event out of my ordination would be a difficult fit. It was not difficult for me to envision the two liturgical celebrations, ordination Mass, and my first Mass, as just two liturgical celebrations. Close members of the family would attend. A few special friends would receive hand written invitations. The first Mass would take place in Alma House at the corner of Berkeley's LeConte and LeRoy Streets, where our main classroom and chapel were located.

But for all my intended nonchalance about the ceremony, ordination got to me like every good liturgical ritual is supposed to. And what a ritual it was, in large part facilitated by the most sensitive liturgist in the class behind us and his colleagues at the Oakland Cathedral. It was literally orchestrated: the orchestra from that cathedral as well as its accomplished chorus all came to the sanctuary of Saint Ignatius Church in San Francisco that Saturday, June 20, 1970. There were a lot of Weber tears shed during the ceremony and Dad would characteristically transpose them to laughter at a Fisherman's Wharf dinner afterward: "It was the goddamn music!"

As the liturgy began, I held it together until the trek down that center aisle and then I was overwhelmed.

The procession into ordination. Dad is facing the aisle just to the left of his hippie son in the photo.

The church's scale, the energy of very eager human hearts in the filled pews, the sight of my classmates in the simple white albs like the one I wore, and the music—all hit home. Like never before or since. Frightening it was, as in whether I would ever get control of myself. And then I did and maintained right through the entire ordination ceremony. Until communion.

While I left the reception of the sacrament completely up to the comfort level of my family, I put unfair pressure on Dad. I had always thought my father got an unfair shake over his marital situation. Even though I was told by one of my official Jesuit examiners[38] to mind my own business, I had personally inquired about Dad's legal status in the Church. He was an excommunicant because he married Gracie without being

---

[38] Applicants to the Society of Jesus were by rule required to be interviewed by designated examiners who would then advise superiors of their judgment on the applicants' suitability for the order.

granted an annulment for his first marriage. I had twice asked superiors to submit the case to Rome and they had no luck. So I tried to educate him about the difference between policy and pertinence, between the reality of the sacrament and the formality of Church regulations. I rehearsed stuff he was smart enough to know for himself about the primacy of conscience. I even managed something as sensitive as what it meant for me to give the Bread of Life to someone who gave me life. I limited myself to one careful letter. Then I let the matter rest.

There was the music to be sure, now infused with the fluid elegance of Mozart's "Ave Verum," and enjoying devastatingly immediate access to our hearts. More, there was the first hands-on experience of the gold ciborium and the host held above it. I didn't experience that I had been transformed by the ordination and the sacrament's effect of a third indelible character on my soul. What I did experience was the end of a long journey that was just beginning anew as I assumed a posture and gestures I had memorized since boyhood. I felt empty, tired, emotionally drained, but I felt powerful because I was surrounded by people who wanted to be with me during this new adventure. And among them, assuming the posture he had learned as a boy in the same church as I, was Dad. He had made his decision. He was in line. For a split second our glances met but only long enough to spark a pact: we couldn't risk eye contact or we'd both lose it. But you can't give someone food without seeing them. So we tried. And this time our faces crumpled in spasms of tears and another denial: with a sideways wave of his hand only I could see, he suggested just forgetting it. But we steeled ourselves and went through with it and perhaps crowned everything we had ever gone through. They didn't teach you in rites courses how to avoid dripping tears into the ciborium.

After communion I was fine. But I was still in for a moment of confusion, laughter, and perhaps the best instruction I ever got in what ecumenism, sacrament, and communication might mean.

It was the custom for the newly ordained men to come to the communion rail immediately after the ceremony and give their first blessings as priests to friends and family. Of course we had long known the prayer formula, thankfully in English by our time, so that was no problem, nor was the gesture, so often repeated in the Church. The emotional sensitivities in the faces of loved ones approaching us did present some challenges. Toward the front of the line of my well-wishers were Dave and Gloria Robb, student friends at the Pacific School of Religion in Berkeley. Before the blessing, they placed around my neck a fresh lei they had flown in from Hawaii, their home state. That was a total surprise and a bit of an emotional derail. But we were comfortable enough with each other that we managed a whispered note of naughty humor on the spot. It was something about how special it was to be "lei'd" on one's ordination day.

But that wasn't *the* funniest or most socially catholic moment of instruction in the first blessing encounters. Saint Ignatius Church crests a San Francisco hill at the corner of Fulton and Parker Avenues and as such is only a few blocks from a much more famous intersection, the Haight-Ashbury. Even so, I easily spotted a group of three beaming young folks in a motley that set their finery off from that of our larger, more staidly attired congregation. I knew in a glance they were more indigenous to the real estate than most of us. When they approached they more than confirmed my suspicions about them and about what ceremony could be. They all laughed. They all had their arms around each other, but only one, a guy, spoke.

"We were just passing through the neighborhood, man, and we decided to cut through the church. And we saw you." Here he gestured toward me, beamed in on the lei, and over laughter from the couple with him he explained. "Well, we don't know what race you folks are running, but we think *you* won." No blessing. A hug. I must have been a sight for hippie eyes. There was the lei, all right, but I'd forgotten about my long hair and beard.

Not for long. The next day's *San Francisco Sunday Examiner and Chronicle* carried a large Section A photo of me with my classmates. The cut line about "new and old" made sure the reader knew who I was, where I was assigned, and that there was something atypical in the ordination. I was already scheduled to teach at Saint Ignatius College Preparatory in the fall. Catholic word in San Francisco travels fast. When alumni and parents saw that item in the press, the school's rector-president got enough calls to warrant approaching me. I assured him I had no intention of working at the school with long hair or a beard. I also informed him that I needed this appearance for a role I had created in our current show. He actually offered to buy me a wig.

There had been a much more startling lack of proportion during the ordination ceremony itself. My friend Thae's husband, the Reverend Bart Murdock, Episcopal rector of Trinity Episcopal Church, sought and gained approval to be present and vested in the sanctuary as a priest witness to my ordination. At communion he was denied the sacrament. He could come to the feast but he couldn't eat.

The calculus of truths underlying any irony seems compelling in this one. In 1534, Henry VIII declared himself head of the English Church excommunicating himself and his followers because he wanted to walk out on his wife. — In 1945 my mother walked out on my father. Shortly after that, I was being taught in a schoolroom that a sacrament was an "outward sign, instituted by Christ, to give grace," while Dad was being excoriated in the rectory office because he wanted to marry Grace. On that June day in 1970, within five minutes a humble truck driver received communion from his son's newly anointed hands. Ten yards away, the son's good friend, an ordained Christian priest— albeit American Anglican—was denied communion, *re-ex*-communicated on the spot. I am not certain who actually passed Bart up with holy communion that day. I am certain that truth can electrify all of history in a moment. The important voltage of that moment continued to generate from a humble schoolroom lesson twenty-five years before.

It was as if even in my ordination there was a discernible institutional mayhem or historical irrelevance. Some customs, proscriptions, expectations just didn't seem viable or comprehensive enough. Five months later I was director of the theater program in the new Bannan Theater at Saint Ignatius College Preparatory. In a fortunate echo of history, the shoes of our earlier *Oklahoma!* production's Mike Figoni were filled by another San Francisco Michael on my production staff. As the year's stage manager, varsity baseball player Mike Bartel very capably eased my job in its strenuous juggling of the logistics any theater operation presents.

I mounted a production of John Osborn's *Luther*, a perspective of the famous reformer's life. One of the crankier members of the Jesuit community wagged, "At least they could be doing the life of a saint." On opening night, before cast members donned makeup and costumes, I presided at a Eucharist in the theater on the set of the Augustinian refectory in the play. I told the students about the older priest's remark. I also told them what my reply was. "We *are* doing the life of a saint." The ongoing reformation of sanctity, ritual, theater, and Eucharist had long been asking me where and when any or all of it could happen. That evening, as the kids, staff, and I gifted our creation back to its Source before we shared it with our audience, I had an answer. And before the school year ended, I knew I must continue pursuing the question and its answer somewhere else.

9.
Launching a Circus

At the start you would never have guessed. On top of a box lettered with "Sam's Sidewalk Show," a balding longhaired guy with a goatee was haranguing passersby on San Jose's First and Santa Clara Streets right next to the First National Bank. It was noon on a bright spring day. Sure enough he was drawing a crowd so he started up a balancing bit with a rapier and a camp-stool. Then he did some kind of escape trick with a chain. He never did stop chattering until he launched into a pantomime and when he came out of that he lit some torches and put them into his mouth with not a moment's hesitation over his moustache and beard.

"Sam's Sidewalk Show," First and Santa Clara Streets, San Jose, 1971.

Those folks who gathered were mid-day shoppers and retired people who lived above the downtown stores. They were all guinea pigs. So was I. It was a mutual test to see whether I could hold an open-ended crowd, all by myself. I had no permit, no space reservation. Such things were unneeded in San Jose those days. A policeman did come up to me at a

128

break between stunts. He kindly asked if I would move my show a little farther from the curb since part of my audience was standing in the street.

It seemed to work. And if I could do it alone, I could certainly do it with a few partners to add variety to a longer performance. By summer, former student Steve Aveson, a friend of his and the brother of one of my actors in the Council Players, joined me for another test: a modest road trip. The journey to that first experimental tour was itself a key pilgrimage.

I had left my formal teaching at Saint Ignatius College Preparatory in San Francisco in April 1971 and was assigned to a period of reflection at my alma mater, the Jesuit School of Theology at Berkeley. That assignment was in part brokered by my former mentor, rector, and teacher, Mike Buckley. I had left the high school before the end of the school year in reaction to what I truly perceived as a superior's breech of agreement. Typically, the incident originated with a parent complaint. The problem was over a line in the spring musical. Without warning, the school's president was contacted and I was ordered to have the principal rewrite the line or cancel the play. To save the play, I accepted that arrangement, and the principal rewrote the line. Still, the president, also my religious superior, ordered that even the rewritten line be excised. I judged that such censorship contradicted the conditions under which I accepted my position at the school.

"In that case, I will cancel the play and the school's license for it in New York. And I'm out of here."

"Well, that's between you and the provincial."

"No I'm leaving. This morning."

"Where are you going."

"Berkeley. J.S.T.B."

I had alerted Mike Buckley and when I arrived in his office, he cancelled all his appointments. I remember that he was very active with the telephone, at one time managing two receivers simultaneously as he confirmed my whereabouts with my rector in San Francisco and the provincial in Los Gatos.

Once he was finished placing my coordinates for everyone concerned, he gave his full attention to me. Calmly. "Now Nicholas. Start at the beginning and tell me what happened."

It was easy. I had been over the same territory a dozen times as I reported to my faculty colleagues and production staff the fairly ugly drama behind the drama. But when I finished the story with something like "And here I am," Mike surprised me.

"Good." It was damned near cheerful. He wasn't startled at all. That wasn't the surprise. It was in his call for an encore. "Now tell me the story again." Immediately I saw that he was making sure about what he heard. I relaxed and repeated, virtually verbatim, what I had just told him. Another surprise when I finished. "Good!" with the same near-cheerful, matter of fact ring. "Now let's go down and have you tell the provincial the story." He personally drove me to the provincial's office, now in the very Los Gatos building where I'd started out as a Jesuit novice. What I had done was pretty serious. Mike wanted to make sure that I represented myself well so I had half a chance for a positive outcome. I couldn't have wished for better counsel.

The result was my assignment to J.S.T.B. where Mike was still rector. There, with the help of prayer and consultation, I was supposed to discern what my next apostolate might be. It was a perfect place for me to be. My class had helped move the theologate from Alma College near Los Gatos to Berkeley in the late summer of 1969, and we were the first group to be ordained from the new campus. I knew the faculty well.

I determined that the most effective place for me to exercise Jesuit ministry was in theater, and since my Council Players company was already in place, I asked to be reassigned to work full-time directing it. The provincial, Father Pat Donohoe, agreed with the plan. I told him I needed a car of some kind and a place to live somewhere near San Jose.

"I can get you the car. Why don't you look around for a place to live at one of the communities serving in the San Jose area. I'd suggest that you start by inquiring at Santa Clara University."

*   *   *

Before I phoned the superior of the Santa Clara University community, Father Leo Rock, Pat himself had called him. And Leo became an advisor and confessor in a lifelong mutually supportive friendship. He assigned me to a dorm room in the Jesuit guest-wing on the top floor of Swig Hall.

The car turned out to be a 1967 silver Pontiac station wagon that was no longer needed by the seminary community in Fresno. None of us saw the circus coming quite yet, but the extra space available in a station wagon was a fortunate provision.

During the weeks that followed, my vision for the work in theater began to develop into something unique. I felt it was a sound vision, but it was rather unprecedented even for the performance arts so I bounced it off my friends up in Berkeley.

One of those friends, David Robb, a student at the Pacific School of Religion, was an accomplished mime who worked with the Council Players summer revues in San Jose's city parks. I would later learn his "War and Peace" mime and present it under the title "Change." David and I talked at some length about the form a tiny and poetic circus might take. The idea was to fashion a format that could fit just about anywhere, entice an audience with circus variety acts, and simultaneously inspire it with snatches of poetry and narrated mime fables. In their door with the circus trappings, and out yours with the lessons in the fables. That's the way Saint Ignatius Loyola would say it. The reflex was very Jesuit: that readiness to render a reflection of the transcendent in the tangible here and now.

One day we happened on the subject of what to call such a production. The name had to carry a light informality. It needed to disarm people as it announced a performance that did not take itself too seriously. Eventually we landed on the idea of a grand-sounding title that would contrast with and mock the show's tiny scale, lending a tongue-in-cheek atmosphere to such a project. Almost without hesitation David volunteered, "It has to be something like 'The Royal Lichtenstein Quarter-Ring Sidewalk Circus and Traveling Taxidermy Show.'"

There it was. I nixed the "taxidermy" bit because I thought it smacked of a rock group. Besides, I did have my heart set on live animals. The overall effect of such a moniker was that of oddity: this wasn't going to be an ordinary circus.

The clincher came in another conversation with a much older friend. Father Charles Hagemann was an Australian who had spent his career as a priest advising students of theology for the California province. Even in his golden senior years he still carried his charming Down Under accent. He was deeper and more complex than many folks realized. Certainly Father Hagemann had his reserved strain. But none of us who knew him well were surprised that Haggy was in the front seat of the first car to leave the old campus of Alma College for the move to Berkeley.

I wasted no time in discussing with him my plans for a future apostolate, unusual though it was. There had been several conversations about it, and he was familiar with the past work I had done in performance ministry. One afternoon that spring, he and I were out for a walk on LeConte Boulevard. I described for him in some detail my vision for the circus.

What happened next still approaches iconic status for me. He stopped abruptly as we reached the front of Starr King Unitarian Seminary. Very thoughtfully he looked up into a tree (or the heavens), rubbed his chin, and said almost dreamily, "Oh, yes, yes, yes! This is what Saint Ignatius would want!"

That did it. We were off and trouping. Well, just about.

*   *   *

There were three young people who wanted to try the new venture out with me. Former student Steve Aveson was first and he brought his friend, Rosemary Hart. Gary Brill was the younger brother of one of our Council Players actors and agreed to join. As for equipment, everything I needed so far was at hand because it was left over: I and my baggage from circus, magic and theater, an extra room at Santa Clara University, the station wagon. From the park revues, the Council Players had a canvas backdrop that could be repainted, and the know-how to put it in the air. There were even a few Elizabethan-style tunics we were holding in storage for another San Jose theater company. We had the Council Players rehearsal and work space thanks to the generosity of Thae Murdock and the parish of Trinity Episcopal Church. And most importantly, we had a concept.

What we didn't have was the most critical factor in the success of every circus that ever started down the road: a route. And as we began we also needed places to play. Here again, I started with what I had: connections. Never in my life have I had access to a network like the one I inherited through the Jesuits, with their array of parishes, colleges, and high schools spread across every region of the country. Through my course of studies I had met people who knew people everywhere in those organizations.

Anyway, that's what I *should* have looked into. But at the beginning I had a bug in my brain that the place this little circus should work its magic was the contemporary equivalent of the commercial crossroads and marketplaces of the past: shopping centers. I still have old letterhead with a line at the bottom: *"A New Concept in Shopping Center Attractions."* To an extent, this *concept* would prove viable, but there were factors against our taking that road exclusively, even chiefly.

Shopping centers, especially indoor malls, are slick and clean. At the beginning we were anything but slick and when we began to incorporate animals, we weren't sparkly clean either. Again, if we were to be outside on a shopping center parking lot we didn't take up enough space to be noticed. Moreover I had no idea how to connect with shopping center networks. I would watch Cliff Vargas take over that market with his magnificent Circus Vargas a few years later and then I realized that all the shopping centers in the country are controlled by a relative handful of development agencies. Get one and you're on your way. By then more and more tented circuses had entered that market.

Of course, there was a fiscal consideration that separated us from the big boys and in that area I was, and am, utterly naïve. Basically, we were a free act. There was no admission fee, and no way to control our attendance if we did have a fee. We wanted to be exposed, next to pedestrian thoroughfares, hoping to engage the attention and time of passersby. Since we were presumably an attraction, the few shopping center management offices that hired us would pay a flat fee. Some allowed us to set out our hat as well, but that was never a guarantee or a sufficient source of revenue anyway. By contrast, the tented shows set up in parking lots and sold tickets through elaborate outlet systems on and off the site.

We did have success with a few shopping centers and we held onto them for the early seasons. We played parks and outdoor festivals, too, but those events were limited by the number of weeks we could play in good weather.

As important as a route is for any circus, for one that has no money and no history and three hungry teenagers as performers, lodging along the way was of equal concern. And here the Jesuit network came into immediate play. I put up a notice on the community bulletin board in a hallway of my former home, J.S.T.B.'s Peter Claver House. I announced my intention to mount a summer tour of the circus and asked if anyone knew of relatives or friends throughout California who would be willing to host us.

That landed us Fresno and Los Angeles almost immediately. As important as the play dates were, we began what turned out to be longtime relationships with families of Jesuit friends, and their cities became ours. Jim Straukamp, who had hosted us with "Slower Traffic Keep Tight" in Sacramento, was on board, as were parents of former students, Jesuit communities, and even a former high school buddy. By the end of our two-month trek, a substantial two-state community would complement the hospitality of the Santa Clara Jesuits, and we had begun establishing a route.

While those arrangements were being confirmed, the exploration of venues in each city also took place. Help came from our hosts, of course, and some contacts I made personally via phone and letter. It was all new terrain for me: the parks administration in Sacramento, Fresno, Bakersfield, Los Angeles, and Phoenix, and shopping centers I had never heard of—Country Club Plaza, the Fulton Mall, Fashion Fair, and places that sampled us once and never booked us again. But it was summer, and between the parks and shopping malls we found enough work to try out our dreams and test our skills.

And were we tried and tested. Finding highways and towns was easy. But getting city directions; finding parking, phones, shopping, fuel; and meeting new people in their homes daily demanded reflexes I had to develop. The repertoire of an hour-long show was simple and the props were elemental. We had that dimension of our lives down thanks to a couple of weeks of intense rehearsal. What we didn't have down were our relationships to each other as more and more of our personalities emerged under the stress and tear of daily routine on the road.

Because we were houseguests at each stop, we were in public round the clock. Consequently, the civil proprieties of table manners, politeness, and graciousness were a constant sensitivity for a Jesuit priest running an off-the-wall ministry with three adolescents. Moreover, there was the harsh strain of our purse. We were operating on the pittance we made as amateur performers. According to one of the few authentic records I can uncover, during those summer months we took in $531.60 and spent $225.94.[39] No one looking at our books twenty years later would believe that.

---

[39] In June 2009, Chris French, a Sacramento alum of our '80–'81 tour gave me a t-shirt that read, "Impossible you say? Nothing is impossible when you work for the circus."

**L-R: Steve Aveson, Rosemary Hart, Gary Brill and I. The first
summer edition of the Royal Lichtenstein Circus, 1971.**

Somehow we arrived home to do a somewhat tattered but secure final performance in the Santa Clara University Mission Gardens, whose palm trees and rose bushes had watched us rehearse our little show months earlier. The audience for that closing date included members of the Jesuit Institute of the Arts, which fortuitously met that summer at Santa Clara. So folks from the entire U.S. Jesuit school network saw us.

There was another gift. I saw a small note advertising a juggling lesson to be given almost next door to me by Bill Cain, a laser-intense scholastic from Manhattan. Some say that modest advertisement was a ruse to meet me. We did meet, and he taught me to juggle. Patiently. Confidently. (His teaching was patient and confident. My learning, not so much.) A humble guy, he was at the outset of his stunning career as theater founder, director, playwright, screenwriter, and brave Jesuit priest. Before all that, he would be a clown in our little circus during the next summer, 1972.[40]

So after Steve and Rosemary and Gary and I stored our props at Trinity Church and said our farewells, I came home dazed about what the hell we had proved, and really mystified by what that might mean I was supposed to do next. Happily, my once-again student, Steve Aveson, had caught a virus called "circus." He would be back in three seasons.

The circus as a ministry had happened in a matter of months. I am so used to the story and the adventures that I overlook one of the most mysterious developments of the process: how I got away with it. I find it funny, really, after all the jokes I have heard about Jesuits, even in sympathetic circles. Why wouldn't a religious order of clowns countenance a circus ministry? After all, even John Quincy Adams was onto their chicanery when he protested Jesuit masquerades and disguises in his writing to Thomas Jefferson.

---

[40] At this writing, Bill Cain, SJ has three award-winning original dramas playing throughout the country: *Equivocation*, *Nine Circles*, and *How To Write a New Book For the Bible*.

As it happened, there was more stealth than chicanery on my part in getting the ministry started. Other than from Father Hagemann, I didn't seek the counsel of older Jesuits or officials till I knew I had a product. There had been reluctance by provincial administrators to imagine Jesuits performing in public. In my third year of teaching I was refused permission to audition for a guest director at San Francisco State. I had been tipped off by my graduate advisor that there was an invitation for me to audition for a given role. But word came down from a provincial advisor that "our men should restrict themselves to the backstage operations." That's the basic reason "Sam's Sidewalk Show" just happened without warning one afternoon in downtown San Jose, twenty minutes from that same official's office.

My sensitivity to Jesuit proclivities wasn't chicanery, but it helped mightily. All of my efforts in the performing arts had been in academic settings: I had directed in Jesuit houses of formation and in Jesuit schools, and I had completed a master's degree in drama. True, I had given some poetry recitations, but those seemed bookish enough. I had formed a theater company in which I acted, but the plays were intended to be performed in churches to stimulate discussion. And that company had become my master's project for the degree. The Jesuit penchant for things academic had been placated. It also helped that among my superiors and peers my work over seven years had won overall favorable reviews.

Especially in the high school communities where I taught, I learned important footwork to protect my feelings and conserve energy for exhausting schedules. The key move was a dodge. I learned that every community has cranks, that Jesuit cranks are articulate, and that some Jesuits will play the "obedience card" with superiors if they don't like what another Jesuit is doing. If one is really busy, such people have to be avoided at all costs. I was very busy. Until I knew what I was doing and that it was producing results, I wasn't in places where I would likely engage such unhappy brothers.

Jesuit obedience is the order's hallmark. That's why such care was taken with a new priest seeking to change what he and superiors presumed would be a career in institutional education. Mike Buckley sensed the need for this care and he communicated it directly to the provincial staff. To their credit they respected him and me and the period of discernment at Berkeley had been arranged. This was important. And when my decision was made, my request was not to start a circus; it was to return full time to the theater company I had begun four years earlier. I really did have continuing theater productions in mind. Only Haggy and some friends knew that I was beginning to see a new form of theater emerging that would bring into play a vital strain of my makeup.

Then there had been experiments by the Council Players. One was an original indoor review called "A Canticle For the Eighth Day." Set in a circus ring and including dance and juggling, its use of poetry and readings was very near meditative. There were my one-man poetry and mime recitals, always including inspiring and provocative subjects. There were the continuing park shows. These efforts were invariably lightweight and portable. They toured. So when "Sam's Sidewalk Show" showed up on First and Santa Clara Streets, I knew I was testing my ability to wrap the charm of my old friend the circus around the heftier menu that theater could serve up.

By the time the modest trial project came home and performed for the assembly of U.S. Jesuit artists that summer of 1971, we knew the product had gained shape. While I had always been slow to think of myself as an artist, we were highly visible and unique, two categorical characteristics of art. But I in no way expected that so many of the Jesuits would encourage us with their enthusiasm. Everyone was still riding the heady surf of Vatican II and maybe the little circus provided an example of what ministering through the arts could be. Our audience at that homecoming had all mined the same rich themes I had in the Ignatian view of Incarnation and the mandate to find God in all things. Whatever they resonated with, my Jesuit brothers from across the country embraced what we were doing. We were on our way to a national route for the Royal Lichtenstein Circus.

*   *   *

"Spellbound crowd."
—Stein, *San Francisco Chronicle*, March 21, 1972

Oddly, in the fall of '71 I had never heard the show business expression, "Take it on the road and tighten it up." That I did that, alone, was something of an accident. My intent was a booking tour, a scheduling of places to play in northern California and Oregon. While I found our future play dates, I also strengthened my resolve, my self-confidence and my instincts as a variety performer. Armed with an atlas, my hodgepodge of a costume, a trunk full of props, and a few animals including a wonderful little dog named Fritzi, I set out as a single performer playing impromptu dates wherever I could find an audience or get one to gather and find itself. My superior, the rector of the Jesuit community at Santa Clara, knew where I was headed, my purpose, and how long I would be away. Not even I knew the details of that journey. The journey was precisely about finding details: encountering them, managing them, submitting to the promising ones.

At one bar and grill in Salem, management put me on a raised platform. Directly below this little stage there was a table and the couple seated there did not appreciate having a guy yelling nonsense while they were trying to enjoy their food. They began to voice their resentment and became obnoxious but at a level only I could hear. That's a straitjacket for the performer. He can't use an outright heckler-stopper because the rest of the audience wouldn't know what motivated it.

On that tour I was using some doves and a duck in a nice box trick. The doves go into the box which then breaks apart in a flash, and instead of doves there's this huge white duck sitting there. I had learned that with a slight nudge at the break-apart, the duck would fly a bit and land in the audience. It was made to order for that situation. He landed right square between the couple's dinner plates. Everyone had a great laugh and I had hooked the couple for the rest of the act.

I made good friends in Eugene at the University of Oregon, which became a regular stop on our subsequent routes. But the most wonderful find was in Portland. One of my very first stops there was at the Student Activities Office of Portland State University, where I met Nina Lowry, the director. I handed her my brochure. "Hi, I'm Nick Weber and I have a small circus that I—"

She cut me off. "A circus! That's just what we need around here!"

And so we booked a show for their coffee shop.

"You've got to at least ask for fifty dollars or no one will think you're any good."

I had no idea how savvy a lady I had met. She knew and dealt with all the major artistic enterprises in a very artsy city. A trained scientist, she read continuously, could sight-read Bach at the piano, and had a very broad taste in the arts. Lucky for me, that taste appreciatively accommodated the humble trappings of my own efforts.

Because that was a booking tour for me, I did not offer my identity as a Jesuit priest except to Newman Communities or Jesuit hosts. I had early decided that for some, the professional religious dimension of my life could be a distraction from what I really wanted to do. But when I told Nina the address on Burnside Street where I was staying, she became alarmed and demanded detail. I had no idea I was in a skid-row area that any Portland resident would know about. I had to do some explaining. But only some.

I was actually bunked in an old hotel with a Jesuit brother who ran a rehab flophouse for guys in the Lower Burnside. I shared with Nina the nature of Brother Fred Mercy's work. He took in guys who were sober and wanted to stay that way, gave them a clean place to stay and even helped them find jobs, teaching them how to represent themselves. But when Nina had to call for me the next afternoon at Portland Jesuit High School, I felt that Father Weber had been caught with his collar on. The time for disclosure was at hand. This lady was too smart. She had trusted me, and if she now sensed I was hiding something or putting something over on her, I would lose a great friend. I had to confess.

"So what have you figured out?" I tried to make it a game as we traveled across town.

"About you?"

"Yes. You have to be connecting a few dots."

"Well, you're probably somehow connected to Jesuits." She was driving, but she managed an unmistakably deliberate glance to make eye contact with me. "Right?"

"You've got it." And then, perhaps with the most confidence I'd ever had in such a moment, the "Full Jebbie": "I am a Jesuit priest. The circus is a ministry."

"Hot damn! I *did* nail it!"

Done deal. Almost from the start she with not a little amusement followed my religious as well as my artistic vagaries. But she was smart enough to realize that I was very sensitive about how the circus was perceived. Promoting the circus as a ministry could significantly lessen the appeal it had for some sponsors and venues. That would be self-defeating. If you knew I was a Jesuit, fine. But the boldface type for everyone's first encounter had to be that I was a clown and ran a circus, albeit a poetic one.

Nina introduced me to her colleagues on all the other major campuses in the city. Moreover, she made sure I met close friends of hers in northwest Portland, Bob and Jennifer Williams, who had developed the touring Williams Toy Theater. They unabashedly mounted marionette productions of Greek, Russian, and Latin classics complete with the likes of Pegasus and Baba Yaga. Importantly, I was welcomed into a small community of artists who were unhesitant about exploring new media, finding new forms, and celebrating unique combinations of the human quests called art.

The stresses and discoveries I had made on my own and the community of support I had found in Portland made the return trip to Santa Clara a long, meditative drive. I didn't feel so lean and alone. The impulse to blindly push myself was lessened. The whole crazy effort made some sense. It might be viable after all. I headed home knowing that I could probably get a show as far as Portland, anyway. Importantly, I had begun to discover the venue that would become our real home: college campuses and school assemblies.

*   *   *

"It started before it started and it hasn't finished yet."
—Bill Cain, SJ, to the Royal Lichtenstein listserve, September 28, 2009

When he wrote those words to us, Bill was referring to the effect the circus has had on his own life, but he was also referencing unmistakable historical facts about the life of the Royal Lichtenstein Circus. Like several of his colleagues in those very early years, he discovered that I was not only making up the route as I went along, I was making up the circus: what it was, what it could be, what it should be, what it had to be. And he and they also endured the back-break and fatigue required to make all that happen. Once during the height of his writing and directing career Bill asked me why from the beginning I had called the work a circus. He knew that what we were doing didn't easily fit such a title.

"You just called it that, right?"

Affirmative. I knew the word still conjured wonder. I sensed that it was marketable and I was utterly certain that it would impel me toward the realization of a dream that one day would indeed look and sound and smell like Circus.

In the spring of '72, I headed north again, alone, working my way toward a big date at Lloyd's Center in Portland. It was a large, well-known shopping center with an outdoor mall but with cover in case of rain. Jennifer Williams had a good connection with the management and I had a pretty fair contract for three days, stipulating three half-hour performances daily. Amid all the backlash surrounding Vietnam and the invasion of Cambodia, I performed the "War and Peace" mime under its new title, "Change." It depicts with humor and pathos an eager military recruit whose dedication and energy visibly dissolve as he watches his first bayoneted victim collapse. He picks up the corpse and carries it off to burial. The piece is strong, and wanting to put my best foot forward I included it in the first performance hoping the management would be present. They were.

Immediately after that first show, I waited for the audience to clear and then began to set props for the next performance, which would be the other half of the hour repertoire I was carrying. I needn't have bothered. After about ten minutes—time, I suspect, for an official meeting of minds—I was visited backstage by a sad-faced Jennifer and a very serious promotional director who lost no time getting to the point. "This really isn't the type of program we were expecting. Our management doesn't think it belongs in this venue and we're going to have to cancel. Of course you will be paid for the complete engagement." Jennifer helped me tear down and load the car.

The gig died, but the circus managed to trust in its own vitality with daring commitments from three young Jesuits cast for the show's 1972 summer season. I was also emboldened by former students who had volunteered to take that same summer version of the show across country, actualizing the first national tour. There was also very vital promise in the resourceful generosity of Santa Clara University student visual artists John Baker and Mary Hildebrand. These talented friends of mine would be producing our scenic backdrops and specialized props. Now the energy of actors would be complemented by the colors, textures, and sculptured décor any notion of circus conjures. A virtual parade of cloth drops, gilt sculptured animal wagons, foam animal heads, and other specialized comic gewgaws emerged from the university's scene shops and studios over several seasons. The hesitant sketch of my dream was now enjoying firmly drawn lines, color, and shape to be animated by other visionaries who believed the dream should come true.

We knew we were in the business of telling stories. Probably we found some degree of justification in that component of our work, because the stories were parables, what *Time* would one day call "low-key morality plays." So we very carefully fashioned narrated mime interpretations of popular fables such as "The Giving Tree," "The Stonecutter," and "Two Frogs." These were relieved and interspersed with music, magic, comic mime, elemental juggling, vaudeville gags, and my balancing and fire-eating bits. The menagerie consisted of the birds we used in the magic, and Fritzi, a dog who did nothing, which in a circus becomes cause enough for laughter. We had nothing recognizable as circus material, enough bravado and showmanship to sucker Barnum, and we didn't know what in the hell we were doing.

Barnum once said that there were three *P*s required for every successful circus: p*rint, parade,* and *performance.* We were usually right in the middle of foot traffic so we didn't really need a parade. And because we all had such showbiz stamina (we were all Jesuits that summer) performance was no problem. But in print I think I made life tougher than it should have been. When I reread the letter I sent on May 8, 1972, to prepare these young Jesuits for rehearsals, I realize I could type a better bargain than I had to offer. It reads like I know what I'm doing. I barely knew even what I *wanted* to do.

Bill Cain and I were at least and at most analogous. He grew up in New York going to theater and became infected. I grew up in California and became infected by the circus. We were both also infected by that derring-do the Jesuits had in taking the world where they found it. We weren't afraid of the stuff of this world and its capacity for making art. We sensed art itself was transformative, somehow potentially holy. When he met me, Bill seems to have found reassurance that a Jesuit priest could use an art to barge right into the marketplace, become a professional with secular skills that enabled him to profess the sacred. When he saw a Jesuit priest vest himself in a clown's motley to celebrate the Eucharist he felt his dreams were possible. That those dreams were dangerously close to nightmares he wouldn't know till he joined out.

His dreams, however, had an advantage. He was smitten by theater, and theater is intricately related to and dependent upon literature. If you were educated in the literary heritage of the western world, you had a grasp of theater's source. If you were a scholar, you could mine that literary heritage for the essential structures that made theater work. Bill was both educated and a scholar. Even as he contemplated moving his pursuit of theater into the marketplace and beyond academic or religious walls, the roots of his art had a definition Jesuit superiors understood.

The history of the circus has almost no connection with letters. That history eludes form since circus has so often functioned as an ephemeral toy suited to the needs of a given culture and period. Its constant is variety. You can't exactly study it in a library. You have to inductively distill its essence from actual performances. Even then you have more of a process than a product. The common ground between circus and theater, the relationship that enabled Bill's and mine, is in their functions as rituals, sharing elements of each other. Happily for me and my fellow Jesuits, the central public movement of our identity was a minutely defined and universally accepted ritual, the Eucharist. It was, in fact, that ritual that brought theater out of the dark ages. Those miracle, mystery, and morality plays? They began with a hunch during a rehearsal for the Easter Saturday vigil around 1000. Somebody in an English sanctuary had a new idea: "Why don't we give the angel's line 'Who are you looking for?' to someone besides the priest who is reading all the rest of the story?" That happened. And so did the development of drama as we know it.

It was my interest in that development that led my liturgy professor in Berkeley to suggest that I consider presenting workshops around the country addressing what a man of the stage, an actor, had to give the priest presider in the sanctuary. I followed his advice and discovered that post–Vatican II Catholics were receptive to whatever insights they could find as they struggled to rediscover the riches of their liturgy. I presented these workshops all over the country at parishes, seminaries, and even a liturgical convention.

Maybe touring a circus with an all-Jesuit cast led by a priest who was a clown had to be seen to be believed. So if the priest clown would also talk to national leadership about liturgy, why not bring the whole package to town and host a workshop? And that's why we wound up in Colorado Springs. We performed. I led the workshop. I have faded black-and-white snapshots to remember our performance. Of the workshop, I have much clearer memories of two friends who were there to learn liturgy. David Pinto would become our regular host and agent in Kalamazoo, Michigan, and Jennie Madrigal would be our continuing host and ombudsperson in Denver until she actually joined out with the show. Both these onetime liturgical workshoppers would be with me right to the end of a twenty-two-year run that was just beginning.

*   *   *

Ideas and images romp with the fragility of air. At the beginning there is only promise, possibility—*maybe, might, what if, hope so*. And that's when you are working in an established form. We were hunting for a form. We had some notion of circus, but no circus. Bill sensed this keenly. He knew that what he had agreed to was a project I was inventing as we went along. It was frightful because we were daily in front of strangers and what we were doing was still strange to us. Often, like children away from home, we were lost, but we had memorized our family name. We didn't know terribly much about our ancestry or our DNA, but we had at least a tenuous identity: Circus.

Fortunately that summer's Jesuit rendition of the Royal Lichtenstein Circus was a messy lab in which we explored the whole concept of circus, trying it on, trying it out. There is a sense in which a circus defies definition because it sets out to be amorphous. It is inclusive enough to harbor the pathos of the theater, the church, the concert hall, gymnasium and fairground. Probably its success depends precisely on how well such myriad human endeavors are married to achieve a ritual unity. Then it can be strong enough to fashion scattered attention spans and isolated hearts into the soul of an audience. We had the variety down; we were short on the unity. In the beginning I'm convinced we thought that if we moved it all fast enough the show would seem to have composition, thematic integrity. But pace very often robbed our individual sketches of their own vitality. It was as if we didn't have time to take them seriously, and even comedy has to be taken seriously.

Exploring such a rarefied process with the shreds and patches I had managed to assemble was made possible only because I had the companionship and sensitive, brainy input of fellow Jesuits. Bill, Mike Moynahan, and Michael Sparough were ascetically trained; they were also educated in letters and they were smart. Their humanity allowed us to find our way through the anger, surprise, and stupidity that attend all wayfaring. So it was that we helped an incensed Bill get over Fritzi's chewing his expensive handcrafted leather top hat. And so it was that everybody found foolish humor in my harebrained ideas.

L-R: Nick, Mike Sparough, SJ, Bill Cain, SJ and Michael Moynahan, SJ. Bill Cain's hilarious "Knife Thrower" pantomime in Colorado Springs, summer, 1972.

Doing our circus on a beach was stupid. For one thing, stakes don't hold in sand and our drop was guyed out to stakes. For another, people on a beach don't have pockets to carry money in, and our hats at the end of the show needed money. And the reason those folks don't have pockets is that they aren't wearing clothes (many)—and that makes it very difficult to remember your lines.—Yosemite was another wild miss. Not only did we not get to perform; bears managed to frighten two of my partners out of a night's sleep.

*   *   *

Through all this reckless prodding of possibilities with a form I barely grasped long enough to recognize, let alone develop, I had gotten lucky. For one thing, there was still magic in the word *circus*. And our "clown-white," the basic greasepaint so many clowns still used, was also the badge of a tribe of performers resurrecting the respectable form of mime. When we began, mime and juggling were enjoying popularity as street arts. Earlier they had properly comprised repertoire of the theater and the circus, respectively. Now, street theater and street performing in general were far out enough to be *in*. Concurrently, college activity offices had discovered that their highly visible central campus quads could be performance venues. In some sense, these socio-historical factors I played with fell into place, but I did nudge them a little.

I suspect the nudging was possible because I was a Jesuit priest. I felt called to serve people by acquainting them with God's word and the blessings of that word. The Jesuits explained the word and the blessings and taught me to see my own gifts with words as blessings. They also helped me bless my skills— even the unusual ones.

And in their network the Jesuits had what every circus man needs: a route. There was a map for a circus pilgrimage. The summer of 1972 brought two and a half months of hard work, fear, doubt, a modicum of satisfaction, lots of laughs, and plenty of the kindness of strangers. And none of us were yet sure what it all meant.

What is perfectly clear is that the entire enterprise came to viability through the pilgrims who joined me in covering that map, mile to mile and day to day. In the beginning, most of them came from the Jesuit network. That there were honest-to-God Jesuits at my side so early on meant that I could probe the merit of my quest, challenge and evaluate myself as a priest and an artist. You can do that with guys who have let Ignatius lead them through that workout on the Incarnation and the huge quest of finding God in all things.

10.
Clowns On the Interstate

"A testimony to all that is good in the circus."
—*Arizona Daily Wildcat*, University of Arizona, November 21, 1972

L-R: Carlo Pellegrini, Nick, John MacConaghy

I would be joined for the first national tour by a former Saint Ignatius student, John Mac-Conaghy and a Santa Clara University junior, Carlo Pellegrini. How could I have missed it? It was so obvious. Guys raised to share a religious dream setting out on a long trek because of a priest's vision. It had to be a pilgrimage. And one of the guys wasn't just Catholic. He was Italian and his name, Pellegrini, means "pilgrim." Even if I had completed the equation, I wouldn't have understood the terms. This was to be a longer and deeper pilgrimage than I could have imagined in my early years of ministry, and Carlo Pellegrini would be there after the long haul he had helped me start. So would the Irishman we affectionately called "Big John."

I didn't run away to join the circus. The circus and I had been living together, awkwardly, for years. And I didn't live "out of a suitcase." Circus people carry everything they need with them in their vehicles, making sure they don't have to pack and unpack too much besides the technical gear of the show. So getting ready to leave out is tense. Priorities become stark: an atlas, flashlight, first aid kit, fire extinguisher, duct tape, bailing wire, toilet paper—things you *really* need every time you need them. Stress was unavoidable as we worried about clothing, props, cash (I had only heard about credit cards), the animals, costumes, and makeup. Coins for pay phones (no one had a cell phone in '72). Don't forget the animal feed.

Our own food came from quick, boring stops along the highways, and at the warm and friendly tables of scattered hosts along the way. There were lots of such hosts, all generous, all excited to be part of what we were still discovering, and all perfectly willing to feed a whole circus at one sitting. In homes that shared our faith, those dining room or kitchen tables sometimes became settings for the Eucharist. And still our identities as pilgrims didn't register with me. What registered? Recipes and addresses. Happy-go-lucky Millie in San Rafael and doe-eyed Memphis Maggie had great pasta dishes. I would be cooking up Millie's carb-celebration of garlic and butter over spaghetti for years to come.

But ducks and doves don't like pasta, so during that first stop in San Rafael I had to go to a pet store to pick up some grain. And there I met one of the loves of my life: Penelope. She was loose, to say the least, and that made her very attractive of course. And all she had on was a diaper and a sun suit. Hold me back. Best of all she was curious about me.

"I don't suppose that monkey's for sale."

Penelope is the good looking one on the left.

"Oh, sure. We'll sell her."

"Dare I ask what you'd charge?"

"About three hundred." It got better and better. Calm enough to roam a store. Broke to wear clothes.

"How old is she?"

"About three years."

I went home with a racing pulse and pulled Carlo into a huddle and an instant business collaboration.

"Oh, we gotta have a monkey. I'll loan you half the price." And we had a monkey. "Penny" was a spider monkey, half-black and half-gold and completely popular everywhere we went.

North to Portland, east to Omaha in a month; east and south to New Orleans in the next month; west through Texas, New Mexico, Arizona, and into Southern California by early December. Circus fans reading our route in their weekly *Circus Report* couldn't believe it. They didn't realize that "the World's Smallest Complete Circus" traveled in one vehicle, so the jumps between dates seemed impossible. Even with one vehicle, though, such distances were insane.

While we were in Los Angeles, disaster struck Carlo's family and our company: his father was murdered at his San Jose place of business. Carlo flew home to Palo Alto immediately and John and I brought the show into quarters in San Jose.

By that time, however, we had managed to secure a December booking at an indoor shopping area in Dallas, and happily our ingenious property designer, Mary Hildebrand, joined John and me to retain that date. (I still had this thing about how important shopping centers were.)—I think we made it home for Christmas that year. With the severity of our dear partner's loss, however, everything seemed subdued, even for circus people. But when late January came, Carlo was ready to troupe with us through the second half of the season: north to Seattle, east through Idaho, Montana and the Indian reservations, and points even farther east.

We were to perform what was basically our repertoire from the first half of the season, but we would look different. Thae Murdock had carefully dismantled one of the borrowed tunics we had been using and made a pattern. The billowing shoulders and multicolored sleeves were no longer the mysterious challenge she had feared. And with a polyester blend called "Trigger Cloth" she found brilliant colors with which she could develop a palette of ensemble costumes that would give each performer his own statement and still tie us altogether. Then I made a daring decision: for the first time, we would all be in white tights. The idea was to add a modest sheen of formality; the white of our gloves and the well-fitted tunics and white tights suggested a theatricality that would not be out of place for a circus. Visually and practically the new look made sense and became our trademark. Everything was easily washable. That was important because our rule was that tights had to be clean, always. Gloves, impossible to keep bright and clean, were shed after each show's opening routine. Bucket and sink washings became *de rigueur*.

Even on a little circus, it's very difficult to know what's going on in the real world. We didn't know that we were being watched by the FBI as we approached the Pine Ridge Reservation in South Dakota. We didn't know that because we didn't know there had been an Indian demonstration at Wounded Knee in which Sacred Heart Church and the Jesuit pastor had been taken hostage. And we didn't know that the FBI had been attracted because the brave and notorious Jesuit felon, Father Dan Berrigan, and his lawyer, William Kunstler, were also trying to enter the reservation. Nor did we know what *Time* was planning for its April 23, 1973 issue. So when we arrived at Holy Rosary Mission in Pine Ridge, I became the embarrassed object of a Jesuit superior's consternation.

As we were settling into our assigned lodgings, someone handed me a message that I was to call a reporter at *Time*. I was a circus man; I knew the importance of press and print. So I lost no time. At a phone on a small hallway table I reached a dial tone and called. The magazine was doing a cover story on the Jesuits throughout the world. They wanted some information on what I was doing, including coming dates where they could obtain photos. We talked and we talked and we talked. Then the stern face of the superior materialized before me. His voice was hushed so as not to be heard over the phone.

"Do you realize you have been tying up the only phone line open into this part of the Reservation? We are under duress here because of the demonstration at Wounded Knee. I have to ask you to terminate this call as soon as you can."

I explained my situation, terminated the call, and apologized to the superior. And there I was come April 23, on pages 41 and 48, heading up something described as "an amiable blend of circus acts and low-key morality plays."

Even in the glow of being covered by *Time* I felt put off by the obvious reserve. But in all fairness, neither I nor that reporter recognized the key characteristic of the phenomenon that brought us together. It was right there in the calm little word *blend*.

It didn't seem important because it might have suggested too narrow a focus on the obvious combination of priest and circus, or ministry and clown. But *blend* signifies process, sometimes chemical, always dynamic, always creative. That's what every successful circus achieves: a grand unity among a variety of images that change precisely because they are unified. And in our circus, with so much interaction between performer and spectator, where clowns, jugglers, and acrobats talked with the audience, the most important blend of all could occur. We showed up in the middle of a busy pedestrian intersection and, as in every valid ritual, asked strangers and friends to gather, while we, other strangers, unpacked a parade of sight and sound symbols celebrating who we all are and what we might become. That's what we were doing, but I didn't know it at the time. I am confident others did, including my superiors, peers, and that string of young people who had yet to come forward and ask something like, "What do I have to do to join you guys?"

*   *   *

Some of those who understood what we were really doing never traveled with us, but they brought a richness into our lives that made their towns our temporary hometowns and their families part of ours. That was certainly true of David Pinto in Kalamazoo. Besides the wonderful bookings that David secured for us, including shopping malls, we were able to meet his family—of thirteen. In those years when we started coming to town, almost everyone was still at home, so dining was a unique happening for us. Everyone was seated at a very large circular table. The center of the table held another circular table, a lazy Susan whose diameter was calculated to leave room for place settings on the main surface and still make it possible to reach servings that were passing by. And pass by they did. That Susan didn't have time to be lazy.

Such gatherings, which always embraced our shared memories, failures, jokes, minor triumphs, and major losses, probably taught me more about Eucharist than I had ever known. I could never be a priest whose first concern in the day was where or when he was going to celebrate Mass. For one thing it was impractical given the intense and sporadic schedule I lived. For another, my spirituality, even when I was living in the formality of a Jesuit community, had long simplified itself to the extent that the Mass had really become a special occasion, not a daily need or event. I knew I was in conflict with the teaching of our founder, Ignatius, who championed daily Eucharist. But shared meals always held something sacred for me, and whether or not we actually reset a dining room table for Mass, such meals as we shared with the Pintos fed into the depth of my next formal celebration.

Of course in sharing any kind of meals we share each other's lives, and my partner clowns were closer to me than I realized. This came home to me when we got up into the mining country of West Virginia and played for the Downtown Association of Wheeling on a Saturday when lots of folks would come to the main street mall to shop.

I always enjoyed such open commercial venues. There was an easygoing spontaneity that embraced the surprise of what we were trying to do: nice, if strange, people showing up unexpectedly to entertain nice people. People are nice. And we were nice, even if I could talk the skin off a tomato. And even if Carlo could still sell you the tomato. Then Big John—quiet, gentle John— would smile-smirk and let you know you really didn't need the tomato skin anyway. He is a nice guy.

Well, this particular Saturday afternoon, I was resetting props between shows. At that time our "offstage" area—in circus jargon, "the backyard"— was an unbleached muslin lean-to Thae had sewn for us. It attached to the main drop batten just to the left of the door in the drop. There we kept the animal cages and magic props. As I came around the edge of the lean-to a couple of not-so-nice teenage guys stopped me to ask a question or two and very quickly became insulting and then abusive. Never in my life had I encountered anyone "looking for a fight." I somehow communicated I wasn't interested in what they were saying and fortunately they left. Very soon, John came up to me.

"Hey, boss! Those guys make you nervous? Tough talk, eh?"

"Well *yeah*, I was nervous. Plenty."

"You shouldn't have been. I was inside the lean-to right behind them with a pipe wrench in each hand."

Gentle John. He'd had my back. I was surprised and warmed.

Then it was the return west through Ohio, Indiana, Iowa, Denver, Salt Lake, Reno, and home.

*   *   *

While in recounting these tours, the distances and the routes seem prominent, performances were almost daily. And everything we did revolved around a timetable dictated by a given day's performance from the time we arrived and parked. If we came into a town the night before the performance was to occur, our hosts had to be apprised of when we were to leave in the morning for setup. Our meals, animal feeding and cleaning, and everyone's sleeping schedule focused on the starting time for the next show. Even when larger vehicles allowed us to pull onto the performance site as soon as we arrived, the parking configuration was dictated by the layout required for setup. Most performances were given midday, so breakfast had to be punctual and substantial: punctual so we stayed on time; substantial so we could last till lunch after the show.

Setup was second nature. From the onset of full run-through rehearsals, our modus operandi was to do the same thing the same way every time. The goal was to save enough mental and physical energy to make the performance sparkle and get to the next stop. No use wasting effort reinventing procedures that were effective. When we were lucky and on time, there was a respite after setup. Since the show was so often in a public place, the earlier setup was complete, the more advertising we gave ourselves. There were scheduled practice times for the skill routines, especially those involving ensembles of jugglers or unicyclists. Individual acrobats found time for their private stretching routines. Then came makeup, which was always done with the group standing around a table or trunk lid littered with jars, bottles, pencils, moist rouge tins, baby oil, and plenty of toilet tissue for cleaning hands and trimming the edges of our clown-white masks.

And then we waited. The exact decision to start was an art in itself. For college shows, we knew we had a deadline. If the show ran overtime, we'd lose our audience during the bigger acts at the end of the lineup. If we started too early, it was hard to get the group chemistry in the audience going. Stragglers could feel self-conscious. There was very often a compromise on when the first clown entered the ring.

We progressed from a silent dumb show with a surprise clown-gag finish into a welcoming poem and then simultaneous spiels that unabashedly announced we were a circus of clowns that didn't hesitate to talk. In rapid-fire succession, a dog act, a skill act, and then the first fable continued the pace and the mix. The idea was balanced variety. The content centerpieces were the fables. Of course the more elaborate skills and animal acts came toward the end. Usually, magic, clown comedy, and lighter skills such as balancing acts came earlier. For years, my fire-eating act was at the end, but some years it yielded that place to the Milk Can Escape or to the horse routine. The sequences were tight; the timing was deft and professional.

But you had to have your ears about you. Just when you thought you'd heard everything from your fellow clowns, someone would find a new expression, noise, or line. Since we had a very open exchange going with our up-close audiences, spectator input was frequent and we developed a supply of funny, easygoing heckler-stoppers. One day as John and I were tearing around in the backyard getting ready for the next piece, Carlo was in the ring with a routine we'd heard a hundred times. Then suddenly, something we'd never heard.

"You know? You have a ready wit. Will you let us know when it's ready?"

It worked beautifully. Carlo later paid the credit to a copy of *Reader's Digest* he'd found somewhere. Part of the shock about that line was in function of a characteristic reserved intensity Carlo carried into the ring. He really was a superb mime and reminded me of Bill Cain. He was so good at conjuring with gesture, I wasn't expecting such a spontaneous verbal turn. What I did grow to expect was an impromptu practice session in some host's backyard during which he would spend half an hour opening and closing a door—which was nothing but air. There wouldn't be as accomplished a mime in our company until 1982, when Eric Wilcox left his college career in Iowa City to join us. He would become a professional mime entertainer and would one day come back to us when we needed all the entertainment he could bring.

No matter how successful a performance or an act was, however, the last act ended and the show had to start thinking about tomorrow. Teardown and load-up took around ninety minutes even when the show moved with heavier equipment and livestock. This was itself a ritual, with every task completed in the same order and fashion every time, but quieter. We were exhausted by the setup and performance; there wasn't any energy for chatter. I recall a priest happening into his church hall after our audience had cleared out. Wanting a good look at the dismantled equipment, he made his way very close to the main drop, which was now flat on the floor. He just stood there for a minute, and he wasn't missing a thing. He watched each performer working silently at his given tasks, and then he offered, "This is religious!"

Something to eat and back on the highway in a vehicle that smelled of its contents: sweaty acrobats, fur, and feathers. Winter months were the worst: you couldn't roll the windows down. Animal cages were cleaned more frequently. Even when weekdays could not be booked, very often church or festival dates would be. So it was travel, setup, perform, teardown, load-up and travel. Four months out. A one month winter break, then four more months on the road.

We were quite literally blazing a trail for future casts of Royal Lichtenstein troupers. Very often the trail led through snow that our blaze didn't melt. We had begun to set a route for ourselves: two cross-country roundtrips in eight months. And no matter how we cut it, no matter how long we stayed out, for our first eight years we drove 14,000 miles annually and wound up where we started: Santa Clara University. No wonder I never saw it as a pilgrimage. All that and we never got anywhere.

How could I be so slow to understand? All those kids I took through Chaucer's *Canterbury Tales*. The whole point was that the road to the shrine was not the important trek. And how many kids did I expose to that perfect sonnet with which Romeo and Juliet first flirt? All that stuff about "palm to palm is holy palmer's kiss," and then he actually tells her to *stand still* "while my prayer's effect I take" so he can smooch. So there it was: we didn't have to get to anywhere. We were the shrine. The real journey was ourselves: in me, the discovery of essential ministry in the intersection of my personality and priesthood; in my partners, new insights into their personalities and new questions about what their educational pursuits should be. All of us had a richer concept of the society we sought to serve and complement.

In that spirit we talked over dinner the night before our closing campus show at Santa Clara University. We discussed how we should celebrate our year together. Without a pause, Carlo set the custom for years to come. "I think the most appropriate way to close the season is to do something we really know how to do: perform the show."

That's what we did. Then tore it down, loaded it into storage at Trinity, said goodbye, and headed to our homes. But I had houseguests in my room: Fritzi, Penelope, the duck, and the doves. That's when it really dawned on me: this wasn't a pious pilgrimage. This was a life.

*   *   *

It was time to begin expanding my personal skill-set, and I wanted to learn how to walk the tightrope. That skill had been my favorite in the circus repertoire for a long time.

I began training on a rope stretched between two trees at a height of two feet. Meanwhile a self-standing rig with the rope at seven feet was being built. Eventually I managed the essential balance during my very first session. The business of tightrope walking is always falling off, but it was clearly achievable. I was quite pleased. The skill imposes a dance on the acrobat, and how the body moves is unlike any other movement. It would be as close to dance as I ever got. But there's a reason that particular skill has become a metaphor for navigating tight spots in life: tricky as conflicting demands can be, we actually do achieve a measure of grace when we resolve them. We rise above a level of mere coping.

*   *   *

I started Joe Reichlin out on the wire in 1987. This stellar trick, he learned by himself.

Late during that summer I discovered an ad for "stinkectomied" baby skunks being sold at a pet store in Reno. I had long wanted to work a live skunk into a clown gag, but they were illegal in California, because they are prime harbingers of rabies. Here was my chance. Without knowing exactly what I was going to do with it, I set out for Reno, bought an animal, and smuggled it back into the state. Aerosol was a fine male with a very broad white stripe down his back. Perfect. I had a vague idea I wanted to have him pop out of a giant deodorant container after involving a spectator with the outsized prop.

I hauled him out to my vet for any shots he needed. Then I bought a small cat's harness and a leash. Back in the dorm room, while trying to put the harness on him the first time, he turned around and bit my hand rather badly. He wasn't ferocious; he just wanted me to stop bothering him.

The next day my arm was throbbing. I couldn't go to a doctor. I would have been fined and the animal would have been confiscated. So I traipsed back out to the vet who I knew would cut me and the skunk some slack. He looked the animal over carefully. I could tell he loved it. Then he looked at me, read my mind, and sat me down in a chair. With the straightforward commanding tone that a priest uses with a severely scrupled penitent, he gave me the medicine I needed.

"Now look. There's absolutely no way you have rabies. If you did, that animal would be dying, and it's in perfect health as you can see. You don't have rabies. You have one hell of an infection, but you don't have rabies."

He told me how to treat the infection and sent me home. Other preparations crowded my schedule, and I decided to spend the months till Christmas getting Aerosol acclimated to the show and letting him grow up. After that we would work with the leash.

My new human partners would include John Salazar, a young comic graduating from Santa Clara University's theater department, and another former student from my last year at Saint Ignatius, Steve Saiz.

The schedule for rehearsals in August was the same, lasting a fairly intense two weeks. I had decided I didn't have the skill on the tightrope to perform a straight act, so I prepared to do it as a gorilla in a tutu carrying a lace parasol. Donning the tutu in the ring was a very funny image. Seeing out of the mask was the major task.

In Chicago the previous spring we had visited "Magic Inc." shop and I purchased an antique classic, the die box, which had a breakaway feature allowing us to develop a storyline about a floating crap game. It was a nice routine with a double surprise finish demanding that Steve smuggle a live rabbit into a performance space that was about two-thirds surrounded.

There was a crazy faux mind-reading act with John in a turban and cape: Professor Zogah, who had "memorized" the phone book. John Baker and Mary Hildebrand continued as our scenic and property designers. John developed two new drops for the fables "Peddler's Dream" (on the importance of holding fast to one's dreams) and "Herman and the Night" (about a curmudgeon who figured out that what he thought was his enemy was a facet of his friend). Mary came up with a wonderful little cannon out of which I "shot" our little dog, Fritzi.

That little cannon would trade off its wheels backstage with a scale model of a modified Gollmar Ringling mirror wagon that Mary also built. This gorgeous little vehicle rolled into the ring, then stopped center, and when one of the side mirrors was lowered, out came Penelope. It was marvelous. Where a kid in the front row had just seen his own face, out came a live monkey. The old joke.

By this time we had befriended a very clever local magician who loaned us an antique Celestina barrel organ that was over a hundred years old. We had a metal box designed for its transport. This humble music box would allow our little show to open with wafts of music just right for the territory we held on the vast acreage of entertainment styles. A clown cranking a little barrel organ. What could be a more fit emblem of what we were about?

For the first time we were able to have indoor rehearsals in the lobby of the Lifeboat Theater, the temporary performing space the university was using while the new Mayer Theater complex was being built. (The old "Ship" had floated into history; hence the *Lifeboat.*) We opened at Fresno Fashion Fair, a beautiful indoor mall, on August 23 for three days alternating two halves of our show. Alas the mall was a bit too beautiful; we were not allowed to use our animals. Then we were off to Sacramento's Country Club Plaza, San Rafael, Oakland, and back down to Santa Clara for a Mission Garden performance and a formal blessing of the show by a fellow Jesuit priest. After that it was the north-to-Portland route, east and south to the Midwest. We were launched again.

But blessing or no, it wasn't an easy tour. In late September, we played Weber State University in Ogden, Utah. While driving around looking for a place to have lunch I didn't realize how far left I was on my side of the street when I began to make a right turn. Another car was attempting to pass in what was effectively a right lane. Our right rear door was hit.

We eventually had lunch, and kept to our schedule with a slightly bashed door. The next stop was Denver, where Jennie Madrigal was waiting for us, and she and her friends knew their away around enough to find a junkyard with our door and someone who could change it out. We now drove a two-tone station wagon—the newish door was gold. But hey, it worked. We never heard anything further about the incident.

In Saint Louis in mid-October we stayed with Jesuit friends at a sub-community connected to Saint Louis University, in a large home on McPherson Avenue. By a stroke of luck it was quite a cold fall evening so I brought Penelope inside with me. (She was my roommate that night, just like at home.) We had the next day off, so we all slept in. But at 9 am one of the Jesuits knocked on my door and popped his head in to say, "You'd better get up, Nick! Your car is gone!"

We had parked the station wagon in front of the house on McPherson Avenue and sure enough it was gone, as was the cargo—and Fritzi and Aerosol and the rabbit. At about 3 pm the police called to say they had found the vehicle where they find several a week. Missing were a part of the gorilla costume (Halloween was coming), the antique barrel organ, and all the animals. But the car ran fine. The magic props and costumes were intact. We had one smashed window, and we still had Penelope.

A very generous Jesuit friend dedicated his time and taxi service to us as we scurried around for a few replacement props we could find to muster the Saint Louis University campus show the next day. I got brave and did the tightrope straight, telling jokes along the way to cover my lack of real tricks. Eventually we found a replacement gorilla head, and a rabbit. I have to admit that I still hope Aerosol bit hell out of anyone who tried to mess with him.

Then we continued south to New Orleans, west into Texas, New Mexico, and Arizona, then east clear over to Miami by Thanksgiving, and then back up through Alabama and directly west home to California for Christmas break.

One day, while I was at home at Santa Clara, the new rector of the Jesuit Community, Father Bill Rewak, told me that the Community wanted to help me replace the station wagon and that I should seriously consider what type of new vehicle we could use and let him know what the cost would be.[41]

This proposal jarred my thinking into line with a well-known fact about circus life: the quality of your show correlates directly with the quality of your

[41] Such generosity was typical of the kind of support I enjoyed from the California Province and widespread Jesuit associations across the U.S.

fleet's serviceability. It may not always be that neat, and perhaps not everyone can articulate it that way, but the basic truth is, you depend mightily on what carries the show down the road. No matter how many elephants you have, no matter how many plates your juggler can keep in the air, no matter how daring your aerialists are—none of it matters if you can't get it all to, say, Holdrege, Nebraska in time for the matinee.

So I began thinking. And I imagined. I took my reflections "outside the box," as administrators persist in saying. And I wound up with a box. Precisely, a cube van: the 1972 model of Dodge's KaryVan. It was the engine and snubnosed cab of their regular van with a box stuck on. You could easily stand up in it, and there were double doors on the back end suitable for loading equipment.

Bill accepted the proposal, including my plans for customizing, and the purchase was made. Then an RV shop with sheet metal expertise took on my customizing proposal. The truck was to be given a second interior sheet metal skin so the walls could be insulated. There would be a 115v electrical hook up servicing a roof mounted A/C, small refrigerator, lights, and receptacles. There would be two fold-down, bunk-sized tables hinged permanently to the walls, each able to accommodate a bedroll. An identically-sized shelf would be permanently installed closer to the ceiling on one side of the van. Thus there were sleeping areas for three people.

The van was to be outfitted with propane servicing the refrigerator and a two-burner cook stove. And there were to be small storage spaces permanently installed at the very rear of the cube. The cab had two seats on either side of the engine shroud, and a third seat was added right behind the front passenger's. In a pinch, we were self-sufficient; we could house ourselves. Though I hadn't had this particular plan before, it was realized just in time to load up for the second half of our tour.

We again shot straight up to Seattle and then headed east through Idaho and on toward Montana and its Indian Reservations and colleges. The new truck handled well and ran very smoothly. But of course at that time of the year in that part of the country road conditions were icy and dicey. Sure enough, coming down a steep mountain pass in western Montana, I hit a patch of black ice under an overpass. The van slid sideways on the roadway, and against every instinct in me I turned into the skid—just like they tell you. Thankfully we straightened out three minutes before the biggest semi I'd ever seen came up the opposite direction. We reached the little town of Saint Regis, pulled into a café, and unwound as driver after driver came in detailing the treacherous adventure they had just had with the same patch of black ice.

There was another watershed and better luck when we finally reached our first Montana date, the University of Montana in Missoula. Because of severe weather we were scheduled indoors in the very stylish student union mall area.

Unbeknownst to me, a young woman who had done artwork for the Council Players in San Jose was studying dance at the university. She talked her instructor into bringing the dance class to see a friend of hers in another form of performance art, and their class made up a very enthusiastic and responsive center of our large audience.

Our performances always included volunteer participation, and that always injected a healthy and spontaneous energy into a given routine. I was doing an old magic classic I had learned from Father Bob, jazzed up a bit for the ring. It involved the vanish of a spectator's marked coin and then the discovery of it buried deep inside a large ball of yarn. Just as I had a hundred times before, I asked for a spectator, and one of the kids in that center section immediately jumped up.

On his way up to the ring he took off the calf-length navy blue overcoat he was wearing. Of course I pushed for the surefire lower comedy with something like "Oh, no more please! This is a family show!" We did the routine while a classmate held his coat for him. My friend from the Council Players days came up after the show and introduced her dancer friend, now an experienced circus volunteer, Mitch Kincannon. We all got together that evening where the show was lodged for the night.

Mitch and I talked a lot about his own dreams. He had already identified mine pretty well. His horizons seemed to be expanding as he studied at the university. But performance was obviously to be a focus in anything he hoped to accomplish. Of course what we were doing included a potpourri of performance skills and opportunities, and I think even in that first conversation, the kid from Scobey, Montana seemed a bit in awe over this little truck show playing at an out-of-the-way school. There was in that first long meeting a depth of interest in what I was doing, why I was doing it, and who I was. I don't think I have ever experienced a more intense conversation.

The next stop was about forty miles north in Saint Ignatius, Montana, an evening show at the Jesuit parish there. Mitch came up to catch the show again. He was hooked on what we were doing. Just before teardown he said goodbye and gave me a farewell gift: his navy blue overcoat. Needless to say we stayed in touch because by this time we had discussed what he might be able to achieve as a member of our company. We would discover that he could achieve a lot, and did. But he needed to finish two more semesters and we needed to finish our tour.

No matter how comfortable your stay was in any given town, no matter how artistically satisfied you might have been or how much press you gleaned there, you knew you had to get to someplace else. That's what such a life demands, and there is no letup. For the director that drive and discipline even muscles into the off-road time when a show is in quarters. Always future places down the road have to be found and cultivated. We had learned early that it's very nearly impossible to remember where you were yesterday while you're on tour.

With hearts full of all those tomorrows that became todays and enough of a kitty to buy some paint, more Trigger Cloth, and a new illusion for next season, the show made it home by the end of May. Once more, our last celebration was the performance itself. But this time I knew I wasn't just returning the props to storage, or transferring the animals to the customized cages in my room. There was a significant component of the circus—our circus—that I couldn't put away. It was inside of me and moved as I moved.

As importantly, this dimension of my personality had begun to redefine my self-concept of priest. I no longer thought of myself as lugging around a hyphen or an "and." I walked and talked and worked and practiced and prayed as a clown who was a priest who was a circus director. I tried to present myself humbly, tentatively. I knew there was an edge about me that said, *Take what you get, all or nothing.* I also knew enough about circus and pilgrimage to recognize both as only processes and promises. So once again I spent the summer harnessing my imagination to an atlas, some coffee-stained route sheets, and the phone.

11.

Humble Ring of Wonders

"A circus with as much for grownups as for children."
—One Main Place, Dallas, December 1972

When I described our public workspace as "this humble ring" in the poem with which I opened so many shows, I was aware of more than the truth of what we were doing and what I had done to make it possible. Lexically, *humble* derives from the Latin notion of earth and soil, *humus*. That's why humility is associated with lowliness, as in "coming back down to earth," and remembering "where you came from." If there's one constant preoccupation for a man running an outdoor circus, it's earth and soil. Rough or smooth, planted or not, soft or firm were all attributes vital to our playing spaces. Unicycle tires, animal hooves, our own footing, what the audience would sit on, how easily and deeply stakes could be driven, and the whether and when of automatic irrigation: these were all parts of an almost daily interface with earth.

Of course the size of our playing space, the ring, was deliberately small and in that sense humble, especially in contrast with the scale of other circuses. But no matter how large a circus ring is or how many rings a circus has, the notion of the ring is itself humble. It leads nowhere. It seemingly defies progress, champions present concentration. As such, rituals limiting themselves to such a space run in circles. Going in circles can lead to a healthy process of self-recognition. An audience encircling performers willing to undertake such a journey in public might walk away from the circle on a straight sidewalk. But when their paths next encounter one of life's necessarily repetitive rituals, perhaps they will bring to it the rounded welcome they helped shape at the circus.

Among the routes each circus season follows are journeys to intimate personal discoveries more important than uncharted horizons. Facing the self that showed up in my life's circle meant facing the truth of exactly who and whence I was. Magazine interviews, television appearances, and hundreds upon hundreds of performances could not for half a day interfere with the earthy tasks of feeding animals, rehearsing and risking new acts, airing animals, unloading freight, driving stakes, cleaning up after animals, loading freight, driving and maintaining trucks and trailers. Those tasks were just the ones associated with the show itself. They presumed the attention I gave to myself. But it was guaranteed that whatever attention I gave myself came within a context of fairly rugged reality.

One of the signs and payoffs of humility is the capacity to say "I don't know." Those words, and the attitude they signal, are the perfect setup for learning. Everywhere I turned, especially in the earlier years of the circus, there were things I needed to learn. Loving the circus was not enough. Building a circus involved me in a maze of specialties, from esoteric skills requiring technical apparatus to animal medicine and husbandry. Most of what I needed to learn had been known for a long time, so I just needed to find the people who could teach me. The spin-off from the generous publicity we had been given was that I could more easily discover my teachers.

For the 1974-'75 season our Santa Clara magician friend, Bill Wizard, agreed to build us a classic illusion, "The Packing Box Escape," which was a variation on the famous "Metamorphosis" of Houdini's career with the added complication of a laced-up canvas "skin" over the outside of the box and the locks. This was the biggest magic act we had yet tackled, and our friend taught us an important lesson involving locks and keys. The rule is, never begin an escape rehearsal or performance with open locks. Always be sure you have to unlock the locks with a key in front of the audience; then you know you have the key onstage. But we learned the hard way.

It was an early evening dress rehearsal on the Santa Clara University campus with an audience of about ten or fifteen friends. My new partners were a returning Steve Aveson and a recent Santa Clara graduate, Dana Smith. We began the escape. Steve handcuffed Dana, put him in a mail sack, tied the top shut, and Dana, thus secured, knelt inside the wood packing box. The lid was put on, the locks were ready (i.e. *open*. Oops!) and snapped in place around the edge of the lid, and then the canvas cover was pulled up over the box and laced tightly across the top. Assistants from the audience helped Steve place a cloth tent over the box and hold it at the corners. Steve entered the tent through the front opening and held the flaps tightly below his chin so that only his face showed. He counted to three, withdrew his head into the tent, and out popped Dana's. The tent was dropped, removed, and the canvas cover unlaced to expose the still-locked padlocks on the box.

This part of the stunt must go very quickly because then the locks are removed, the lid taken off, the mail sack stands up, and there would be Steve waiting to be unhandcuffed. Done up to speed it is a marvelous effect and Dana and Steve always did it justice.

Except that evening. We had gotten through the routine to the point where we needed to let Steve out and there was no key to unlock the padlocks on the box. Embarrassed, we had to lug the crate with Steve in it around to the privacy of one of the backyard tents to free Steve without revealing the secret. Later there was a backstage laugh on me. At the moment when I realized we had no key, I panicked. I had completely forgotten that no matter what, Steve could get out the same way he got in and Dana got out. But we learned how important it is to have locked locks at the start of every run-through.

There is another very practical tip performers working this act should know and nice people don't talk about it. It's—well, humiliating. Whoever gets tied up and locked up first should be careful about what and when he eats. Split-second timing is essential, and the box is completely enclosed. The magician is inheriting that space immediately after his assistant is out, and a partner's vestigial flatulence can be torture. We learned that the hard way too.

The packing box escape was a hit everywhere. Not for nothing did "Metamorphosis" help build Houdini's reputation. It is so much more than an escape, since there is the surprise of the assistant's revenge. We still have iconic photos and memories of a very appropriate volunteer from the audience checking the locks. It happened at the University of Detroit Mercy, and Father Dan Berrigan, arguably American Catholicism's most famous jailbird, a recently released convicted felon, examined the restraints. I'd guess about half the audience noticed the ironic fun.

L-R: Dan Berrigan, SJ and Steve Aveson. April, 1975. University of Detroit Mercy. (With permission, *The Varsity News*)

In September of that season, I shared a date with Catherine Deneuve and it was all over *People Magazine*. Well, all we shared was the September 2 issue with her beautiful face on the cover and my mug inside. The *People* people had decided they wanted to begin a column titled "Spirit" and had asked me for an interview. It was a generous article with straightforward reporting and several good photos.

Balancing the glamour of the article came a humbling lesson. At least one reader didn't catch the spirit *People* represented me as pitching. Four issues later, on September 30, a letter to the editor was published.

> *Who the heck does that "Jesuit clown" think he is anyway? "I'm allergic to materialism." It's a good thing for him that others still believe in materialism or the good father and his "pre-evangelical" circus wouldn't be able to jaunt around the country "living sort of naked." Or hasn't he figured that one out yet? Maybe the light will dawn when he sponges his next dinner and lodgings from his next family.*
>
> Colette Lettinga
> Des Moines

As a matter of fact we were headed to Denver, so the next lodgings we sponged were from my extended Jesuit family at Regis College. Of course we sponged the next meal from Jennie Madrigal. Neither the Jesuits nor Jennie were known to "believe in materialism." But I was learning. I hadn't been paying attention to the possibility of other views. They would continue to temper the enthusiasm with which I characterized such an unusual ministry.

That season we also performed the rising cards illusion. In the audience three cards were chosen from a regulation deck. Then those cards are seen to rise one after the other from a giant deck placed in a large brandy snifter onstage. We could hand out the giant cards and the large brandy snifter for close inspection immediately after the third card rose from the deck. But early on, I was gifted with a humbling lesson, and it came from the audience.

At the start of the season, we performed the rising cards in Fresno's Roeding Park, right next to the zoo. I didn't yet have the expertise at judging audiences that I thought I had, and I also presumed everyone was as dedicated to the success of the show's repertoire as I was. When I brought the large brandy snifter down to the front row for inspection I made a grand mistake. I didn't just show the handsome glass prop, I put it into the hands of a little kid sitting with his friends, front row center. Within five seconds those kids achieved more surprise and comedy than we managed in an hour show. They and the glass were gone. We never saw them again. The audience overcame their embarrassment for us, laughed a smile onto my stunned face, and we went on with the show. The illusion had worked perfectly. It was a beautiful effect. We replaced the brandy snifter, but I had been humbled enough to learn another lesson. I never took my hands off that glass again.

Another beautiful effect materialized in Washington, D.C., and it emanated from a humble circus man's honesty. We were booked to play a civic birthday celebration in front of the District's City Hall. Long before setup began, I was walking past the truck, which was parked in a huge bed of bright yellow daffodils. The van itself was incongruous; and there was my partner, Dana Smith, with a bucket of water and his face close to one of the side mirrors, shaving. One of those moments in my life where I thought, *That's Circus.*

*   *   *

During the winter break back at Santa Clara University, a friend introduced me to a lady who raised miniature horses. From her I bought a magnificent little black stallion and immediately named him "Othello." He was completely fresh, unbroken, with not a clue about taking commands. And I didn't have a clue about teaching him to take them. It was humiliating enough to make me more than eager when I learned there was a professor at Santa Clara who knew all about horses. The plan was to let Othello spend the second half of that season just getting used to us and our daily routine. Serious training would take place in the summer months.

In May of that season, we visited some of our college dates in Ohio, and wound up at Chatfield College in Saint Martin, a small school run by a group of Sisters called the Brown County Ursulines. A wonderful Sister Dorothy, in full traditional habit, was in charge of feeding us and was very generous. On the evening of our arrival, the school's lay bursar offered to show me the sights of Saint Martin and in the brief course of our few stops we entered a dark tavern. My life stopped for awhile. At one of the tables sat a man feeding a small bear cub from a Pepsi bottle rigged with a nipple stuck on the end. Nothing else mattered.

"Where'd you get that little bear?"

"Up at Ladderback's place, that plumber in Xenia. He raises 'em. Got two more. Little females. He'll prob'ly sell you one."

"What'd you pay for it?"

"Five hundred."

That was it. The next morning we owned a little bear (having circumvented the lion chained to a tree in Ladderback's front yard). But she had to visit the vet first. We had been advised to have the claws removed. That lion and the tiny bear's claws were nothing compared to the anxiety my most outspoken partner was experiencing.

"Have you thought about this? You do know that animal is going to grow and that it is wild. Are you prepared to take responsibility for raising and controlling it?"

I don't know how I answered him. I had thought about it ever since I saw a bear in a black-and-white Bunuel film. I didn't even have specific circus bears in mind. But I knew circus menageries included bears. I knew nothing about bears and I didn't know how quickly I would humbly recognize the need to learn.

We picked her up the next day on our way west to make our date at the University of Dayton. We had a beautiful furry little bundle, still very much asleep from anesthesia with her tiny paw-ends wrapped in bandage. The wire cage we bought could wait for now; she was comfortable in a small cardboard box riding between the two front seats. Her name? We had found her while visiting the Sisters of Saint Ursula (*little she-bear*) and one had been very nice to us: Sister Dorothy. Our little bear would bear her name. That night we smuggled our new recruit into the married students housing apartment where we were staying at the university. She had awakened and she was hungry. It took us weeks to adjust her diet so her stool would firm up. It's fun wondering now what Penelope was thinking about all this

*   *   *

"A marvel: full of joy and good humor, raising just the right kind of gentle havoc. Such gentle fun and rare wit marry in one marvelous hour."
—Philip Zaeder, Associate Chaplain, Yale University

That summer we prepared for our Bicentennial Edition since half the tour would occur during 1976. I opened the show with a musical bottles act, playing "My Country 'Tis of Thee." Early in the show we presented a classic bit of magic with three silk handkerchiefs that pass through a newspaper tube and come out blended into a perfect American flag. That's what everyone expected, anyway. The performer "accidentally" drops the blue silk and the flag comes out in only red and white. Finally the performer hears the yells from the audience, sees the dropped blue silk, and pushes it through the tube with the defective flag. Voila. We immediately flew the flag up to a mast centered on the top of the main drop. Later in the show we would fly what appeared to be a spectator's boxers below the flag to represent the tiny nation of clownery. We mounted "Miles From Giles," a fable about a slow-witted mean giant, complete with an outsized puppet and drop. And another new fable was based partly on a pun, "The Truthful Lyre."

In the skills department I retired the tightrope for awhile and learned how to walk barefoot up a ladder of knives, and one of my new partners mastered foot juggling and a straitjacket escape. There is no gimmick to walking on real machetes; it hurts like hell when you start out. I almost gave up, but then, when I knew what to expect as soon as I brought all my weight to bear on a placed foot, it became manageable. Not pleasant, but manageable. It's really part of traditional sideshow repertoire, but so is fire-eating and magic. We brought these acts into the mainstream ring entertainment of our show. I took a risk thinking I could present such acts straightforwardly. That was a mistake, and the audience helped me through the correction. Listening to their reactions I learned a key lesson. We could get away with anything as long as we paid attention to our primary identity: we were clowns. Even the dangerous stuff called for comic settings. So the jokes developed and were delivered as integral parts of the routines.

Besides the new bear, our performing menagerie had grown to include "Othello." This little guy had never been taught anything about work and he gave us a run for our money. He looked very sharp in an all-yellow harness and halter set. But even though we would like to have worked him at "liberty"— that is, without a lead—we didn't dare. He could run faster than any of us.

It took us fifteen years. This is as close as we came to a liberty act. Bucko and Dan.

To me the horse complemented the show like nothing else could. It was in those days that I felt comfortable calling the show "complete." There was a historical reason for this. The circus as we know it has nothing to do with ancient Rome or Nero. The word of course means *circle*, and the circle of the ring is directly related to the horse. In the mid-1700s a former British cavalryman, Philip Astley, exhibited horses traversing with and without riders around a ring 42 feet in diameter. Probably, the diameter of the ring was determined by experiments seeking the smallest circumference a horse could effectively gallop. The ring itself consisted of a simple wooden curb about a foot high. It was a guide for the animals and, properly trained, they would remain within the circular space without attached leads. Then, along with equestrian feats, other variety entertainment of even ancient marketplace and more recent fairground origins were presented in the same space. Most likely, Astley's first competitor, Charles Hughes, named this entertainment *circus*. So the shape of the entertainment, the circular ring, is directly related to the horse. For me, the circus is inseparable from "horse."

Penelope, our spider monkey, was by seniority queen of the menagerie, and she seemed to calmly accept the new smells and sounds the horse and the bear brought with them. But monkeys are curious, so Dorothy and Othello were constantly monitored by this magnificent little black and gold creature with the huge dark eyes and five hands. But once, Penelope wasn't paying enough attention at a time when Dorothy was. The little monkey was being carried out of the truck when just the end of that marvelous prehensile tail, a virtual index finger, glanced across the grill of the bear cage and Dorothy nipped it. It was gashed. Treatment, stitching, and daily changing of bandages as we moved from town to town and vet to vet didn't prevent gangrene. Finally amputation of the tail's tip was imperative. There is nothing quite like the sadness you feel when you fail an animal, especially one who makes your way of life possible. Once the pain was gone and she recognized the new configuration of her tail, Penelope went on with her part in our life. She didn't express fear of the bear or other animals. I think she recovered faster than I did. She had taught me something about safety around wild animals. Humiliating as it was, I didn't learn.

In Chicago that season I wanted Jay Marshall, the professional magician and author who founded Magic Inc., to see our very original take on the little magic silks classic, "Mismade Flag." So I was very excited and proud that this American magic legend accepted my invitation to come and see us in a dorm lobby at Loyola University. But during the act before that routine, the white silk in the set was nowhere to be found. A third of "Mismade Flag" had vanished. This embarrassing mishap occasioned a new backyard rule: no props, under any circumstances, were to be set on top of the bear cage. Bears have long tongues. The learning never stopped, and so often the process was energized by surprise.

The biggest and best surprise of that season happened on my birthday. When we arrived in Caldwell, Idaho, Mitch had come down from Missoula, Montana to meet us. And it was during that visit that he committed himself to joining the show. In several senses, Mitch was perfectly suited for the life we led. Of Scotch and Irish origin, he grew up in the rugged plains of northern Montana, which are almost in Saskatchewan. His father, like mine, operated heavy equipment. Raised Catholic, Mitch was at once inquisitive and questioning. Above all he was sensitive, keenly observant, and kind. He had thought he wanted nothing more than to perform as a dancer, but when he ran into us he found a wider performance model and a style of theater that called to more of his talents.

Although he was unequivocal about his decision to join us, it was very clear that Mitch wanted to be a substantive contributor to what he understood us to be doing. Without his using the words, I sensed that his goal was to explore the possibility of a creative partnership extending beyond performing and beyond a season. To the point, he wanted to apprentice to the show for the second half of the current season, and then perform in the following years. He volunteered the plural word *years.* I knew he understood my relationship to the Jesuits, and my life as that of a religious order priest who was a circus man and a circus man who was a religious order priest. There was no doubt in my mind that he understood that his part in the circus, like mine, could not be a way to *make* a living as much as a way to *do* a living. All of us worked for our keep, and we kept together for the work. That he wanted an apprenticeship was a signal. He sensed how difficult it would be for us to take the year's established repertoire and read a new man into it. More importantly, the apprenticeship meant he was going to approach this methodically. Both of us paid attention to that plural, *years.* There was another signal. I knew that when he left the University of Montana, he would be ending a significantly personal set of choices: a career, a training program and a set of colleagues. The Royal Lichtenstein Circus and what he could help it become was a new life choice for him.

Mitch went back to Missoula and we moved east to Pocatello. But while the show still faced half a season of adventures with its present cast doing an already proven repertoire, I knew I had to explore new territory and new procedures. The four-year-old system I had been wed to had to seek out its roots and discover a method that would incorporate new personal investment, new ideas, and new dedication to possibly better systems and better seasons. Mitch Kincannon would not perform with us until the '76–'77 season, but he would be present for work on New Year's Day of '76, ready to begin learning everything he could about the show. Then, humbly, he would work on the second half of the current season in whatever capacity he could. I was damned if I was going to waste a second of his time.

*   *   *

"An ultra-creative blend of circus, mime, ballet, parables, nonsense, a few animals —and magic."
—*The Cincinnati Post-Times Star*, May 4, 1973

On New Year's Eve 1975, Mitch's plane arrived punctually at the San Francisco Airport, where I picked him up for his first visit to California, his first sighting of a palm tree, and that evening, his first trip to a tented circus. (Circus Vargas just happened to be in town.) Mitch was set to become part of the Royal Lichtenstein Circus and, as everyone—especially the Jesuits—soon realized, part of Nick Weber's priestly ministry. According to plan, he immediately took on the detailed schedule of my life, largely dictated by animal husbandry, property maintenance, and the business of booking solicitation, travel details, and publicity.

The conversations we had begun two seasons before about spirituality and my take on ministry would continue through what became some of the most demanding and rewarding soul-soundings I have encountered. Jesuits are handy with distinctions; Mitch became handy at discerning which ones were warranted or justified, and I was his lab. I never for a moment had reason to doubt that Mitch worked for and lived in the same circus I did. He came to own what he knew of the Jesuit way of doing things, and in the best of senses, the Jesuits, especially at Santa Clara University, owned him. He shared the other student-space in my dorm room; he ate with me in the break-room of the Jesuit Community.

Mitch Kincannon in "uniform" as our house manager

After the winter recess, when we were back on the road, Mitch did not have to be asked to cover bases for me; he found them and often covered them before I knew they were a concern. He mastered the route book that guided us from town to town and from phone number to phone number. He knew how to find every kind of animal food, and each animal's needs and schedule. In Missoula when I first met Mitch, he kept excusing his sloppy driving habits. In those days he could be more attentive to conversation than to the vehicle. In a year, he would become our best driver. Perhaps the happiest talent he developed was his manner of speaking with overcautious religious sponsors. The first few times I knew he had been cornered into sharing his own take on the merits and spiritual warranty of the circus, I eavesdropped in case he needed help. But he had his feet on the ground. He knew what we were and what we weren't and everyone around him knew he did. I had a spokesperson I could trust. It became clear he had as consequential a stake in the work as I did.

That summer, we moved once more into the routines of menagerie maintenance, prop construction, and equipment repair. There would be two substantial innovations for the coming season: a new costume design and a major escape illusion that was as dangerous as it was cumbersome. The costume choice was to give us a new look and that alone made me hesitant because I was partial to the tunic silhouette and thought it would become part of a trademark. But I agreed to the suggestions of our generous seamstress. It involved a Renaissance-styled white blouse with ornate cuffs and a multicolored slipover vest. Both pieces were washable and lightweight. While the new apparatus for the escape was eminently washable, it was by no means lightweight. Our version of the legendary Houdini Milk Can Escape was a one-hundred gallon stainless steel tank. It was ruggedly constructed and lasted through several seasons. The new wardrobe design was retired after one season.

Stage magic's appeal is to be found in the set of archetypes literary artists have manipulated from Homer on. The magician tells his stories with objects, or human assistants used as objects, rather than with human personalities and characters. And every one of his stories, like literary ones, is a variation on a limited number of themes: appearance (including productions and multiplications), disappearance, transposition, mutilation-restoration, and escape (including variants such as levitations that escape gravity). I suspect that of these archetypal themes, the one that more directly correlates with literature is the escape.[42] *That* certainly was my own conviction when I developed the patter for the climax of the Milk Can Escape.

"And once more ladies and gentlemen, living proof that there is only one story possible to the human psyche and it has two chapters. Chapter One: Getting Into Trouble. Chapter Two: Getting Out."

And out would come the performer, dripping wet and out of breath as we moved back the screen to reveal the can intact with padlocks still locked and in place.

The Milk Can Escape is difficult to stage, and it is strenuous and dangerous for the performer. There are safety principles on which the effect is based. Thankfully, William Wizard our insightful magic consultant and designer had complemented the Montraville Wood–Harry Houdini work with safety features of his own. But the facts remain that one hundred gallons of water have to find their way onto the stage and off, and a human being is submerged inside a filled heavy steel container to be secured by external locks. In our situation, the audience was usually more than halfway around us and in fact enjoyed 360 degrees of visibility. No one could access the can to assist. Nor was there any way to remove the water, which the audience had seen poured into the can, bucket by five-gallon bucket. The can rested on a solid piece of thick plywood—often outdoors—so there was no trapdoor access. Before any water was poured, volunteers from the audience examined the can, the lid, and the locks.

The young man who was to inaugurate our staging of this illusion was Kevin Duggan, a Santa Clara University graduate who was with us for two seasons. An avid soccer player, Kevin had a trim athlete's build and cheerful good looks that belied the fact that he was pulling a fast one when he did magic. In everything he did, there was thorough preparation and meticulous rehearsal. How inventive he was we were yet to find out.

---

[42] The French concept of *denouement* is that of release from crisis as a plot or *noeud*—literally *knot*--unties itself.

What none of us realized until the first "wet run" of the Milk Can Escape was how impossible it was going to be for the performer to communicate with us on the outside, should he need help. The water insulated against all sound. Besides, music would be playing and we and the audience would be counting aloud to sustain tension. What if the guy was in trouble and needed to be let out? Independently of procedural failure, there was the stark possibility of sudden illness: stroke or heart attack or severe muscle cramping. Eventually we settled on our counting as a less-than-perfect safety mechanism. From rehearsals, we knew the shortest and longest escape times. We averaged them, and established the count at which we would presume there was trouble. If by that point I had not felt Kevin touch me through the cloth screen I was holding, I went in with the key. When he actually appeared was up to his dramatic sensitivity, but he was to signal me as soon as he was safe. This worked well. I only had to rescue him once. But that was too many times.

One hundred gallons of water weigh a lot, so the Milk Can Escape was our finale. With the can unlocked and open, pumps were submerged attached to hoses and the water drained so we could handle the prop and finish teardown. Since this was often performed on carpeted floors and second story venues, we saw a lot of janitorial mop sinks.

Another class of magic found its way into our repertoire quite regularly, and that involved the transposition of a coin or a bill that had vanished. Here again magicians invoke a theme with reasonably close resonance in everyday life and literature. It is a universally shared experience that money always changes hands and often disappears. So there is commonly a tense tracking of its travels by everyone. With us a marked coin or bill went up in smoke, or vanished from a handkerchief and then turned up inside a huge ball of yarn, a loaf of bread, the center of a fresh lemon, or the innermost of a set of nested locked boxes.

Admittedly, such manipulation of real, borrowed currency allowed me the development of patter touching on the place we give money and things material in daily life. One way or another we were always envisioning our tiny circus as an antidote to the materialism and rampant consumerism of our culture. If not a clear illustration of our effectiveness, certainly one performance of the nest of boxes hilariously exemplified how automatically driven we can be around money.

The performance was for a formal $135 per plate "Bal Du Cirque" at the Riviera Country Club of Pacific Palisades to benefit the Hathaway Home for Children. Guests could come in circus attire if they chose. Others wore tuxedos or evening gowns. It was a glittering audience to say the least. (Herve Villechaize, aka "Tattoo" from *Fantasy Island*, was seated ringside wearing a brilliant sequined scaled-down set of a ringmaster's top hat and tails.) One of the guests volunteered to help with this classic old feat and proffered a quarter which we had him duly mark for future identification. Then I vanished it "accidentally." Feigning embarrassment I asked the volunteer if he'd help me with one more trick in which we would contact the Spirit of Circus Past. This involved unlocking a chest, inside of which was another chest, locked, inside of which was yet another locked chest—but surprise. A quarter is taped over the keyhole. The spectator is asked to remove it and examine it.

"Is THAT your quarter?"

"No!" This was always delivered half triumphantly.

"It isn't? You're sure?"

"Yes, I'm positive."

"Well, since that's not your quarter, I'm going to ask you to give it away. On the count of three, I want you to toss that quarter high above the audience's heads. Ready? One! Two! Three!"

And up the quarter went. It was still airborne when formally attired members of our audience jumped out of their seats. There was actual scrambling around on the floor to recover it when it landed. At $135 a plate. Adults in tuxedoes. I asked where the *Hollywood Reporter* was when we needed it.

When order resumed, my volunteer opened another chest, and then another, inside of which was a ball of yarn in which was the marked quarter. I will always wonder whether the person who did get the tossed quarter enjoyed the trick's finale as much as gaining twenty-five cents. That routine was always surefire. We had practiced enough to render every step of the effect entertaining, especially the misdirecting tossed quarter.

Once we discovered we had a method that worked for a magic routine, we just about set its mechanics in stone so that we could count on everything happening the same way every time. We all learned, however, never to presume we had heard Kevin's final or definitive take on a routine's patter, especially at times when he had a chance to address the audience directly. He was always thinking, always inventing.

Sometimes, outdoors, that water for the escape was very cold. Just imagine working outdoors in the northwest in winter. One day, everything seemed normal. Everyone could see their breath, though, and everyone began to hold their breath with Kevin as he lowered himself into the tank and we all saw the displaced water overflow into the shallow kids' wading pool in which the can rested. Kevin looked right at the audience, daring them to ask. Forget goose bumps, his nipples had turned blue. Then it happened, and he'd been waiting.

"Is it cold?"

"Is a frog's ass watertight at twenty fathoms?"

The tension was jettisoned. All of us were laughing so hard we had to strain to get focused on what we were about to do. It was one of the nicest surprises and most tailored comebacks I had ever heard. It goes without saying we were entertaining college kids.

Kevin Duggan:
"Go ahead and ask!"

The last breath

On Lincoln's birthday, the promotional office at Portland's Downtown Meier and Frank Department Store presented us in their toy department for three half-hour performances. It was before one of those "sets" that we experienced a classical wrinkle from the tradition of Houdini and all escapists: a challenge. A local escape artist named Brian Corrigan, who claimed to be the only true escape artist since Houdini, made a distinction between escapes achieved through magical device and those achieved through skill and insight. (Somehow he assumed that some insightful skills were not devices.) Alluding to numerous explanations of the Milk Can Escape as dependent on a mechanical gaffe, the challenger asserted that Houdini himself avoided the word *escape* and substituted *mystery* for the act. In fact, in Saint Louis in 1907, Houdini's own publicity called the feat a "death-defying mystery" and an "escape from a galvanized iron can."[43] Our advertising indeed referred to Kevin as an escape artist.

Mr. Corrigan submitted a letter challenging Kevin to escape from a pair of handcuffs he would provide, with an award of $100. Copies of the letter had been sent to the local and state newspapers and he came to our venue with a radio host in tow. Clearly this was a publicity ploy for his benefit: the letter was typed on the backside of his flyer for a performance the next day at a suburban mall.

Refusing the challenge meant that we would be assumed to be "willfully defrauding the public by presenting feats of illusions as escapes"[44] by a magician from Portland, Oregon. We had a week of college dates left in the greater Portland area, so my decision wasn't completely automatic, but it wasn't too difficult.

"Thank you for noticing us. But you have to understand that we are entertainers first and foremost and not interested in recreating turn-of-the-century type publicity stunts."

---

[43] Kalush and Sloman, *The Secret Life of Houdini*, Atria, 2006, p. 216.
[44] Letter hand-delivered to Nick Weber, February 12, 1977, downtown Meier and Frank, Portland, OR.

Eventually, he understood that I was trying mightily to extend a professional-but-summary dismissal. If he stayed, we didn't know it, but I hope he would have enjoyed our presentation. Because, for all his research and skill, he had overlooked the entire *raison d'être* for his cherished talents: Houdini escapes were entertainment, and entertainment is an art.

We were off the next day so of course we hiked out to Beaverton Mall to catch his 2 pm show. And my suspicions were sadly confirmed. It was quite definitely a display of physical prowess and expertise. He had a substantial crowd in front of his almost bare platform. As a straitjacketed Mr. Corrigan bounced and rolled around on the floor, one older gentleman was straining to see. Finally he relayed what he saw to his wife at the rear of the audience. Perhaps he captured the mood of most of the crowd.

"I cain't really see, Myrtle, but there's a whole lot of thumpin' goin' on!"

There was laughter from those in earshot because that was all that was "goin' on." Sadly, there was no poetry, no purpose, no variation on the barest skeleton of the archetype: getting into trouble and getting out. He may not have used mechanical means but his product bore all the repetitive deadliness of a machine anyway.

We were visited under much more gracious circumstances in Billings, Montana, at Eastern Montana State University. Mitch had once been a student there before going to Missoula. His wonderful family came down from Scobey to meet us and see what their son was up to. His mom, dad, brother, and sister were all in the front row. If that weren't tension enough for him, however, he had a costume malfunction just before we were to begin: his tunic's zipper stuck at the beginning of its track. There was no way we could get it to move.

We had a large audience jammed into the student union lobby. Of course college kids are on schedules, so you have to start somewhat punctually, and here we were with a stuck zipper. I actually threaded a needle and basted the two edges of zipper track together right up his back. (The day would come that Mitch would return to Billings where a friend in the Montana State Theater Department would tutor him in the construction of our costumes. He became an expert circus tailor.)

Mitch came from rare stock. Don, his father, like mine, dealt with large agricultural equipment. Unlike my father, he was quiet and modest. He was always more than willing to explain anything you didn't understand about his trade and his part of the country. I remember Mitch's mother, Irene, as a titan of energy and healthy curiosity, with a philosophically inquisitive spirit modestly seeking explanations. I have always imagined her as at once a gift and a force to be reckoned with in her community and parish. Both Don and Irene were certainly gifts to the Royal Lichtenstein Circus, always encouraging, always concerned. Very often they would lend a needed hand or generous check to be sure we felt secure beginning another season.

Having Mitch's family in the front section of our audience meant we had four faces beaming back to us what we were all about. Of course they had an emotional purchase in what they were seeing, but that only made their enthusiasm easier to read.

Of all the lessons I had ever been given in magic, learning to take care of audience enthusiasm was among the most important. I had learned it at Jay Marshal's "Magic Inc." in Chicago when I purchased the die box we used in the season of '73–'74.

The die box effect is one of a category of transpositions known as sucker tricks. The magician's equivalent of fiction's "red herring," such a routine will deliberately lead the audience to the incorrect understanding of how the trick is done only to establish that solution as impossible. In this respect, the die box is one of the most devilish of sucker effects. When I had purchased the effect, a visiting magician called me aside. He told me that he had worked ten-in-one sideshows for years and asked if he could lend me some advice. How could I have refused?

"You of course know that you're going to turn the audience on its ear when you reverse everything they're thinking. And most guys really come down hard with the end of the trick and a mighty 'Well, you're wrong!' close. I've had a lot more success pretending to arrive *with* the audience at the end of the trick. So I say something like, 'Well, that's what I thought too. Imagine my surprise when I found out—' and then you reveal the shock finish."

His advice applied to far more than magic. It was the very best understanding of the psychology of performance itself. The audience's energy is what calls for the performance as much as any performance can attract an audience. The compelling forces are mutually engaged and enjoyed and those forces are the real magic.

As a priest spending most of his time performing in something as secular-seeming as a circus, I paid attention to audience energy. My ministry counted on my ability to feed and satisfy that energy; it demanded that along with the allure of bare variety entertainment, we serve up the substance of deeper human truths. Any man of faith placed the source of such truths squarely in the realm of divinity. Of course, truth is always served in matter and form, substance and delivery, message and medium. We came to see our entire event—noontime, playtime, freetime, strangers amid strangers re-exploring the terrains of childhood—as a sacred hall of mirrors in which we and our audiences exchanged reflections of the best of each other and became better mirrors waiting for the next recess. Both *how* we saw and *what* we saw were precious. The seeing was all.

In the early years I was still teaching priests around the country. Typically a workshop or lecture would treat the common grounds between serious actors in the theater and the priests in the sanctuary. There are many, of course, but the most germane have to do with belief, whether you were behind the old communion rails or the old footlights. And the handiest handle for the mode of belief vital to both priest and actor is called "make-believe." Shocking as that sounds to the person of faith, both vocations are vocations to work at belief, to make it functional in themselves as servers and legible for those they serve. I would tell young priests, "You must show me what you believe. Then you won't have to bore me by telling me what you believe." I have bored myself silly telling (rather than showing?) actors the same thing. I even bribed priests. "If you read the Gospel passage well—that is, if you believe what you read and show your belief, you won't have to preach a homily." Of course I had no control over what they had to do and didn't have to do, but they liked the idea.

In the circus, we were in part stage magicians. But our hope was always that what the audience experienced when we fooled them was an honest effort to surprise them. Hopefully they could recognize such a feat as just one component in a show that in itself was a surprise. Perhaps that's one of the privileges we stumbled upon, a supreme chance to surprise. In the experience of surprise, we humans become vulnerable to alternative and more intense perception. With luck, such perception might uncover more of the genuine in spite of our day-to-day skirmishes with the illusory. I have led a life of lucky enough perception, but one surprise revelation held more light for me than any other.

12.

Finders, Leavers

Our mail would catch up with us in weekly batches forwarded to a reliable sponsor. In May 1978 we played the University of California at Davis and it was such a mail stop. For me there was a handwritten letter from a stranger who gave no return address.

> *Dear Father Nick Weber,*
> *If you are the Nick Weber I think you are, you may want to know*
> *that your mother, Doris, nee Britten, Weber is dying of ovarian*
> *cancer. You might want to visit her.*

Of course the signature was of no help. There was only a postmark: "Paradise, California." That postmark and one of our bibles, the *National Catholic Directory*, were helpful indeed. I called each of the few Catholic institutions in the small town and happily located the woman who was kind enough to contact me. My mother was in the hospital in Ashland, Oregon, the small town where she had lived for years.

Dominican friends who ran the Newman Center for Southern Oregon State College in Ashland agreed to do some Sherlock Holmes work. I needed to determine whether I would be welcome at this time in my mother's life. My friends obliged and returned the happy word that I would be more than welcome. I headed north for the third time that season, and I found my mother, returned to her home, three months before she died.

Never at ease with extreme emotional moments when they have to be shared, I fretted about what the first gestures of the reunion would be like. Would we recognize each other? Probably not. Was an embrace likely? Such contact never came easy to me. Even my usual forte went pianissimo: I had no idea what I would say. I had never spoken about this relationship, taking my cue from Dad, who never once brought the subject up with me, neither during my childhood nor later. But here was an occasion far deeper than arbitrary convention; our meeting would literally rumble up from the level of blood and guts. This person had given me life at the great risk to her own that only a parent recalls.

She watched me approach the house and answered the door herself. In the moment it took to push the screen door out of our way, our bodies took over. There was no rule except the desperate awkward rush to physically cover lost distance. Happy and confused sobs blocked any paltry word that tried to interfere.

Eventually we managed a joint stagger into her modest living room, where she introduced me to her longtime husband. Jarring as it is to recall, by the time we were all seated, the original emotional outburst had completely subsided. Tears and those first flushes in our faces had cleared. It was as if the stage had to be ready for the important matter of this scene, catching up, the exposition the principal characters needed. We all took long looks at each other, looks that radiated the unspoken scores of questions we both intended to ask and answer. My mother and I were strangers.

She was not shocked by my appearance. She had followed my career in the press. She knew of my ordination and she knew something about the circus. What she did not know was how physically close we had been to each other at least several times in the past few years. She worked for a long time as a librarian in the Southern Oregon State College Library. This meant she would have walked right by or very near the Royal Lichtenstein Circus set up outside the student union in clear view of the library.

My mother, wearing a simple kerchief covering a head bald from chemotherapy, could only whisper. The treatment had taken her voice, too. Sometimes her husband would repeat what he didn't think I quite heard. She was nonetheless active enough to tend the lunch she was preparing for the three of us.

To restore our lost narrative the conversation frantically struggled in reverse, tracking our lives from the present to the turmoil of the mid-Forties. We had time, so there was no need for the forced perspective that literary artists bring to bear upon works for the stage. In my heart, however, this was a wringing trek through two acts, each with its own arc. The second arc would be a peak moment of the afternoon—and of my life.

Of course the conversation turned to Dad. Even with my long blondish hair and goatee she saw his features in mine, and she knew I had grown up around him. She knew about Gracie. She couldn't have known how attached I was to Gracie, how easy it was to call someone else "Mom." I would never tell her that. Eventually, though, the point of our separation had to be replayed and I had paltry data: what Beth had told me, and a white plastic radio my mother had sent me on an early birthday.

Beth's capitulation of my mother's rejection of both Dad and me was disarmed succinctly. This did not surprise me. For years I had reconstructed a scenario in which, to some degree, the Weber family had carefully guarded me and my potential for succeeding in spite of this early trauma. The strict German Catholic reflexes in my grandparents' home moved into full protection mode, and I was to be isolated from whatever they perceived my Episcopal mother was up to. So deconstructing the harshness implied in Beth's reporting was simple. But it was complicated by some hard evidence that surprised me. After the gift of the radio, which was a boyhood treasure through the years I had it, my mother had received a letter from Dad. And here it was in her frail hand in Ashland, Oregon. She had done some homework uncovering what had to be a harsh relic.

"You've probably never seen this."

Handwritten on two sides of a page of personal stationery was a blunt request that my mother not attempt to contact me in any way. The reasons adduced were my psychological stability and my emotional health. It was a polished piece of prose, logical, lean and just about literary. It was in Dad's hand and bore his signature.

"Thank you for letting me see this. But I can't imagine Dad writing in this style. He doesn't think this way and he doesn't speak this way."

"You're right. I have always suspected that the Webers had an attorney compose that for him." This information supplied a charged recasting of my childhood memories.

That she was whispering meant I had to pay very keen attention to her face as she rasped the words slowly. In fact, I didn't hear her most important question of the visit. Each time I knew I wasn't getting the tired, strained whisper, I glanced to her husband for help.

"She wants to know if you sing."

Then he gratuitously continued opening a secret trapdoor in the stage platform that held my life.

"Music and singing have been a big part of her life." What a time for her voice to have failed in our conversation.

Good trapdoors are invisible. This had been one of the best. As if by the most sophisticated of theater technology, a wonderfully warm and intensely intimate radiance rushed up through my body and grabbed hold of my heart and intellect simultaneously. At the speed of light rushing to fill darkness, I knew why I was who I was. Up to now, I recognized as my family's traits only competitive business, the outdoor pursuit of hunting and fishing, military life, sports, and heavy duty equipment. None of these spoke to what shaped my life purpose: a laser lock on making things, and wrenching from my lonesome untrained sensitivity, stuff I could recognize as at least clumsily beautiful. I finally made sense to *me*, thanks to this frail, bald, near-mute little person sitting across from me. Through very ordinary historical happenstance she had long ago launched and left my life. Now in the context of an extraordinary private revelation, she was repeating both the launch and the leaving. Even life and death were mysteriously one, but happily for me, so was I. Together. Whole.

Pastorally, I was concerned that she felt comfortable. Experienced enough as a priest in the real world, I never presumed anything concerning an individual's stance toward faith, no matter what I knew about their past. I made my life in the marketplace. I was hardened enough to expect that my own faith stance might account for nothing at the deepest level of any personality. My initial parries into such matters as belief had long been very general. I asked after my mother's concerns about God and her religion. Unsurprisingly she had not practiced her Episcopalian religion all that much.

I quickly dealt religion out of the discussion and seized on faith as the topic of her last days. In so many situations, religion is not the comfort faith can be, and many folks remain confused and uncomforted by it. Literally, religion is a pattern of connecting—linking with objects of faith. The pattern is prescribed and learned by rote and, when practice becomes awkward, abandoned. Faith is a fundamental reality in a person's mind and heart. Pattern or no, religious practice or no, there is a connection between a person and the person's source or ground. It is even deeper than belief. Belief can be formulated, verbalized, whereas faith is so often nonverbal in the barely conscious area of "habitual hunch" and consistent tendency, where "I just know" lives. Because it can't be easily named does not mean it is unreal for a person.

Besides my friends at the Newman Center, some Episcopal clergy had contacted her. I suggested that she talk about what she feared and what she hoped with anyone she trusted to understand and care. They didn't have to be clergy. Her husband or anyone who cherished her could help hold those doors open. Our real hopes and fears are so often closeted by the busy partitions of everyday preoccupation. I also knew that the more she shared such concerns, the more easily she would find competent direction. Loved ones would seek it out for her. But she'd done some competent seeking on her own.

"Don't worry. God and I are alright with each other." The strength of the statement belied the whisper's frailty.

I shifted to doctors and encouraged her to demand as much relief from pain as she could. I was already on my way to a very liberal attitude toward the use of morphine in terminal situations. The day would come when I could see morphine as ministry and pain relief as pastoral. She seemed comfortable and confident with her medical support staff.

Sons appearing out of nowhere don't usually presume to give their rediscovered mothers advice, but I felt assured that she might be receptive to what I said to her. She was intelligent; I knew she heard and understood me. And in the glow of an awkward last look into the past, washed with the gracious conversation of a champagne luncheon, I sensed she might value at least something of what I had suggested. And when we said goodbye, I left assured our reconnecting had held some useful substance for her. More selfishly I left assured that I had a right to be who I had become.

I suppose we said goodbye. I honestly do not remember anything specific about the exact leave-taking. Way before we sat down to lunch, I was obsessed with two very personal realities. First, I had known on the trip north that just my identity as her flesh and blood who happened to be a priest would coax from me some awkward effort toward comforting advice, whether or not she expected such advice. Second, the staggering revelation about where I had come from would mean taking on the sinewy reality of my artistic life with enlightened assurance I had never known before. She had handed me an insight into what my life had a right to be. Just in time she revealed what I would now strive to more confidently embrace for the rest of my life. It was as though she made up for lost time and gave me life once more, just as she gave up her own.

It sounds dreadfully heartless, but that's all I recall about leaving. If we did somehow manage "Goodbye" it was more than we managed the first time. This time I was the one who left. Except for the insights and the personal revelations I describe, there is little of an emotional hangover from that dramatic event. As was the case in the first parting, however, I think there was, at some level in my consciousness, a determination to control again. Again, there is no emotional memory. Of course she would get the last leaving. And weeks later when a shaken caller delivered the details of my mother's death and obsequies, I felt no need to be part of such a curtain call even after that climactic final scene. In general, I do not like last bows and I avoid all obsequies I can. But even in this case there was never the slightest emotional draw to be present.

Such control, such an ease at displacing emotions and emotional memory, has its limitations. Even in the grip of selfishness, tears have a blurry way of reconnecting us with those we have tried to displace. It was twelve years after my mother left my father and me that I was surprised by tears as a senior in high school and cried myself to sleep remembering that my mother "had left me." This time, it took twenty years. A box of photos found its way to me when my mother died, and most of them stayed in that same box. One had found its way onto the top of a bookcase. Last year, I walked into my living room and saw, as if for the first time, that portrait of me at the age of five. And I dissolved. That was how she would have last seen me before she left. Until Ashland, I had no pictures of her. Until Ashland, I did not know I was her only child.

That day and that visit were at once a re-entrance and a re-exit. The entire experience was as full as it was sparse. In that, it resembled its counterpart in my younger days. There was no conscious emotional residue or hangover.

**Doris Britten, the mother
I never got to know**

Especially at the level of everyday awareness, there is more to human affection and attachment than flesh and blood. It would be Gracie who asked for the full report, just as it was Gracie who reported that Dad wanted no information or conversation about the reunion he knew had taken place. That streak of dispassionate control and repression can definitely be a matter of inherited flesh and blood. Because of it, I was able to return to rehearsals at Santa Clara University and the administration of a circus the next day.

13.

More Than Human

"…and always comes up smiling."
—C. B. DeMille, narrator, *The Greatest Show on Earth*, 1952

Our personnel called us; we didn't call them. Over twenty-two years, nearly one hundred young people found their ways to our phones, mailboxes or the edge of the ring and asked to join out with the circus. I didn't have to run away to join a circus, nor did I ever have to look far for performers. Both media representation of our work and the performances themselves won new personnel for us.

An extraordinary person volunteers to train and work in such an environment. But *extraordinary* is a long word that can cover a lot of territory. In the case of the Royal Lichtenstein Circus, *extraordinary* meant adventuresome, talented, imaginative, resourceful, and generous. Usually these young people, men and women, were either in college or recently graduated. Some were just out of high school. Most of them in the early years had only the performance arts skills associated with theater programs. Some didn't even have that. The ones who did have some theater behind them, such as the Santa Clara University alumni, were possessed of crisp comedic skills. Such performers were joyful challenges to me: everything seemed new each time we performed. Perhaps more than anything, they taught me the value of an actor's honed reactive skills. A large part of acting is reacting to one's fellow characters and the events of a plot, and even the simplest clown gag consists of a character involved in a plot.

Many of our later applicants, especially those who heard about us through school counselors or other performers, brought readily adaptable circus skills with them. When we started out, more and more people interested in joining us had learned to juggle. Some were already accomplished street performers, skilled at unicycling and juggling and comic patter. A few had worked in mime. There were those who, knowing they were applying and had been accepted, sought out training in a given discipline they wanted to bring to our show. Some who had spent a year or more on the show and valued the experience would invite a best friend to join. Ringling Clown College alum John Hadfield brought along his brother Paul.

The Hadfields with brother Paul aloft

There were very few times when there were more applicants than we could place. Circus has a way of winnowing the weak of heart out of the waiting line. Nonetheless, each year's show had to be fashioned from the talent base we had. But minimally, right from the outset we could present juggling, clown comedy, magic, storytelling, and my balancing and fire-eating acts. Most importantly, everyone was healthy and very eager to learn. When people joined us with a technical skill we didn't yet include, they became teachers. Not long after the first unicyclist showed up, I bought unicycles for those who wanted to learn. I coached others in wire-walking. A gymnast would coach in elemental ground acrobatics. In this way the more advanced skills found their places into our repertoire. Without our knowing it, a new kind of bonding took hold of our ensembles as everyone became a potential teacher and a student. And no one learned more than I did.

In the beginning, at Santa Clara University, we put our shows together in two weeks. Gradually more and more time was added. By the time we relocated to our training quarters near Santa Barbara, we took seven weeks. Mornings and afternoons were divided into rigorous training sessions for the skills, and the evenings were devoted to staging rehearsals for magic and the fables. The animal acts worked in the afternoons and evenings.

The community aspects of our endeavors were not lost on me. If the circus was a ministry serving a larger public, I knew there had to be a special spiritual resonance between me and these dedicated personnel who were the circus itself. Circus as a sacred endeavor, a celebration of unity and expansiveness, rendered its people not only special but in some basic sense holy, no matter what their religious backgrounds, if any. Everyone in every cast knew I was a priest. How they understood that was not as important as how I understood it. For me, it meant that in a reality that included the dimensions of sweat and heartache, triumph and graceful failure, these performers were part of that priesthood. Beyond the promised board and room and minimal expenses and winter break airfare, I owed them a vision of something sacred even in their gritty struggles with dirty props and stubborn, smelly animals. Sometimes I succeeded. Most of the time I tried. But never did I limit my understanding of their own sacred work to some of the consecrated notions of sacred that had become, for me, lifeless scorekeepers of a given sect.

The apparatus of an intelligent Catholicism was always nearby. We were, after all, living under the auspices of Jesuit sponsorship. In the institutions housing our rehearsals and feeding us were Jesuits who valued our work and who befriended the performers. During training and rehearsals, there was always time for weekend formal worship. While I meticulously enforced the entire timetable of circus rehearsals and performances, however, I tried to develop a sensitivity about the performers' readiness for structured faith expressions. I early on realized that everyone was in a customized, sensitive, often very private posture vis-a-vis religion. Everyone was part of my priest-hood; but they had a part in shaping their contributions.

Even a small circus is truly a celebration of the best in human potential. The driving concept in such an enterprise is a stretch: *longer, higher, bigger, farther* are the side-coachings at rehearsals for a ceremony that will make the same demands of an audience's imagination. And the most outstanding personalities I was privileged to engage in the Royal Lichtenstein Circus were those who broke through my own complacency, asked me to stretch my own imagination and join the circus they knew they could make. Of the dozens and dozens of extraordinarily generous people who were our circus, some distinguished themselves by way of invention, courage, persistence, and generosity.

Joey Colon always seemed to amaze even himself.

You can ride a unicycle?" Dumb. Joey Colon was a Manhattan street performer who could learn or do anything. "Can you bounce it up steps?" Just the image fired the performer's imagination, and our best carpenter went to work. Beautiful steps and a beautiful trick. "But how do you get down?"

"Watch!" and he rode directly down with a spectacular, balanced braking just as he met the ring curb. That was Joey Colon, already a fixture in Washington Square Park.

"You did the Roman rings as a varsity gymnast? Can you do the routine up in the air where circus people do?" And we had new rigging and a spectacular display of skills many of our audiences had never seen. That was modest Jens Larson, a Dartmouth graduate who had met up with me the season before in New Haven. He wanted to join us.

One morning in training quarters I just happened to catch him pressing into a perfect handstand. "I didn't know you could do a handstand." Well, duh. He did it every time he did the Roman rings act. "Have you ever seen the rola-bola? You know. The rolling cylinder with the board on top? The handstand can be central in those routines." And he and our show both had a new act. Most importantly, I had a friend who would remain as dedicated to what we were doing as I was.

A few of our performers worried me when we visited another show. If they really liked a given feature in some act, it would mean hours and hours of practice back in quarters till they got the trick themselves. That was the case with Joe Reichlin adding Coke bottles to the rola-bola stack-up of planks. In his tightwire

**Jens Larson on the
Roman rings**

display, Joe would kneel sideways to the cable and pick up a handkerchief with his teeth. Kevin Curdt would include not only an ankle-hang in his trapeze routine, but a toe hang as well. He eventually learned to ride his tall "giraffe" unicycle through a slalom of traffic cones—even backward.

When I had taught Jennie Madrigal at the Colorado Springs liturgy workshop back in the summer of 1972, she was a youth minister working for the Archdiocese of Denver. She and some priest friends ran a youth service called "Spirit's Runway," and she would later devote her talents to campus ministry and even prison ministry. In this last capacity she almost orchestrated a clown act a little too risky. It is funny now, but it could have been chaotic, at least.

Jennie had gotten us booked into the Federal Youth Prison Facility outside Denver. After we were cleared by security, the guards escorted us to the field where we would set up, and then they disconnected our distributor so that the van couldn't be used as an escape vehicle in the event of unruly behavior. They also asked us to surrender any objects that might be used as weapons. This was getting serious. Of course we had a sledge hammer and pipe wrenches, which we gladly turned over. Everyone went about the task of setting up for the performance, forgetting that a magic feature in the show involved six authentic butcher knives. Needless to say, that trick was, uh, *cut* from the show.

Eventually Jennie trained and worked for the Denny's Corporation, first as a restaurant manager and then as a district supervisor. We only saw her once a year, usually in the fall on our way between Portland and the Chicago area. But we always knew when we got to Denver we had an enthusiastic fan and friend ready to feed us well and run the odd errand for us.

One year, the mail brought word that Jennie was no longer with the Denny's chain and was seeking a different type of work venue. She was deliberately and methodically trying to discern where her talents were leading her. Mitch and I finished reading the letter, looked at each other, and watched each other's light bulbs come on simultaneously. What about asking her to join us as a staff person? Mitch by this time was juggling house management duties with minor roles in the performances, but most of his time went to booking and follow-through with sponsors. He could use help already, and we hadn't even imagined the concession operation that was coming.

Jennie Madrigal, house manager with an electronic connection to the backyard

In November 1987 we made our proposal and mutually worked out the details of a job description in subsequent correspondence and phone calls. She was corporate-trained and she knew how to protect herself and us from unforeseen conflicts. Money never entered the discussion any more than it had for Mitch. Jennie Madrigal became part of the Royal Lichtenstein Circus in June 1988, and most of her concentration was on relating to our sponsors and house management issues. Gradually she learned the techniques and resources for booking the show and cultivating future sponsors. She had no hesitation in shouldering her part of day-to-day chores behind the wheel and in the cookhouse. She was a superb driver and in our reduced version of a restaurant, her Mexican heritage made for some mighty fine enchiladas. One day she would even marshal us into our new roles as concessionaires. But the real timeliness and benefit of Jennie's arrival on the Royal Lichtenstein Circus would eventually register beyond anything Mitch or I could have predicted.

What a circus audience sees pales in comparison with the chemistry of a circus in rehearsal, its troupe uncovering its potential. Those preparations for me were not only exhilarating; they were the healthiest calls to humility and mutual respect I ever endured.   Surrounded by the strains and struggles of young people bent on enriching our little circus, I was gifted with a priceless realization. Priesthood itself was not a gift as much as it was a call to giving. My job was to give my meager gifts away so that other folks who trusted me could develop other gifts to give away. Everything any of us put ourselves through at rehearsals to get a partner or the director to say "You've got it!" really meant "You're going to be able to give something else away."

Rich as those weeks of training were, and rewarding as our giving tours were, we also had much to give up. Security or feeling secure were not states of body and spirit to be taken for granted. There were slick roads and bumpy roads. Always long roads. There were burnt bearings, burnt nerves, burnt food, and even a burnt truck. Of course there were flat tires, but flattened egos as well. There were cancellations, unexpected storms moving in, and perturbed performers storming out. Tension extended beyond the tight wire and moods extended beyond the menagerie. Unexpectedly, tears would well up in our private, sometimes-selfish hearts and eyes. Still, somehow, by the day's first entrance into the ring, our hearts and eyes acknowledged only the wide open hearts and eyes before us.

*   *   *

Some seasons began with a sturdy foursome in the cast and after the "shakedown loop" of San Jose–Fresno–Sacramento–San Jose would be depleted by half. Then, improvising a two-man show and hitting the usual route, the stalwart diminished cast of the already diminutive circus would chance upon a fan who noticed the lack and volunteer to join. And join immediately. And stay for more than one season.

Jealousies, irritations, and personality conflicts that could not be solved in the context of a fast-paced tour sometimes resulted in abrupt departures from the cast. When people collaborated with us and "got with it," they were depended on. If they "walked the show," you quickly found a way not to depend on them. Adjustments were made because they had to be made. The show didn't have to go on. It just did. Most of the time. Verbal agreements were the extent of an arrangement to join out with the show. There were no formal contracts. A conversation, an invitation, acceptance, and determination of a date for the beginning of rehearsals usually sufficed. Almost all those commitments held for at least a season, and the series of those twenty-two seasons calendared my life as a priest struggling for grace within a clown's motley.

The canonized aphorism that grace builds on nature has probably never been tested in the same way twice. Certainly the road-test my life has given it shouldn't be tried at home. A clown priest's cosmetic makeup is easy to duplicate, but the experiences through which I was supposed to build myself gracefully were a bit extreme. A Jesuit in a circus ring, or in tights, or in a bear cage— or in jail, had to have coaxed even the Holy Spirit to start working with a net. While that sounds funny, it reflects where my relationship with the Spirit was after a few years on the road.

Growing up with God, my characterization of the divine was as loving, remote and controlling—but available through long distance. God was a father who created me and a brother who revealed himself as Christ and savior. I believed they loved me in some mysterious way. But both these figures were somewhere else, physically and historically, even though I could reach them through certain formulae. They knew absolutely every move I made, every thought I had.

When the poetry of a fellow Jesuit, Gerard Manley Hopkins, told me that not only was the world "charged with the Grandeur of God" but that the Spirit broods over a bent world "with warm breast," I took a deep breath. And by the time another of my religious brothers, Teilhard de Chardin, described for me the possibility of a noosphere and a milieu that was of God, I knew the breath (in Latin, *spiritus*) I had drawn was God's, and that I couldn't help it. I had let the Spirit in and I began to live the truth of our order's founder, Ignatius, who really did believe in the Incarnation and that God was to be found in all things. Just as the oxygen I breathed supported every cell of my body, this new quickening I accepted enlivened all of me, all the time. It made for an enlightened transcendent embrace with everyone and everything.

In Emeryville, California, Little Sister Josefe enlightened me about light itself and introduced me to a new love affair with a whole family. The Little Sisters of Jesus could do that to you, especially if you loved the circus and its people as they did. When the small Rome-based group decided to begin its first U.S. community on a circus, they had asked me to suggest a show. I encouraged them to contact Circus Vargas, then arguably the finest example of a three-ring circus in the country. They were with the Vargas show for eight years. The charism of their ministry was service to migrant groups. On a circus, they worked shoulder to shoulder in regular behind-scenes jobs, paying their way. On their own time, in every way they could, they ministered to the religious needs of other circus personnel. Before long, they had established a network of priests coast to coast who could and would come to a circus to preside at Eucharist and administer the other sacraments. I became part of that network, and when the show was in Emeryville, in June of 1978, I was nearby.

The occasion was the baptism of a baby born in a semi-tractor rolling out of D.C. a couple of months earlier. Dad was an elephant trainer, mom an aerialist. This little boy had entered a community of exotic risk and hard work. But no one chooses the setting into which they're born. Each of us makes do with the communities we find and those we find make do with us. Both these adjustments are the stuff of lives. For a young priest there couldn't be a more critical and timely opportunity for pastoral formation than in a baptism.

I was keenly aware of the havoc circus life wreaks on its own. Below the raucous and flashy level of spectacle, their life is a sometimes ceremonial, sometimes mundane flaunting of caution. Here miracles are virtually teased from

the jealous claws of nature as time, talon, gravity, muscle, and incisor are inge-
niously courted. So I knew the need show people have for constant help
reweaving the tattered fabric of their religious lives. Here was my chance to
give a few of them something in return for the dimension of my vocation they
had given me. I cared for them. I knew something about the non-glamorous
side of their lives. I shared faith with them. I had become a fairly good teacher.
And I was scared to death that I would fail. There was so much I wanted to give
this little community as it welcomed their tiny newcomer, so much I wanted to
help these heroes of mine get right. Yet from the outset I got almost all of it
wrong.

Inside the tent, the arena for the tiger act had already been set up in the center ring, so the ceremony would take place in ring one. Not a moment's
thought was given to using a space next to the inside concession joint or in
front of the bandstand. Important things at the circus happen in or over the
rings. The heavy vinyl fabric of the tent was double-ply, so it was dark and it
would be an hour before the show's generator was cranked up for the day. No
sooner had I voiced concern over our need for light than I noticed one of the
littler Little Sisters dragging a large metal elephant tub into a shaft of light
beaming through a hole around the first center pole. Now there was not only
light, there was a table.

"We'll have God's light, Father." It was Josephe.

That shaft of light went right to my heart and mind. I surrendered. It was
all right to fail; I just had to be willing to be taught. With luck, being wrong
becomes a preamble to learning. A cloth covered the table. The family came in
and the priest introduced himself to the parents and their newest star. Mysteriously, with one shaft of light, a candle, and perhaps ten people, that tent, with
its three rings and seating for five thousand people, was full.

Certainly, a very focused love was in place. The father casually lit the candle with his between-cigarettes lighter. A lady from the concession department
brought in flowers for the table, and the cookhouse boss had warmed the water
a little. The godparents were looking over their responses in the ceremonial
booklets. Without realizing it, I handed my Greek fisherman's cap to one of
the Little Sisters, and another of their tiny community helped me put the stole
over my head. Three young Mexican girls and their mother began singing "De
Colores" cued by Little Sister Joel. And I relaxed. I remembered whose work
and play this was supposed to be. I let myself be moved.

The early morning surprise delivery of this little boy had been a holy and
sanctifying event itself. Now, who he really was to be for his parents and their
community was named in a public way with Names connecting everyone there:
workingman, humble parents, aerialist, concessionaire, sisters, cook, acrobat, and
priest. At once, with the help of a child startled to tears by water as he once was
by air, all of us were reintroduced to our own fragility, our hope, and ourselves.

Halting memory and ragged Spanish and English recitations helped us tell each other who we were in the creed of those long ago Apostles, who were by name and work, troupers like us.

I extinguished the candle, removed the stole, and replaced my cap. Trays of cookies, hot cocoa, and coffee were brought in from the cookhouse and the celebration continued. The tent was still very full. Right on time, the diesel roar of the generator signaled the beginning of the workday and the big-top lights came on. Horses had entered ring three for a morning workout at the other end of the tent. Before long, the baptism party collected the food remnants and the flowers were sent to the baby's house trailer. I picked up some of the simple props and books to carry them back to the Little Sisters' trailer chapel. Behind me I heard a male voice, husky but polite and a bit shy.

"Say, Father!"

It was the baby's father.

"I wanted to give you something."

Oh, God no. You are a poor man and I cannot sell what is not mine. Besides, you've already given me part of my soul, man.

Too late. The man's billfold was open. From a leather fold, he extracted a black fiber, much like a paintbrush bristle, about five inches long. He held it out to me.

"I can tell you've been around these shows a lot. Know what this is?"

I smiled and shook my head. Something more to learn.

"You really don't? It's a hair from an elephant's tail. If you find one, it's very good luck. I've carried this one for twelve years, Father. I'd like you to have it."

Overwhelmed, I took off my cap, but not to shake hands in gratitude. I instantly knew exactly where I was going to carry this talisman. Above the narrow front brim of authentic Greek fisherman caps two buttons hold a piece of woven cord braid the width of the brim. Right on the spot, while the elephant handler watched with pride, I wove the hair into that black braid. It was as invisible as it had been in the billfold. I put the cap back on knowing that I loved these people and I loved this world they made possible. Because I had risked loving them, my clumsy life as a priest clown was becoming as comfortable as the hat on my head. Graced with an intensified awareness of what circus meant, I returned to rehearsals for a coming season in the ring of the Royal Lichtenstein Circus.

*   *   *

The circus ring is a symbol of inclusion. I was called to hold onto a unique band of young people, and teach them how to embrace their audiences in turn. There was no better way of loving my fellow performers than allowing them a share in my best dreams for the brief miles we were together. Dreams, however, risk becoming nightmares. We had our share of those. Besides performance mishaps, there were auto accidents and tangles with local officials labeling us suspects. One of the most debilitating nightmares was anger with a fellow performer or a sense that your dream has disappointed a companion.

Our use of motor vehicles progressed from an overstuffed and over stacked station wagon to a cube van. We and the nature of our menagerie outgrew the van, so we added a two-and-a-half ton van with more of a kitchen and a couple more bunks. When our music box was replaced by a band organ, we added a small trailer to the smaller van. When we added still another two-and-a-half ton van to this odd fleet, we retired the small trailer. But that many tires, three engines, and three transmissions ask for trouble. Most of the time our vehicles, even their customized additions, did exactly what they were supposed to do. Once, our funky makeshift quarters saw us through an emergency in high style.

During a severe delay on the eastern slopes of the Bitterroot Range going into Montana, we all climbed into the independently heated and illuminated dining room our van provided to enjoy freshly made coq au vin. Outside, a queue of stopped traffic had to wait over an hour in very icy weather while the highway patrol removed a jackknifed semi.

Somewhere early on, my habit of prayer had greatly simplified. I readily bought the methods of centering based on breathing, so that connection with life in the Spirit could only become as intimate as it was pervasive. This made hours behind the wheel sometimes holy, when the other blessing of conversation flagged. But it also informed more strenuous times in mechanics' shops or at the side of the road. I championed everyone's need to find the surprise of the Spirit even in a flat tire, or a burnt clutch.

Once, though, we really had to hunt to find the Spirit's presence in two vehicle mishaps occurring in immediate tandem, one involving more than delay and repair. Just before Christmas we had played Strake Jesuit High School in Houston. We were going to spend the winter break at the Jesuit novitiate in Grand Coteau, Louisiana, rather than travel back to California. Two generous Jesuit scholastics in Houston had volunteered to bring the cube van over to Grand Coteau the day after Christmas. Two days before Christmas, someone else took the cookhouse van on ahead to Grand Coteau, and I drove the animal van over the night of Christmas Eve. Just east of Houston, the vacuum assist for my truck's brakes gave out. All I had for stopping or slowing was an extremely forceful application to the mechanics of the brake pedal itself. I fell in love with the right lane and wide shoulders. It was one of the most frightening journeys I ever made, and I was alone with the menagerie and band organ riding in back. Late at night, I rolled into Grand Coteau and parked beside our cookhouse.

The morning after Christmas brought more bad news. My friends, the scholastics in Houston, had trouble getting the cube van engine to start. When they removed the shroud for a look, the carburetor belched flame. This was an interior engine between the two seats in the cab. I had not told my helpers that there was a fire extinguisher right next to the driver's head. Fearing injury they jumped out of the cab and the canvas curtain dividing the cab from the cargo area caught fire. Instantly the rest of the vehicle was engulfed. Mercifully, neither of the young men was injured.

Emergency fire equipment reached the scene in excellent time so our major props were saved. But the rubber ring mats were gone, as were the ring curbs and some costumes. The truck was not salvageable.

In selecting a replacement vehicle, a classic enlightenment by the Spirit occurred. Finally seizing on the wisdom of all circus people everywhere, we would tow our quarters, cargo, and menagerie in trailers with interchangeable towing hitches and trucks. The chances were always greatest that trouble would arise with the towing vehicle. Another towing vehicle could get what we needed to the next performance by what all show people know as "double jumping." It took a disaster, but we finally got it.

*   *   *

Because of our daily travels, we were strangers everywhere we went. Very often we were camped in residential areas, and at night especially that could attract the attention of the Law. There were many opportunities for making the police understand they were talking to part of a circus.

Once when we were staying with a Jesuit friend's family in Hawthorne, near Los Angeles, I couldn't sleep. So I went for a late night walk. After a hot chocolate in a cafe, I headed back on a quiet street. Suddenly I was engulfed in bright light. *What was I doing? Why wasn't I walking over on Hawthorne Boulevard? What had brought me to Hawthorne?* I had nothing to say but the truth. Finally I got an anemic reprieve.

"Well, Mr. Weber, I'm going to let you continue on. You haven't done anything wrong. But I want you to realize that if something in this neighborhood should happen, you would be the prime suspect.

Once police found me taking our miniature horse Dan Rice for a night walk. That seemed to make even less sense, and the officer was really sarcastic.

"Okay, so what are we doing with the little pony on a neighborhood street?"

I countered, daring only a mimic of his rhythm, not his sarcasm. "So the little horse is with a circus that it is playing in the neighborhood tomorrow and is parked in a resident's driveway overnight."

I had a similar encounter one night on fashionable Saint Armand Key in Florida. By then I must have had a better routine for explaining myself because it didn't take so long. Just an ID check. But even that is unnerving when you are in a strange place.

Sometimes the run-ins happened in broad daylight, right on our performance site. In Greenville, South Carolina, while we were performing at Furman University, a downtown bank was robbed and the getaway vehicle had
been stolen from the Furman parking lot. We were informed that the FBI
wanted to talk with us. Our good friend, the university chaplain, Jim Pitts, suggested that they should also talk to the president of the university who had just
managed to afford a new car. Then he remembered that the *Sesame Street* arena
show was in town and suggested they interview Big Bird.

One of my partners and I were roughed up in New Orleans by a rookie cop.
We were on the Saint Charles streetcar returning to the trucks at Loyola University. That campus is right next door to Tulane University, so the car was
jammed with unruly college kids returning from a night of partying in the
Quarter. The operator signaled for police help. My partner and I were
exhausted and hadn't spoken a word to each other the entire journey. Somehow the students all knew to let themselves out the rear door when they saw
the cops come through the front door. Suddenly we were the only ones left on
the car and the cops had to save face, so they started lecturing us. Eventually I
was sent to the rear of the car so they could question us separately. When they
ordered my partner off the car, I objected and they ordered me off. It got
rather abusive outside next to their squad car. Thinking I could rely on some
vague rights I might have, I made an extremely wrong move and asked for a
badge number to make a complaint. No magician could have produced two
sets of handcuffs faster. And we landed in jail.

My one phone call was to the campus security folks who knew us at Loyola University. They found some bail money for our rescue. On the way out I was recognized. The young man who was discharging us brightened and all but shouted, "I
know you! You're the guy who brings that circus to Tulane every year!"

We were booked for a court appearance in two days, our date for Louisiana
State University, one of the biggest crowds of the year. In luck, I had breakfast
the next morning with a young Jesuit scholastic who was a lawyer. He was convinced the case would be thrown out and agreed to represent us. So we continued on schedule and the charges were dismissed. The paperwork revealed
that we were the younger cop's first arrest.

*   *   *

Negative dealings with the outside world weren't as upsetting as misfires
among our own personnel. Our work brought us the need for mutual dependency and trust. So usually, when someone left, there was more than a physical loss. Even with folks who never developed an easy presence on the show,
their departure could trigger reflection about what we could have done better
for them. One man quit because I reminded him for the second time that he
simply could not overfill our onboard water tank so that our living quarters

were flooded. Another person left the show after a midday teardown, got in line at the local Greyhound station, and then decided he really did belong back at the circus. He made it back before we left for the next town.

I asked a few people to leave the show. One had invited me out for a talk over breakfast and then proceeded to tell me everything that was wrong with the show. He was just out of high school and hadn't yet trouped for six months. I determined that I really didn't need to hear what he was saying, and, recognizing his unhappiness, asked him to leave the show. He was caught completely off guard. But so were all of us. We had no idea he had been so negatively disposed toward the show.

Some performers resigned during the mid-season break, which of course made it slightly easier for us to compensate. But losing a performer who was doing a fine job in the ring was never easy. And to be honest, I took it personally very often. I knew there was a better way to do my job and that I wasn't clever enough to find it. Some irritated or disturbed cast members would seek for help with sponsors along the way, knowing I trusted these friends who had supported us in visit after visit. Some would use these friends as intermediaries with me. That was a smart solution, but my vanity also took a beating with the realization that I was too intimidating a boss. For a priest, I could be very non-pastoral.

Very rarely but far too often, we accidentally risked serious injury to a performer. When that happened, there was the added trauma of a cancelled performance and the loss of an audience's energy. Such energy was an uplift we always calculated into our well-being. One of the most dangerous accidents happened in Cascade Locks, Oregon. We were scheduled for a morning school assembly and arrived the snowy night before. Well ahead of dawn, I was up cooking breakfast and Mitch was doing his morning animal chores. Suddenly I heard a scream that could only be our little dog, Jingle Bells. I ran through the snow over to the animal trailer. Jingle Bells was beneath the step leading from the animal compartment of the vehicle. Mitch was coaxing her to her feet. He was nearly hysterical.

"Gas fumes! Must be the heater!"

He had gotten Jingles out as fast as he could. She was barely conscious and he placed her in front of the door. Then, in removing a second dog, Scotty, he had accidentally stepped on Jingles. That's when I heard her. My mind jumped to the spider monkeys.

"Open the back doors of the trailer! We've got to be sure the monkeys don't pass out!"

With that, the front door of the trailer opened. I had forgotten all about the two *humans* who slept in that unit. Kevin Curdt stumbled down the step from his door, fell to his knees in the snow, and shouted an Election Day anthem into the freezing dark air.

"A vote for George Bush is a vote for the death of America!"[45]

Kevin Curdt works an Iron Cross into his trapeze routine

Then he collapsed face-first into the snow. By this time his close friend, Carlo Gentile, was outside and apparently okay, and it was then that another performer recognized what had happened and sprinted off to find a phone to call paramedics. Kevin was taken to the hospital for oxygen but everyone else and the entire menagerie were fine. While we lost the day's performance, thankfully Kevin was returned to us for a round of laughs about his gassy politics.

He would return the following season, too, as did Carlo. Kevin was my shotgun, keeping me awake on long-hauls, reading directions, forcing me to reconsider a piece of literature. He and Carlo embraced the reality of circus like few I know. There was something about the circle, the ring, which they had sounded in depth. It stayed with them. Kevin continues to keep me awake via email from a California office, directing me still, forcing the deeper meaning of a line in Shakespeare and, vitally, reminding me that the ring's embrace is just that, an embrace. Carlo and his wife are professional circus people who years back set up an electronic embrace that keeps all the former members of the circus in touch via an

Carlo Gentile's version of Monsieur La Plume

online listserve. Kevin and Carlo have kept so many of us in contact over the years, ferreting out even some who left in disappointment. Perhaps more than I, they grasp what is behind the symbol of the circle we and the animals traveled. They understand and feel that folks belong together, especially folks who have made vital the humble ring-shape that captured their love.

To be sure the show could keep going in a healthy way, I once even helped Mitch walk the show. In 1979 we agreed that we needed some distance from each other, and he landed a job with Circus Vargas where our dear friends the Little Sisters of Jesus, Joel and Priscilla were working. Mitch would be driver and groom for a magnificent large dog act in center ring.

---

[45] It was the day of the 1988 federal election. The reference was to George Herbert Walker Bush.

Of course we kept in touch through weekly phone calls. By early October, the Vargas show was in Atlanta and we were playing Rockhurst College in Kansas City, Missouri. Mitch was ecstatic because after that evening's show, the Vargas company was going to watch a center ring screening of Cecil B. DeMille's *The Greatest Show on Earth*. Mitch had never seen the film.

I was devastated. "That was going to be your Christmas present. I wanted to be there to watch your reaction the first time you saw it."

"Well, I guess you'll have to get creative and think of something else."

That was Saturday, October 6. We had the weekend off and were staying with the Jesuit Community at Rockhurst. I distinctly remember reporting the conversation and my disappointment to partner Stevie Coyle, a Santa Clara University alum, superb musician and comic who knew and loved both Mitch and me. Without the slightest strain or hesitation, he calmly said, "Why don't you fly down there and watch it with him? We have enough cash and you have enough time to get back."

It was the most elaborate practical joke I ever played. And it worked flawlessly. That very evening I walked down the Vargas midway wondering where I was going to find Mitch. Suddenly, there he was talking to someone in the concession wagon and he had his back to me. It was a perfect setup, and his reaction made the whole endeavor a clown-magician's delight. There was more in the bargain than watching my favorite film with Mitch as he encountered the DeMille images for the first time: all around us were performers and staff whose parents were in the film.

After that season with Vargas, Mitch toured Europe and then backpacked through Asia. By this time the show and I had managed to keep our own adventures on schedule. We had to increase our company size to compensate for Mitch's absence. Still, nothing was as easy as it had been.

*   *   *

During the spring of 1982 we were working our way home and had booked an elementary school assembly in the Los Angeles area. Because the show was scheduled for an early performance in a gym, we arrived the night before and the others chose to load the show into the building while I prepared dinner. I can't remember what was on the menu, but I remember a sheepish performer coming into the kitchen area of the truck to deliver some bad news.

"There's something wrong with the packing crate trick and they want you to look at it."

"What is it?"

"We can't figure it out, but it's not working right."

For some reason it couldn't wait. There seemed to be panic. Only a limited number of things could be wrong with the prop. It was mysterious. Disturbed and angry that the problem wasn't expressed more explicitly, I went in to investigate.

Just as I approached the wooden box in the backyard area, someone took the lid off. A quiet second or two passed and then everything exploded. Even in the days of Houdini's "Metamorphosis" version, that illusion has not enjoyed a more effective reaction than it received that night. The "problem" with the packing crate that night was that Mitch was in it. When he popped up he knew he had paid me back for the Atlanta surprise. It was a classic and elaborate touché. Mitch was back for ten more years in the joyful project that had brought us together.

*   *   *

His timing couldn't have been better. The show was bigger than when he had left. I'm not sure it was grander. I couldn't tell at the time, but from my perspective later, I realized I was beginning to be tired. I welcomed ten more years, but of course I couldn't know what they entailed. I did know we could no longer be lugging so much freight so far every year. I also knew our audiences were changing. Colleges themselves were changing, and college students seemed to have less time for midday playing. It might have even been the notion that we would have to adapt that began to tire me. Reinvention is more demanding than invention.

Besides the wear and tear of such physical artistry as circus directing and performing, there may already have been a new source of distraction demanding energy I didn't have to spare. Now I would describe it as a *de*-invention. Our tiny effort was born in the zestful wake of the Second Vatican Council and the calls for an enlivened sharing of the Easter treasure with the only world we really grasp, the secular one. We were, in a way, an effort to find more places at the table, regardless of who could read the menu. Now I sensed a tightening in the official church—an edging back to manners, ID checks at the dining room door, dress requirements. The expansive vision of an expansive pope, John XXIII, was shrinking into a divisive myopia affecting membership and authentic participation. There was bureaucratic reaction that seemed over-concerned with outdated proscriptions even though officials knew—as one of my superiors used to quip—the toothpaste was out of the tube.

But on we went, buoyed with the knowledge that several of our alums were finding their successful ways in professional performance, and that we still knew how to hold an audience wherever we found it. We also had the vital, enthusiastic support of the California Jesuits, and Jesuits across the country. Our unusual ministry was not only accepted, it had been tried and found vital. I had no doubt that this gift exchange between us and our audiences was powered by an indwelling presence I had begun to breathe easily enough to share.

14.

Core Complements

"A circus man was always on the lookout for likely horseflesh."
—David Carlyon, *Dan Rice, the Most Famous Man You've Never Heard Of*
(N.Y. 2001), 121

Wherever or however we met the young people who worked with us, one of the conditions of circus life they knew they would have to embrace was the constant presence of animals.

Over the course of its existence, our little show presented five dogs, four monkeys, three pigmy goats, four macaws, three horses, two bears, three domestic cats, and more doves, ducks, and rabbits than that elephant we never had could remember. These animals literally lived with us round the clock. Some of them did fairly impressive things in the ring; most of them were comic surprises.

One of the skills you develop as a talking clown presenting an animal is the ad lib that picks up after a mishap. Once, Mitch was working a little white poodle named Pepe on the high-dive ladder. Pepe was at the very top platform ready to jump and Mitch was jumping up and down shouting, "Jump! Jump!"

"Look who's jumping." We had a nasty ringmaster. But the joke stuck, and as Pepe got older he didn't have to jump anymore. Climbing the ladder was enough.

I was virtually self-taught when it came to circus tricks and animals. I had been around animals all my life, but training was something about which I had more enthusiasm than skill. Basically, I learned that you discovered what an animal could do. And besides watching your own animal, you could gain this insight from watching already trained animals. Then it was necessary for me to discover what the animal *liked* to do. If I could work its potential and its preference into something like an entertaining behavior, I coaxed, tricked, and begged it to do the maneuver and immediately rewarded it. That's the most successful motivator I know: rewarding preferred behavior. This is tedious and boring for the animal. Short sessions were in order, and we had three a day when an animal was beginning. Still there was failure, balking, runaways, flyaways, and frustration.

Bears, dogs, monkeys, and cats are usually trained from the start to go to a specific place in the ring. It's meant to be a secure place for them should there be confusion or interruption. "Seat" is a universal American command, and it's arguably one of the two most important things an animal, especially a wild one, is taught. "House," the command to return to the backyard enclosure that is the animal's home and safe haven, is also vital.

Bears walk on their hind legs naturally and with considerable ease. One of the most laughable details in the library of misleading propaganda from such interest groups as PETA is how circus bears are trained to walk on their hind legs. According to such poppycock, red-hot steel plates are placed under their front paws, causing them to recoil and (voila) find themselves on their hind legs. First of all, who wants to work with a bear with blistered front paw pads? And second, as often as not a baby bear cub will look for breakfast, lunch, or dinner by standing up on its hind legs to give mom an extra nudge. Bears have good balance on their hind legs.

Having bears walk on their hind legs is an attractive movement, but it is also a way of controlling them. While they're up, they can't run very well. Preventing a run is also a reason we worked our bears up on pedestals. To run they would have to climb down, giving us time to realize something was amiss.

Bears do not see well, but they are very smart, very curious, and have a sense of smell exponentially stronger than ours. Moreover, they could be the best poker players in the world; their facial expressions rarely change. All these factors coalesce to make the bear the most dangerous wild animal in a circus. You cannot smell or hear what might alarm them. Nor can you tell what they're thinking about doing. Unlike a cat, whose eyes and ears change, and other animals who visibly change their focus, the bear gives no clue before a strike with a claw or, as damaging, with those jaws. So we paid a lot of attention to the "seat" and "house" commands.

With our second bear, Jill, the "seat" command could have resulted in a calamity. Jill was a magnificent Himalayan I bought when she was already grown. She had never worn a muzzle and never would. Nonetheless, she came to us trained to know that in the performance situation she was supposed to pay attention to a human trainer. She knew only one real trick: taking a monkey biscuit from the trainer's mouth.

"And if she kisses you once, will she kiss you again?"

Jill and I in our daily PDA

So, with that steal from the old mouthwash commercial, Jill and I smooched twice a day in public, leading a famous bear trainer we had all seen to a rather frightening comment.

"I wouldn't do what that guy does with that bear for two million dollars!"

But the kiss isn't what almost backfired. She and I began our act in that posh setting of the Riviera Country Club for the Hathaway Children's Home benefit. In came Jill on her hind legs wearing her red sequined tutu as usual. I gave her the command to "seat" on a pedestal stage right in the ring. As she was momentarily preoccupied with getting her bulk up on the pedestal I noticed something that caused my heart to leap to my throat. Directly above the pedestal was a huge, illuminated, cut-glass chandelier. It would have been easily in Jill's reach once she was on the pedestal, especially if she rose up on her hind legs. I had a second or two advantage in having seen the attractive nuisance first. But I knew I had to work overtime to distract her with her very next move, which was to mount and roll a large barrel to the opposite side of the ring. I could tell the very moment she noticed the chandelier. It held her attention for just a bit and then the smell of the monkey biscuit treat prevailed and off we rolled to the other side. A very close call.

Our second horse, another miniature stallion, was light gray. He looks almost white in some photos. We named him Dan Rice after the famous talking clown who had a "one horse show."[46] Dan was already ring-broke when we bought him, so he also knew he was supposed to watch for commands. Other than circling the ring at liberty he hadn't learned any behaviors proper to an act.

We managed to teach him to jump through a large ornate hoop, to place his front feet on a small tub and pirouette, and to navigate the perimeter of the ring with his front feet walking the curb. He would run under a table on which our little Keesapoo, Jingle Bells, was waiting to jump on his back for a ride. His last trick was to walk on his hind legs before exiting the ring.

---

[46] The Dan Rice Circus traveled on a riverboat on the Mississippi and is thought by many to have been the first circus the Ringlings ever saw when it played their hometown in McGregor, Iowa. On the way home, legend holds that Al Ringling suggested, "Why don't we have a circus?" Later the Ringling family moved to Baraboo, Wisconsin, where their circus matured and grew on its journey toward becoming the largest such entertainment in history.

Probably the most successful entertainment we ever achieved with Dan Rice happened by accident. It was funny and we reinforced it. One day, for whatever reason, he stopped dead in his tracks and would not repeat his jump through the hoop. Of course I talked to him and explained what the objective was and that he had already done it. No response. It was already funny. Then I stumbled on something that opened up the joke.

"Look. I'll do it for you." Through the hoop I went. Surprisingly, he followed me, teeth bared, as if he wanted to catch me and bite my butt. Needless to say, we kept that in the act.

There was some "professional" consternation about transporting the horse and the bear in the same vehicle since the horse would fear the bear. Wrong. He loved the dry dog chow that was her staple diet, and once he got too close to the grid on her cage to mooch some of her spilled dinner. She tore just the very tip of his ear. We cleaned it up to prevent infection and assumed he'd learned his lesson. Wrong again. He went right back and we pulled him away and built a barrier. He had no fear of her whatsoever.

How complicated was my relationship with these animals. Ours was not an easy life and it was shared, 24/7. Once during the middle of the night I found myself sobbing in a New Orleans large animal hospital, staring through tears at a puzzled and pained Dan Rice.

"Please don't die." I heard myself say.

I continued to stare at him, held by those dark eyes, big like only horses' eyes can be. Then there were words both of us imagined: "Don't leave me."

And I was escorted away by an emergency surgery team who would open his gut to relieve and repair the damage of severe colic. Truth to tell, the level of passion and respect I felt toward our treasured livestock often revealed itself as wedded to a deep selfish fear of losing them. Dan Rice made it, and somehow we both had more reason to share his act with our audiences.

And then horse people told us we would have nothing but trouble if we stalled Dan and a little roan named Bucko together. Bucko was a gelding and they would supposedly fight. That was wrong too, at least for our animals. They got along fine.

There had been another love story with a horse earlier on. Our first miniature stallion, the handsome Othello, was purchased over the Christmas break and rode with us for the second half of Dana Smith's season. Dana developed a relationship with the animal and managed a schedule of walks and exercise that any horse needs if it is to spend hours riding from one place to another. The extent of this relationship and the adventures of this young man and his charge have only recently come to light for me.

I had no idea how much time Dana and Othello were together. I think that in a way Dana was afraid I might disapprove. And recently Dana has admitted some of the risks he and Othello took. There are, however, two bottom lines to this chapter in the Royal Lichtenstein Circus menagerie story. First, and most importantly, Dana probably saved Othello's life with the exercise he was able to give him. I know now that Dan really needed much more exercise—and he was performing every day. Second, I can only wonder how much more luck we would have had with Othello as a performing animal had we known how Dana talked to him. I'm not alluding to some type of mystical "whispering." There had to have been patterns of commands—not just words, but rhythms and gestures as well. In reality, I fear that Othello came into the ring hearing and seeing the phonemes of a second, broken language: "horse Latin." His first language he learned with Dana.

Kevin Duggan took over as Othello began training sessions for his first working season. Dana is so smart that I cannot imagine he didn't communicate with Kevin about Othello's patterns. He probably tried to communicate with me and I sadly didn't learn. Surely Othello was confused about our goals, and clowning was easier for him. I do believe animals understand the approval of applause. But perhaps like us, they enjoy laughter more. And Othello got laughs.

*   *   *

The concern with keeping monkeys—well, one of the concerns—is being sure you lock the cage. Once we were on our way down Foster Boulevard in Chicago on our way to the "Magic Inc." shop. Suddenly I felt something brush against my leg and before I knew it Penelope had seated herself on the dashboard and was having a grand view of traffic. We managed all right, but we probably endangered the drivers of passing cars with such a lively distraction.

Then there was the day Jennie Madrigal severely frightened a small child seated in our front row. In the final seasons most of the show took place upon a stage platform that pulled out from under the animal trailer and connected to the back of the prop trailer. The monkeys had already finished their act, and I was in the middle of something probably three numbers later when I notice that Heidi was walking out onto the stage all by herself. No costume, no diaper, no lead. I could see that Jennie noticed her right away, so I continued what I was doing. Heidi very quietly made her way down to ground level where the audience was seated. Monkeys *do* have very good eyesight, and that's how she told Jennie what her intentions were: she had a laser-like focus on this little kid's snow-cone in the front row. Jennie calmly got to the side of the kid before Heidi, snatched the snow-cone, and handed it to the monkey.

"I'll get you a brand-new free snow-cone, honey!"

As Jennie escorted the slurping Heidi back to her "house," it was obvious to everybody what some part of monkey heaven must be.

One of our finest audiences was to be found on a hillside next to the campus chapel of Lehigh University in Bethlehem, Pennsylvania. The chaplain who sponsored us on campus very generously put us up in the Bethlehem Hotel overnight. It was cold that night, so I didn't dare leave Penelope in the truck. We smuggled her cage in with us.

Such smuggling in later years would become de rigueur for us. To play some venues the only access was through passageways where animals would not be acceptable. All our cages were on wheels and all of them were fitted with covers. One of the funniest smuggles occurred for a load-in to a carpeted and ornate ballroom at the University of Iowa in Iowa City. The lady in charge of the facility happened by our setup and asked if we had animals in our show. Of course we affirmed that we did.

"Well, there's no way you can have animals in here."

"They're already in here, ma'am."

After an explanation of the protections we installed for floor surfaces, she acquiesced. In fact, our animals never touched the performance area floor when we were indoors.

The most nerve-wracking smuggle was in Jackson, Mississippi, where we played a conference dinner at the Holiday Inn. The only access for load-in was through the kitchen. We spent a lot of time during the day cleaning everything anywhere near the animals. Then we made sure to spray everything down with Lysol. It's probably a medical anomaly that the animals survived the spray. In we went, right through onto the ballroom floor.

There had been some publicity about well-known circuses presenting trained domestic cat acts. Dreading the plethora of stories about cats and their independent spirits, I decided we should begin with kittens and actually train them, with command to "seat" and "house" the clearly determined behavioral objectives. I wanted cats that would remind folks of their big cousins, so we found three tabbies and named them Gunther, Gebel, and Williams after the superstar trainer on Ringling Brothers and Barnum and Bailey Circus. I even wrote to let him know we were doing it.

I had to be away for part of that summer, so Mitch had the duty of seat breaking the new charges. He spent about six weeks teaching them to leave the old mirror wagon we had used for Penelope and walk up ramps to high pedestals, one for each of them. It did look good. They were sluggish, of course, and used every possible distraction to avoid the task at hand. But they worked pretty well. That was six weeks of work, just to get them seat-broke. We had to have a trick or two once we got them in. Cats are sure-footed, so a "bottle walk" seemed possible. In that behavior the animal navigates a journey along a row of elevated pegs from one pedestal to the other. Cats jump easily. So we worked them leaping from one pedestal to the other, even through a hoop, even through a hoop on fire. I bought some fresh baby beef liver. I could tell the moment they smelled the open package in the barn.

As a matter of fact, the peg walk was tough and took awhile. But the jump through the hoop? Five minutes. On fire? Sure. Through, turn around, and then back through. No problem. Jim Jackson would take the tail right after the fire hoop and "blow it out." A nice clown touch.

The trouble came the following summer. After a season of performing, I didn't work them in the summer like I did the other animals. So they figured out they didn't have to work. All we had left for the act was the jumper, Gebel. And early on in the season even she would balk about doing the return leap. So I developed a cover joke. I was always on the side of the ring toward which she wouldn't jump, and I'd spot some good-looking male student sitting fairly close and having a good time.

"It's no use coaxing her, Mitch. She won't jump in this direction!"

"Why?"

"'Cause this guy's too ugly!"

Worked every time. Then one evening we were doing an after-dinner show at Connecticut's Fairfield University in the large open patio outside their student union. That night it struck me that maybe we ought to let some girl have the joke. And there sat a perfect candidate: very pretty but casually groomed, not self-conscious. She was having a ball. Gebel set the whole thing up and balked right on cue.

"It's no use, Mitch. She won't jump in this direction!"

"Why?"

"'Cause this girl's too ugly!"

The girl's face changed in a flash to a blushing horror, and she lost no time energetically flipping me off. The crowd's reaction was definitely mixed, with a significant groan undercutting any laugh. I could not hear whatever the girl might have said. I never tried that variation again. So much for equal opportunity.

*   *   *

Discovering what an animal likes to do and will do demands constant attention. You can miss important unwitting clues they send you. Sometimes these develop into quite witting *cues*. Archie was a green and red macaw, a beautiful bird that came to us quite young. I never tamed him up to touch. All our work together was done with a hand perch I carried for him to ride to the next prop. If I or anyone had tried to pet him, he could have broken a finger. (A macaw's upper bill is quite solid keratin and bone; together with the power in the jaw it is able to split wood.) Since his predominant coloring was a brilliant red, I decided to have Archie play a fireman.

We built a little fire station on a table that rolled into the ring on casters. It was a two-story brick building, but the lower floor area was really the garage into which a large toy hook- and- ladder rig rolled from behind another brick wall. A pole came down from the upper story. So as Archie was introduced I rolled the fire truck into place, released a trapdoor in the upper chamber, and Archie came down the pole with the aid of his claws and his beak. Then he crossed to the truck and climbed to the topmost part of the ladder while I rolled him across a green parkway to a tiny trash barrel "on fire" courtesy of a red light inside it. All this time a revolving red emergency light rotated at the side of the fire station. When the fire was out, a switch was flipped and both the trash barrel and the emergency light went off. Our design worked beautifully and so did Archie. The scale relating Archie, the toy engine, and the miniature station seemed perfect.

The flaw was that I hadn't made my mind up about how to get Archie to handle a small water hose and aim at the "fire." As it happened, I didn't need to bother. When the hook-and-ladder truck stopped, it left Archie standing on the topmost rung of the ladder, directly above the little trash can. During one early practice session, as the truck stopped rolling I noticed that Archie raised himself up a little, fluffed out his wings, and relieved himself right onto the trash can. I wasn't sure that was the first time this had happened. Maybe not. Believe me; I paid attention the next session. Sure enough. Bingo. And there was just enough time after the truck stopped rolling to fit in a setup line.

"Put out the fire, Archie! Put out the fire! Good bo-oy!"

We had one of the best tricks in the show. People actually admitted they revisited the show just to make sure it wasn't an accident. Everyone wanted to know how it was done. Who knew? You can be sure we never changed that parrot's diet or feeding times.

We were working outdoors at the Wine and Harvest Festival in Paw Paw, Michigan, September, 1992. Archie finished his great trick and then directly flew off the performance area into the air and disappeared.[47] That's the type of moment you realize that Irving Berlin had "been there" when he wrote that show people "smile when they are low." There's nothing else you can do. You have an audience to entertain and a show to finish. Because I kept going with our show, most people in the audience thought Archie had a scheduled return flight sometime before the show ended. We all wished. He landed on an electrical pole. After the show the local utilities company let me ride up to him in a cherry picker, but he knew he was the trainer now. He was putting me through a funnier act. I couldn't get my stick-perch close enough to him. So I gave up, hoping his instincts would get him to food and warmth. It was a sad loss.

We were staying with David Pinto in nearby Kalamazoo, so it was easy to run an announcement in the local papers, and we would be in the Michigan

---

[47] Of course parrots can fly, so in situations like ours the custom is to clip their wings to prevent escape. In mid-September 1992, we and Archie were overdue for a clipping session.

area for a couple of weeks to come. Finally the call came in that a man had coaxed him out of the cold with some grain. I never thought I'd be so glad to return to Paw Paw, Michigan. I paid the man's rent for the month.

*   *   *

One must learn to pay attention to what threatens an animal. Of course I had to learn slowly, usually the hard way. Jojo, our magnificent spider monkey, hated dogs, even our dogs. Monkeys are very alert, and anything perceived as danger throws up vibrant red flags to their nervous systems. If they can't escape and they feel you're to blame, they attack. You. For whatever reason, Jojo thought any dog barking was barking at—and pursuing—him.

Once I was in the barn at Santa Barbara, and I had the feed trap open at the bottom of his cage ready to hand him a fistful of monkey chow. I paid no attention to the fact that one of the dog kennels was right next to his cage. Then a workman on the property entered the barn to talk to me and the dog began barking. While I tossed a greeting over my shoulder to the workman, I simultaneously put my hand through the feed trap to give Jojo his dinner. Such pain. He clamped down on the knuckle of my right index finger and severed the extender tendon. Off I went to emergency care, and lucked out. The doctor on duty was training for a specialty in hand surgery and was in immediate touch with the best hand surgeon in Santa Barbara. Fortunately again, the surgeon was apprised of some important circus medical wisdom that is not always shared by doctors. Physicians should not even think about closing up a wound from an animal bite. Such a lesion will always infect and must be able to drain. And there is only one bite that is more bacteria-ridden than a monkey's: a human bite.

In March 1990 we had a 7 pm show at Incarnate Word College in San Antonio, Texas. Fine performance. Everything went right. I decided during load-out to clean the monkey cages before they went into the trailer. I usually did that while holding the animal against me with one arm. Monkeys usually feel very safe in that position, as human babies do. I finished cleaning Jojo's cage and opened the door to put him back in. This was always a bit dicey as Carlo Gentile, who had to return him during each performance, well knew. But we were in unfamiliar territory at night, and there was a detail that I again neglected to remark: a dog was barking. I hadn't learned the lesson. There was no way Jojo was going to let go of his secure grip on me. When I applied some force, he struck. I was only wearing a T-shirt, so he ripped into my right upper arm down to the muscle tissue. By then he and I both knew he had to lose the battle, so I secured him and let some folks know to load his cage and calm him. Then a partner placed a tourniquet above the gash and Jennie hauled me into downtown San Antonio looking for an all-night emergency care center.

Point taken: both these strikes, no matter how understandable, were my fault. Entirely. I had responsibility for the animal's protection and minimal comfort and had failed. That had been a rule for me for a long time. I didn't always practice it, but I sincerely believe it. Sadly, though, I could no longer take a chance that a spectator or one of my partners would be at risk, so Jojo lost the tips of his two eyeteeth when we got back to quarters. A sad compromise.

The decision to disarm an animal is a tough one. If you want to exhibit wild animals, they ought to be able to have their teeth and claws. Years after we got the first bear I felt I had copped out by agreeing to have her declawed. Jill wasn't declawed, and on separate occasions two of our performers got scratched.

*   *   *

Some conventional wisdom holds that horses are smart. My conviction is that they are easy to train into a rut and happily they don't usually explore a way out of a set pattern. I love them a lot, and I respect them for their beauty and what I perceive as their loyalty, but I'm not sure how much is going on between those beautiful ears.

When we retired the circus, the new home for the animals was a small zoo run by a veterinarian friend of ours in Belleview, Florida. We had known Dr. Mark Wilson for years and he knew and cared for our animals. Mark was truly a find for anyone with a collection including exotics in that part of the country. He not only practiced, he taught young interns who wanted to pursue careers in animal health and management. These college-age students got to know our animals and care for them, and one day an intern challenged me.

"That Dan Rice. Don't try to tell me he ever performed in a circus. He's nothing but a little biting hay burner!"

Our old discarded ring curb was piled under a nearby tree, sadly rotting. I knew it could still be put together. What I didn't know was how much Dan Rice could put together.

"See that yellow and red striping over there? Those are pieces of the ring we used. They're all there. And that little tub is a horse prop. Put it all together in your free time and I'll run the act."

They couldn't wait. There was the ring and the tub. I didn't have a crop so I used a short piece of bamboo as my pointer and went and got my old pal. We hadn't worked the act in over a year. I brought him into the ring and started. We got through the pirouette on the tub and he dismounted and turned to the rear of the ring, as always, but I was gloating over the reaction of the interns. Suddenly I was pushed to my left as Dan needed to get by me to finish his act, the front foot walk about the ring curb. He was on automatic; he didn't need me or my pointer. Then up into the hind leg walk and out. Perfect. He loved monkey biscuits and the zoo had plenty of monkeys to feed, so of course Dan got a fat paycheck. All of us were amazed. Except Dan. It's just what he did.

The Animal Welfare Act of 1974 began a definition of minimal standards for the enclosure and treatment of performing animals. Government agencies stipulate cage dimensions and materials, ventilation, availability of water, and medical care. Between the Department of the Interior and the Department of Fish and Wildlife the movement of exotics, domestics, and indigenous wild animals are meticulously monitored.

Licensing, inspections, and codes became part of my life. Even a poodle trained to roll over and play dead as part of your livelihood together must be certified. Such a dog, pet or no, can no longer legally ride on the seat beside you en route to the next gig. A specified kennel is in order. It takes some study to navigate these requirements, but most of them are useful and beneficial for the animals.

I remember a Fish and Wildlife officer who had answered a neighbor's complaint that we had a bear. There was no problem since we were licensed. But when he finished his visitation he all but ordered me to keep Jill's cage locked. The possibility of "animal rights vandals" trespassing and releasing even dangerous animals was a real one. I knew there had been such an insane release of laboratory primates, including large ones, from the University of California at Davis.

*   *   *

There was always an unwritten custom for our first night in New Orleans: everyone was expected to have a Cajun dinner in a restaurant and then attend at least the first set at Preservation Hall. All on the ringmaster, of course. (I make pilgrimages to few physical shrines. Preservation Hall is one, and Baraboo's Circus World Museum another.) I felt obliged as an educator to make sure my partners knew something substantial in the lore of the French Quarter. On subsequent nights they were on their own, and we usually had the better part of a week booked in the Crescent City.

Accordingly, in the fall of 1975 I parked the van in a lot in the Quarter and with Tommy Crouse and Kevin Duggan headed for dinner and then Preservation Hall. I'm pretty sure we stayed for at least a couple of sets. Then we headed back toward the parking lot. About two blocks from where we had parked, Tommy let out a scream and took off running straight ahead. By the time I figured out the problem, I could see that our truck was surrounded by people and that the back doors were open. As we drew nearer I could hear Jingle Bells barking.

Police milled about, and a couple of guys in tan uniforms ran around with a pole and nets. Off to the side stood a couple in formal evening wear. A cop came up to me—I must have been the one who looked most anxious.

"This your truck?"

"Yes, sir."

"What're you doing with these animals? There's no ventilation on that truck."

I explained that we were a small circus and that we were headed for our lay-over for the night, where the animals would be aired, fed, and watered. I also called his attention to the A/C unit on the roof, which would be activated when we hooked up.

"Well, you can explain all that to the head of the SPCA there," and he gestured to the formally dressed couple.

As I waited for that conversation, I noticed that they had loaded Jingle Bells into an animal control truck, which was why she was barking nonstop. And they had dislodged the bear's cage and angled it so the main door was facing out the back end of the van. Puzzled, Dorothy was staring at this crowd that was definitely not recognizable as a circus audience.

I explained to the SPCA director that we were a small circus. I confessed that given the humidity and New Orleans temperature I had misjudged the ventilation issue. He said he wanted to hear from me each day we were in the area so that he knew where we were and that the animals were safe. He was most reasonable.

While I was talking to an official about returning my dog to her kennel, a very "pretty" young man walked in front of me, his shirt open to the navel. A policeman put his arm around this guy's shoulders, and as they passed I noticed a revolver stuck in the back belt of pretty boy. I was suspicious he was under-cover vice working the Quarter's gay prostitution scene.

"If you want that cash we found in the cab, you'll have to go over and sign for it at the precinct house!" The cop gestured across the street to a sure enough police station. So over I went. I was given the bag of money with no request for ID of any sort. But I was treated to the entertaining bellow of a uni-formed curmudgeon sitting in the corner of the station lobby.

"I don't care if they've got a tap-dancing giraffe over there. You guys are running around like a bunch of high school girls on graduation night!"

Making sense of what happened took some well-placed questions to some pals of ours in campus security at Loyola University, where we were bunking during our stay. I had inadvertently parked in a New Orleans Police Depart-ment lot, across from their precinct. At shift change, they came over to their cars and found this white cube-van rocking. Bears pace in their cages, and they are heavy animals. We had no idea that vans like ours were used by pimps in the Quarter to provide ready privacy for their "clients." And this one was rock-ing. So vice was alerted. When the doors were forced open, they saw they had been had. Call the SPCA! The director and his wife were out for the evening. But they came anyway, after animal control was alerted.

How fortunate for everyone that those animal control "Tarzans for the Day" only attempted to mess with Jingle Bells.

*   *   *

I can conceive of a circus without animals, and I respect the many shows that have been realized so artistically with only human performers. For me, however, the history of including performing animals in a circus performance illuminates vital archetypal dynamics. They are archetypal because they originate at the most profound levels of life. They are dynamic because they relate to how we behave. And they are vital because they so readily complement, enable, and enrich any fully human endeavor.

What was sensed in the didactic fiction of Genesis is the need to accept our partnership with animals in the pursuit of life on the planet. We are actively together in this venture whether we avoid each other, eat each other, feed each other, teach each other, or help each other. And all that activity presupposes the truly precious spiritual pursuit of communication with each other. (This pursuit far outweighs the importance of a supposed command to "subdue" or "rule" the animal kingdom.) Such experiences are as deep as they are perennial. The fact that they may seem remote in today's society only forces the need to question suburbia's expansive need to pave, industry's deforestation reflex, and the absence of live animals in our children's lives.

I am convinced great circus is a ritual that dramatically calls forth and depicts at once the inventiveness and the strength of human endeavor. I am also convinced that such invention and strength includes our relationship to animals who really can imitate our attempts to defy gravity, nudity, weakness, and boredom.

But I'm odd. After all, for three years I ended my day on the Carson and Barnes Circus giving a huge rhinoceros a loving pat on the cheek while I wished him a goodnight.

*   *   *

"When [Merle Evans] put down his cornet for the last time with the Ringling show on December 4, 1969, this 'Toscanini of the Big Top' had played an incredible 18,250 performances without missing a day."
Hoh and Rough, *Step Right Up* (VA., 1990), 194

Unquestionably, of all the exotic components making up our circus, the menagerie demanded the most constant care and concern. The animals were the neediest of the performers and those needs cried for attention year round.

Sometimes people ask if I would do it again—that is, create such a uniquely fashioned circus. Most already know I cannot possibly imagine such an enterprise without animals. But if I can raise my thoughts above the memory of so much fatigue and worry, I muster the affirmative—with a surprise.

"I'd start with the music."

*   *   *

For over twenty years, the various realizations of our "quarter ring" contained a rich panoply from the repertoire of circus skills. There rolled, jumped, and danced before our audiences a gamut of juggling routines, aerial and ground acrobatics, unicycling, wire walking and balancing. But whenever even a part of such a kaleidoscopic display was served up over music, we knew we had reached another level of circus quality.

It's not that I am a musician. That in itself is something I'd change had I the larger project of life itself to do again. But I carry reflexes from years of theater and circus directing that are intensely cued by even the idea of music. Precisely as an idea, a musical phrase probably connects more directly to the brain and subsequent physical reaction than most other concepts, remembered or imagined. One can choreograph in silence and away from the theater; one can design the order of behaviors in a horse act in silence and away from the training barn. Both projects are stimulated and accelerated when accompanied by music that is only remembered or imagined.

Like everything I learned about circus, I learned circus music and how to use it the hard way: by doing. I was in college before I caught on to a myth about circus music. It does not follow an act's performers, human or animal. And performers do not follow the music. When everything is right, they meet each other and the effect is overwhelmingly satisfying to the performers and the audience. But the hard work is done early on. Looking at the "charts" an act submits to a musical director on a show fortunate enough to have a live band, one sees abundant evidence of almost mechanical selectivity. The act has rehearsed to only so much of a given piece before switching into the rhythm of a different piece or a different section of the same composition as the performers change a trick or image in their act. This may go on through five to ten more sections for a seven-minute act. Thus when a juggler completes his repertoire with a given prop type—say clubs—the chord accompanying his "style"[48] is played, and when he picks up the props for the next section of his act—say hoops or fire torches, or juggles ping pong balls from his mouth—the music will be different, quite often because his rhythm is different or he wants a different mood. When fire is used in an act, very often Khachaturian's "Sabre

---

[48] A circus performer's "style" is the energetic pose he assumes at the end of a given trick or act. This pose is meant to cue applause from the audience.

Dance" is played. If there are distinct highlights—say, very difficult catches—
a drummer will hit the cymbal. The same is true of most professional acts that
have cared enough to set their routines to music. Even those using "canned"
accompaniment will have edited tracks with cuts from one rhythm to another
and one piece to another.

I have worked a horse to the senior Johann Strauss's *The Radetsky March*, and
I have seen a huge liberty horse act on Germany's Circus Krone work to that
same piece. It is hard to imagine better music under trotting horses. But even
in that genre, the horses, by design, assume different behaviors, different patterns, different gaits, and a good act will change music accordingly. The music
directors, even if they are digitally editing recorded music, must learn the act
and select the music type and amount that a given figure in the ring demands.

Only once in my life have I seen a flying trapeze act really use the support and
design suggested by John Hall's *Wedding of the Winds*. But there is no more pleasing a combination. Even the practice swings during an act's warm-up can meet
such music without much effort. Similarly, the *Blue Danube* waltz is wonderful
trapeze music.

While working as a clown on the L. E. Barnes and Bailey Circus I was accompanied by the show's live band playing Karl L. King's "The Walking Frog." I came
to two conclusions about the comic quality of that piece. First, it would be difficult
to find a better way to announce joyful craziness; second, it lets every nerve-end-
ing in the performer know he has the entire world's permission to be totally zany.

All seasoned performers and directors know these things. And they know the
tedious labor that goes into making the performance and the music "meet" as one
in the performance space. Such psychology is as old as the oldest of rituals, because
it works on all levels of apperception. From the stark fidelity of note to syllable in
Gregorian chant, through Bach's disciplined leanness
to the even unnecessary ornament in Mozart's *Great C-
Minor Mass*, composers sought and found that rewarding juncture of music and sanctuary gesture. More
mechanically, perhaps, parade ground marshals discovered it in the military march.

It has been my joy to help engineer such moments
of "meeting" in our little ring. Early on we had
nothing more than a tambourine underscoring
threaded razorblades coming from a performer's
mouth. Then Bill Cain brought his wonderful
recorder and a wistful haunting mood to a narrative.
Moyna brought his banjolele to warm us up in an
overture letting everyone know we'd "be comin'
round the mountain." Nanci Olesen was a flutist
with showmanship who could ad lib needed music
on the instant.

Nanci Olesen added
musical charm to my old
paper tree routine.

When the Frankfurt crank organ arrived, it played on punched rolls and I could actually see the music quantitatively. I literally got my hands (and scissors and tape) on *The Radetsky March* so I could edit exactly what and how much I needed for each trick. I "cut and taped." So by the time the big full sound of the Calliola arrived with its data also supplied by punched rolls, I was ready to do some serious "arranging."

Kelly Robertson joined out with us in the summer of 1986. She was a practiced juggler, primarily a ball juggler, but was willing to expand her skills and investigate new ones. A bit timid of falling from the rola-bola platform, she told me she'd prefer to work with both feet on the ground. And how she worked. She was always drilling the juggling material. I knew she was a pianist and had a sense of music, so I watched her ball juggling routine until I had the sections of it pretty well in my mind and then I selected her music for a solo.

Our custom-built Calliola band organ from Stinson Organ Works

Unrolling yards and yards of music, right on the floor, I began "hunting" for what I thought would be the right sections to support Kelly's act. I cut and taped those sections together and played them for her. There were a few miscalls so we corrected where there was not enough music or too much. When we thought we had it right, I made a practice tape for her. She beautifully "met the music" with virtually every toss and catch. The juggling *was* music; it was easy to imagine the balls as notes in the air. Another really beautiful and refined moment had found its way into our ring.—Kevin Kurdt was also meticulous about meeting his music, especially in his trapeze work and the devil sticks routine. I honestly think he found some of his moves in the accompaniment to his acts; the music taught him.

Toward the end of our story I had the privilege of meeting the late Dr. David Harris, a Methodist minister and university professor who had founded "Circus Kingdom" in 1973 as his own pastoral outreach through circus, and he did get to start with the music. A brass player, he connected with an international network of young musicians, mostly accomplished brass players, to learn classical circus music.

I could not get over the richness that band provided to the performance ceremony. Including their pre-show and intermission work, those musicians would rip through upwards of sixty pieces in a show. Nor could I get over what the music was doing to young people who were basically college athletes.

Chests were out. A position change for a subsequent maneuver became a stride, if not a strut. There was contact with spectators that competition audiences never see. There was not just good form, there was large-scale performance.

Moreover, I have reflected on what happened to our show when the Calliola entered our lives. Scale had to change in the ring. Our parameters would necessarily remain the same; we still had to fit anywhere. But the ring had to be fuller, and not just with more performers or more stuff. Performers had to be willing to use their space to the maximum, consume it. The music's rhythms, tempi, and pitches secretly picked up our feet in a different way and set them down in cadence. We were given permission to turn the most utilitarian movement or prop shift into performance, into a continuity with the tricks before and after such a move. The music evoked more of our private spirits and called us to prance, to march, to dance. Fluidity seeped into the pores of our stop-and-go series of acts, and a variety show became recognizably the ritual it had wanted to be from the start.

That's why I would begin again with the music.

15.

Stress, Strain, and Sacrament

In the mid-Eighties I was becoming more sensitive to the risks we were running. The risks hadn't changed. I had. Perhaps some nerves had been exposed in whatever demands I had been making on an already sensitive psyche. I knew I was tired in the ring. I had begun to think about whatever *depression* might mean. I'd only heard the word used, but never applied it to myself.

For whatever reasons, my sense was heightened about just how liable we could be. One night, after a long and strenuous rehearsal period, we opened at a church very close to training quarters. I lost my temper in the ring when a patron moved onto our side of the safety rope to give his toddler a better view of a monkey. Frustration and self-hatred kept me awake that night. How could that poor guy have known I had just heard about a child seriously injured in a tangle with a circus bear cub? All wild animals are wild. Always.

By 1988 the country's litigation and liability fever had reached such a pitch that it was affecting us dramatically. Besides the increase in auto insurance rates, the humblest of our sponsors were demanding liability coverage, some of them demanding the per diem warranty coverage of a full blown carnival: one million dollars. By that time ads for entertainment brokers appeared regularly in our trade journal, *Circus Report*, so we found coverage. My problem was that I didn't want to spike our performance fees so that we were out of range for many of our regular stops. It was time to eat my words about having "a circus that would never sell anything." We had to become concessionaires. The insurance demanded that we define our legal entity. John MacConaghy, a former student and charter circus alum who was now a business attorney, helped us become "The Council Players, Inc. d.b.a. the Royal Lichtenstein Circus."

By the time I reluctantly made the decision, we were already on tour and in Sacramento, California. Physically, the trial concession stand was only two sheets of plywood hinged together and stood on end. We painted them white, inscribed "Circus Candy" in bright red at the top, and ran strings with clothespins across the boards for hanging the bags of "product." A simple cafeteria table set in front of the display boards served as a counter. Of course our first wares would be cotton candy, the staple of our trade.

It was easy to rent a professional machine and purchase the needed sugar and cones and plastic bags, as well as the coloring and flavoring agents. What was not easy was actually manufacturing cotton candy. It was yet another area where we didn't know what we were doing.

Our performance site was the tennis court area of Loretto High School, a Catholic girls' school. High cyclone fences surrounded the courts, and the concession was right next to one of those fences. A supply house rented me a "Tornado" model machine, and we soon found out that it was suitably named. Once that candy started flying out, there was no keeping up with it either to get it onto a cone or into a bag. It didn't help that there was an afternoon breeze up. Eventually we realized that everything was in the wrist, turning the cone and moving it around the circumference of the spinner pan at the same time. Jennie Madrigal caught on first and became the best of all of us. That first day, we did eventually cover our display boards with bagged candy, and we made some money before and after show time. But we had also covered the cyclone fence next to us with a blanket of pink floss that was decidedly not bagged.

I found out there was a smaller, slower "Econoline" machine available and bought it. That brought the flying sugar under control and we learned our new craft. Eventually, we bought our own Tornado and, with the advice of concessionaire friends in Saint Louis, bought a professional popcorn popper and ice shaver for snow cones. Our offerings eventually included cotton candy, popcorn, soda, and snow cones as well as souvenirs. For the 1989–90 season we went out with a flashy illuminated stand that really did help pay the bills. But that candy demanded hard work. On school assembly days, Jennie would often have to crank out between three and five hundred bags of cotton candy before the show. Of course everyone else had to pitch in both to make the product and sell it. To cover our liability insurance costs, we had learned a new dimension of our business.

*   *   *

Besides our concerns for the public and our need to attract them, we were not immune to the internal frictions within our own tiny community. These were a different but serious caliber of liability. There were misunderstandings to correct and occasional losses of personnel. The night after I lost my temper, I lost a performer. An aerialist walked off the site during teardown with not a word of his intentions or destination. He just vanished into the Los Angeles night. Thankfully he had connected with his parents, who were on the performance site with him the next day. No promises or pleas could assuage my fear of assuming more risk by readmitting him to the cast. At least someone could now know where he was.

*   *   *

Perhaps the stresses to be expected in running a circus were only part of what I knew was tiring me. The stingy atmosphere of the country's obsession with liability suits and ordinance was a very real fact of our lives. But for me, there was more consequence and challenge in a constrictive air closer to home. I was a Catholic priest in the Jesuit order. It was not lost on me that people wondered how my talents and the grace of my ordination could be squandered on a circus ministry, when the number of available priests was dwindling to the extent that parishes were being closed. I was also a man who had befriended a large number of very devoted and talented women, lay and religious, who were sure they had experienced the call to priesthood that I had.

We were to play a date in San Antonio. The local Serra club, a group promoting vocations to the priesthood, asked me if I would give a talk on vocations while I was in the area. I agreed and the date and place were stipulated. The circus would perform as part of the package. I sensed they hoped to use the example of our creative ministry as a drawing card. Everything went off without a hitch. But my sponsors let me know they disapproved of my take on the vocation crisis. It wasn't that I denied there was a shortage of vocations. I had suggested there was a shortage of enlightenment about what a vocation was and who could have one. I adduced as evidence the number of women I knew with priestly vocations. The Spirit I worshiped was making a statement that begged theology and demography to engage.

I was not at all unable to articulate my own sense of church and Jesuit failure. By accident, thinking I had asked to be off record, I was once quoted in the *Wall Street Journal* criticizing the use Jesuit superiors were making of some of our best talents. The reaction was not happy, of course. One Jesuit friend remarked that I had depicted the rest of my brothers as having their heads up their butts. Even had I spoken on record I could never have even felt that, let alone said it. What I did feel, in response to his remark, was something that begins, "If the butt fits…" But until now, that too has been off the record.

There was, to be sure, more than cable making up the wire I walked. The balance was a dance sometimes stressful but always worth the risk. Into the context of pastoral and literary discussions of clown wisdom and the holiness of play, a stream of deadening and stringent documents and letters emerged calling for the rightness of rite, and the obedience of ritual makers. In short, clowns had no place in the liturgy. It was official. On November 10, 1985, the Los Angeles Archdiocese (mine) published a clarification of the 1978 "Environment and Art in Catholic Worship" statement by the U.S. Bishops. An upper case banner shouted "THE MINISTRY OF CLOWNS IS NOT

Penelope and I in the Oakland Cathedral, Summer 1974. She only joined me for the recessional out of the building.

APPROPRIATE TO LITURGICAL WORSHIP." Once more, the circus provided my corrective lens. For me, a much more substantial "clarification" occurred when a clown friend died.

The event was at San Jose's Town and Country Village shopping center on May 19, 1989. One of my early Royal Lichtenstein partners, Father Mike Moynahan, joined me as I presided at a Mass of the Resurrection in the center ring of Circus Vargas. We were celebrating the life of a well-known performer, William McCabe, "Billy the Clown." Everyone close to him knew that Billy worked till the end of his life, even contending with a disorienting disease. The congregation was around the altar table in the ring. Some clown performers were in makeup. The homily I gave after the gospel reading was in the form of a letter to Billy.

Dear Billy,

The last time we talked, you were in makeup. That's how I knew you best and that's a sign, I think, of how rushed our lives have been, and how real a clown you were.

I guess I mostly want to thank you for your life, especially for Billy the Clown. Somehow, I think, you figured out what a lot of us missed: the clown, alone among circus performers, gets to relate personally, eye-to-eye, hand-to-hand, and one-on-one with the spectators. It may be the hand-off of a ticket stub or coloring book or balloon, but it's the closest any performer gets to the individuals of the audience.

And the clown-gag, when it's best, addresses the spectators' lives and turns values and prejudices upside down, revolves them and, when lucky, sends folks home with a better outlook. You know what they call someone who revolves insights and prejudices, Billy? A revolutionary.

Why did you put up with all the miles of boring highway, breakdowns, bad weather, artistic flare-ups, lovers' quarrels, and continual readjustment of acts because someone else walked the show? You walked too, didn't you? Why did you come back? Maybe you felt, even thought, there was no place else. But why?

Billy, I have wondered how folks like you handled the strangeness of the Circus. We really aren't "Town and Country Village" types, you know. We aren't even the San Jose or California or U.S. type really. We're a motley gang of strangers that a lot of townfolk still want to see. Thank God. Did you stay with it, and come back to it, because with this band of strangers you felt less strange? And do I guess rightly that more than anything, you prized the clown's most wonderful privilege of being the closest of all the strangers to the townfolk?

We are all strange to someone and to some place. What a magnificent thing you have done dear clown, friend, if you helped even one child, indeed one adult, let alone a million, overcome their fear of strangers and enter into the strange world of bigger, stranger than life wonders displayed in this tent. Isn't that what the Circus is all about after all? Don't we come here to shift horizons, imagine a bigger life? And isn't that a holy thing? You know, now, don't you? You know better than any of us, that the whole God project, Creation, religion, and the pursuit of goodness is to welcome so much wonder into our wanderings that we finally discover who we are: the children of God's dream. Let me guess that now you know that was the kind of clown walk-around Jesus took us through for three years. And wasn't he strange? All the way from the Father. But he never feared a stranger—none of us. Indeed he told us to keep reaching for more strangers.

Don't for a moment, brother clown, feel badly about those performances near the end when they had to aim you around the track because you'd lost your orientation. Don't feel badly at all. It was hard and messy and challenging, but it was about as pure an art form as you can get: the clown as revolutionary who doesn't know where he is at the very moment he is trying to free people up from where they are. It was wonderful, Billy. They didn't know that you didn't know they didn't know you didn't know where you were.

Enough, dear clown. Thank you for your life and for the gifts you made to the American Circus. Thank you for your faithfulness to children in hospitals and burn centers. Thank you for opening us all up a little—for making us a little more willing to risk the stranger who, after all, holds God out to us.

Unusual as such a homily and setting were, I remain convinced that I would never have said those words had I not been a Jesuit, a Catholic priest, and a professional clown. That I had a life at all required that none of these facets of my personhood could be strangers to the others. I was secure. I knew I was unusual, but I was secure.

One of my ordination gifts came years before the ceremony of my ordination. During my childhood, adolescence, and early ascetical training, our Roman Catholic community cherished the event of the Eucharist, a very physical centerpiece of our faith lives, as a miracle.

Simultaneously, another part of my younger formation was the practice of stage magic as an entertainment art. I knew there was no such thing as magic. It was all mechanical trickery that only pretended to be beyond natural cause. There was never a question that such an art in any way connected with what I practiced as a Catholic. I deeply resented even the possibility that a Jacobean-era magician satirized the Latin words of consecration in his expression "Hocus Pocus," a corruption of *"hoc est enim corpus meum."* I identified what he and I were doing artistically as trickery; as a believer, I experienced the central moment of the Eucharist as a miracle. I didn't know how it was done, but I knew I didn't know and I knew there was no one who did. It was a mystery. A known unknown.

Thankfully, new discussions began to catch up with my instructors by the Sixties. There was honest concern that in practice the celebration of the Eucharist had long centered on an attitude very akin to magic. The understanding was that when the priest said a certain formula over the element of bread and then the element of wine, each was changed, into the real body and blood, soul and divinity of Jesus Christ. For centuries, what happened, however it happened, was called *transubstantiation*. Nonetheless, that was no more than a name, a label.

But the process or reality that name represented was unknown. When an unknown is known to be unknown, philosophers call it a mystery. Sadly, many of us blindly adopted the word *transubstantiation* as an explanation of the mystery, and in some sense an actuality. We did not know we did not know what we were talking about. Our notion of Eucharist lived in the area of myth. I was a stage magician; I knew when I didn't know about how something worked.

Fortunately, philosophers and theologians who were unbiased by church authority and specious medieval reasoning began to really examine the entire context of the celebration of the Mass. They revisited the historical setting of the scriptural texts from which the rite derives; they refined their understanding of the early Christian ritual making; and they brought the light of cultural anthropology to bear upon human gatherings, celebrations, and feasting. I know those pursuits went on. I know intense contextual concerns emerged about what happens at Eucharist. I watched, studied, and learned a developing, changing set of Eucharistic prayers. I knew I was called upon to humble myself: I didn't know how this power I would be given worked. As importantly, I sure as heaven didn't know how Holy Orders, the sacrament that conferred such a power, worked.

So at Billie's memorial Mass, by the time I got to the prayer, "And let perpetual light shine upon him," I should have been in the goddam dark. But I wasn't. That's because by that time in my life as a priest, my entire notion of Eucharist took all of its illumination from other people who knew they needed each other for light. They helped each other see. And what they saw was a need to celebrate and nurture who they were because they were for each other the Christ, the Light of the World. As in Circus and Theater, so in Church; a few of us are trained as lenses and mirrors—albeit faulty— to help everybody see this magnificent vision. And when they see who they really are, they celebrate and take food and drink to sustain that Life and Light. It's celebrative food and drink used for festivals through uncounted millennia. Only now, because of the

Life it sustains, it is transformed. So besides being a lens and mirror, the priest also waits table. Latin again, *ministrare,* to serve.

Anyway, that's what I retained from a foggy, adventuresome, exploratory atmosphere as I was being reeducated and trained. It's the most sense I could make of a ritual I treasured and wanted to revitalize as a priest. Such an interpretation was certainly not beyond objection. It was ragged, too figurative. And it got me into ungracious exchanges.

In the days when I was giving lectures and workshops on liturgy I had a seminary audience I would never forget. We had reached the question portion of the evening. Everything had gone well with a group of perhaps five hundred folks, still catching up with the reality of what Vatican II might entail for worship. An older monsignor prominently ensconced in the front row pushed for a more traditional reading of the gospel warrant than the one I'd given. It became clear that he was disappointed that I was deemphasizing the miraculous dimension of the Mass.

"Monsignor, I understand that you were trained in the interpretation that at the precise words of consecration a miraculous change takes place. I was taught that. So were we all. But I don't think there's a seminary in the country taking that approach now."

"What would the Pope say?"

And I replied as if Rhett Butler had the floor, embarrassing as it seems now. "Frankly, Monsignor..."

*   *   *

It must have been very difficult for some to believe that a guy who lived as I did cherished the Church as his only home. From the outset of the circus ministry there had been constant chatter with superiors and hierarchy depicting me as egotistical and irresponsible toward my calling. Tempers were not restrained. Once, a copy of an angry letter found its way to our mailbox.

April 21, 1974
To: Bishop Cunningham, Bishop Harrison, Bishop Foery
Rev. Nick Weber, A clown to attract more clowns...

Don't we have enough clowns among our clergy now? Don't you care that the laity are fed up with Walt Disney productions instead of the Holy Sacrifice *of the Mass? Don't you care that the Doctrines of the Church are being mutilated and destroyed??*

Don't you care that attendance at Mass has dropped drastically? Well, we the laity care. . . And we think it is high time that you and all the Bishops "picked up your staffs" and started using them.

Put these self-serving egotists in their place and bring forth the real men of God to guide and lead us in the practice of our precious Catholic faith.

If you, the Bishops, will not lead your flocks, then we, the laity, will have to take the only redress left to us —close our wallets and checkbooks and withdraw physical and moral assistance. It is our sincere prayer that we will not have to resort to this.

Mr. and Mrs. Robert N. Brown

Fayetteville, New York

That was the first (and I hope the *only*) time we were ever lumped with Walt Disney Productions. And it was also the only time I imagined a bishop striking me with his crosier.

In the practice of a priest's ministry I am sure I was not distracted. It was not always a predictably and formally correct practice. That was because I was bent on making sure the ministry effectively met its goal: the people I was serving. In its guidelines for evaluating sacramental ceremony the Church had long distinguished validity from licitness. A sacrament or rite could effect its communication of grace without hitting all the bases of Church regulation; it could be valid even if it were not licit. For me it was more than a Jesuitical distinction for overcoming scruple: It was an invitation to radicalize[49] my understanding of sacrament and rite so that ceremony could adapt to its context. This was undoubtedly made possible by the atmosphere in a Church that had admitted a need for revisiting centuries-old customs and rubrics. Crudely stated, things in the early Seventies were loose enough to let an unusual presider slip through a few cracks.

The media of course fed on the quirkiness of a priest dressed as a circus performer, monkeys and fire eaters in a cathedral, circus baptisms and confessions and funerals. But the media didn't count. All that counted was whether the folks trying to practice their faithfulness were paying attention. I was paying attention to that. In that area of ministry I have never been distracted. I felt that I was obliged to help God's people be wakeful in churchy situations rather than numbed by rote. I firmly believed that in adjusting the prism of the holy in some minor human way, I could allow people increased light and life in their practice. And this goal of directing such serious wakeful attention in the groups of God's people entrusted to me demanded my own unfailing attention. From the vantage of a life journey that has taken me professionally into so many simultaneous specialties, even rarified ones, I can confidently appreciate the concentration I had as a priest. When it came to pastoral practice, I was focused. My faith, my habits, my work, and my talents seemed to coalesce in applied mission and service.

Two of my Catholic actors in the Council Players eventually married. We were still in touch when their first child was born, and it only seemed

---

[49] *Radix* is Latin for *root*. *Radical* means *basic, pertaining to fundamentals.*

appropriate that he should be baptized as a Roman Catholic but on the property where his parents met and rehearsed for years: Trinity Episcopal Church. I figured out how to make this work legally through appropriate registration, and that was my first baptism.

A former student and his fiancé wanted the celebration of their marriage to reflect the breadth of their love of the world as well as their community. They wanted the celebration to play out against a scenic backdrop readily available from the vantage of Mount Tamalpais in Marin County, California. That was my first wedding.

Everyone in our family knew that my sister Susan's wedding was not going to be at all comfortable if celebrated in a parish church. She and her groom decided on the nicest of our relatives' backyards and somehow managed permission from the parish authorities for me to preside at the occasion behind Uncle Arthur and Aunt Nancy's home. We had the requisite trellis and even the Wagnerian "hit" for opening such occasions. The setting allowed all of us to be comfortable; the weather did not. With the grandparents sitting in the blazing hot Sacramento Valley sun, we needed to get radical. A wedding is the public celebration of something that has already happened. Celebrations can be long or short. I took one look at Gramma Weber and opted for short. A reading, some remarks about what we were there to witness, the exchange of vows, a kiss, and out.

That's the way it happened, but Gramma wasn't happy. "It was so fast I didn't even know they were married till they kissed each other."

I would one day streamline another ritual for Gramma Weber. In November 1976 we had just finished a performance at Southwestern University in Georgetown, Texas. I was handed a message even before I could get to the truck to change. I was to call Dad immediately. The program director offered her office and phone.

"Butch, your grandmother has died. We're trying to decide a date for the funeral but want to know if you're going to be able to come home. Where are you?"

"Texas. It's no problem. I can get there."

By this time the tears were profuse and the sensitive young program director had a box of tissue right at my elbow.

"Who's doing the funeral?"

"Well, the parish is. They've got the priest all set. They just want to finalize the day."

"The hell!"

"What?"

"I'm going to be priest for this service. You *do* realize that she and I have never been to Mass together since I was ordained. This will be the first."

The pastor who instructed my grandmother when she converted to Catholicism actually bragged about the job he'd done. "Well, sure and we didn't make a theologian out of her now, did we?" What he did was make an Irish Jansenist out of her. She simply would not abide the thought of a celebration of the Eucharist in her dining room, and she was beyond getting out of the house. So we hadn't concelebrated Mass since I was ordained.

I was the presider at the Mass of the Resurrection for Elsie Rose Weber. For some reason the lights were never turned on in the church. There was no incense available. For that omission there was a "reason." An associate pastor explained, "We quit using incense when we heard the pastor *explain* the use of incense around the casket. He actually said, 'Now we use incense to drive the devils away from this old lady.'"

I made some remarks at the cemetery. They were atypical of graveside remarks. After all, by that time we were rehearsing in the utility yard of the Santa Clara Mission Cemetery. "I know graveyards are ordinarily seen as sad places. They aren't sad for me. I actually build and rehearse a circus in one. And I think most of you know I fell in love with the circus because this lady we bury today once told me stories about her own love of the circus."

Allowing the mysterious reality of sacramental power to penetrate the language and my clumsy performance of ritual gestures took concentration and energy. The circus was easier, not because I understood it better. I just had more opportunities to practice its formalities. But even as a ringmaster or announcing clown, I habitually sensed that I was helping a gathering focus on important spiritual presence, the sacred dynamism that their life really was. That took almost measurable energy. Wherever I addressed such public ministry, I know I felt stress.

As a working man, I knew I had to enlist the aid of a physician to ensure my health. As a Jesuit, I was obliged by rule to manifest to the provincial the state of my overall physical, psychological, and spiritual health. Both these checkups were annual appointments scheduled for times when I was off the road.

Because of Jesuit regulations, the circus as a ministry made its way into my notes for provincial visitation almost from the beginning of my priesthood. The unique ministry became the frame and the substance of my talks with five different provincials over the years. The personalities of these men couldn't have spanned a wider range of attitudes. The first, who really enabled me in my life's work, was adventuresome but not quite sure it would succeed. (Who was?) He had used the expression "We haven't had much luck" in referring to another Jesuit's experiment in performing arts. Another provincial was a cautious, wise man whose introversion and lack of joy made conversation about a circus—even a Jesuit priest's circus—seem out of place. Conversation with still another was easier, but I didn't feel he connected with what we were doing.

John Clark was enlightened, connected, even affectionate. I think in that relationship there was support and trust such as I had never experienced with a provincial. He was keenly sensitive to the work of my partners. Once when we arrived for the winter break at Grand Coteau, Louisiana, there was a letter from him in the circus mail. It was addressed to "The Cast of the Royal Lichtenstein Circus." His salutation included the individual names of that year's troupe.

Anyone who survives for 5½ months under Father Nick Weber's rigorous standards has certainly achieved much. Of course, I have always found Nick very bashful, quiet, unassuming, humble, passive, docile, and patient. I am sure you have had the same experience.

Seriously, I write to tell you how much we Jesuits are indebted to you for the unique contribution you make to this important ministry of our Province.

Then, after telling them to enjoy their mid-season vacation, he continued, tongue again in cheek, "*Sit back. Rest. Tell Nick he is supposed to do all the work at Grand Coteau.*"

Once, when I trekked to Los Gatos for my yearly meeting with Jack, he took me to lunch downtown. The meal came and before we lifted a fork he suggested we pray a blessing on the meal. His closing floored me. "And let us remember Mitch and pray that he have the grace and strength he needs to continue his generous contribution to this good work. Amen."

While the subject matter of a Jesuit's manifestation of conscience can juridically include serious matters of confessional concern, they are usually carried on in a more casual atmosphere in which both the superior and the subject are free to explore only what seems more germane to an individual ministry. In my case, that could have taken hours. I always left these meetings with John, feeling there was a continuing platform underneath my creativity. What I didn't realize, from early on in my priesthood, was that the spirituality I had adopted, my almost effortless reading of the literal Spirit into all aspects of my life and life itself, was horizontal. Hierarchy, even a divine hierarchy, as in decreeing Father and anointed Brother–Lord–dying (for my sins) Son, had less and less traction in how I lived. The Ignatian reflex of *tantum quantum*—"If it works use it, if it doesn't, don't"—applied even to the sacraments. Moreover, if the divine hierarchy I had grown up with held less meaning for me, then the religious verticality reflected in terms like *superior* and *subject* seemed absurd.

Such developments in my spiritual outlook most certainly bore on the vows themselves. I gave almost no thought whatsoever to poverty. I grew up without money or many possessions, had never been interested in wealth, and now managed thousands of dollars a month running a national business on a shoestring. Still I failed. Repeatedly, in my handling of even meager earthly treasure, I was a selfish and hoarding steward. — I gave lots of thought to chastity. I am a complete sexual male, after all, and I spent most of my time traveling. That requires long hours of solitude, even in the company of fellow passengers, even with a Spirit that, after all, quickens all of you. And anyone who's ever been alone knows how ready a bedfellow lust can be for solitude. That's why there is a vow and such elaborate hierarchical apparatus to demand and ensure abstinence. Without hierarchical focus, such apparatus and discipline can fail. So did I. Repeatedly. And then I kept on trying—repeatedly—grasping what discipline I knew. — Obedience is also correlative to hierarchy. The superior's voice is the will of God. Do what the superior wants and you are pleasing God. During my life as a Jesuit priest, I had assurance that the superior wanted the ministry I had developed and embraced. – Nonetheless, such support didn't warrant my egocentric demeanor of independence from hierarchy.

Fatigue drove me to seek regular physical checkups in the Eighties. All my vitals were right on the mark without any medication. My parents, Gramma, and twenty-five years of balanced diet, exercise, and labor had contributed to an adequate "machine," as Dad would have said. But I felt tired; I was missing energy I wanted to rely on. I brought up a word I had only overheard in passing discussions: *depression*. I had no idea what it meant clinically. I was privy to no literature. It sounded vague, and what I was experiencing was vague. So I brought it up with my physician.

"You should know that depression is a disease that is in large part caused physically. Just as your eyes are blue, there are other congenital factors that contribute to whether a person is depressed or not. I mention that because now we have medicine to treat such physical factors."

Oh, no. I didn't want to go on pills for the first time in my life. I was hesitant and he could sense my internal stammering.

"I just want you to know what's available. Everything else is fine. Just go on with your regular activities, and if there's a time when you feel you'd like to try some type of pharmacological remedy, just let me know. Call me wherever you are and I'll get you the medicine. It's just a matter of a pill."

I liked the guy. He was a friend. I think his advice was very honest. But he was an internist, and I might have needed a different kind of doctor then. Perhaps a psychiatrist. At any rate, he was there if I needed him. I went back to my circus work breathing its dust and magic and spirit. For a few years that was medicine enough. At least I thought it was.

16.
Which Arrows?

"When in consolation, prepare for desolation."
—Ignatius Loyola, *The Spiritual Exercises, Rules for the Discernment of Spirits*, #323–24

The circus will always be an institution synonymous with youth. Our circus flourished not only through the talents of our young people, but also through their idealism as volunteers in a format beyond the limits of commercial entertainment. What better guarantee of life in a "lively art" than idealistic youth. With a shock to all of us, some of that youthful glow about our project was about to dim.

We had just returned to Santa Barbara and I was in the laundry room putting clothes in the dryer when Mitch abruptly came through the door.

"We have to talk."

That was always a command, always serious. The conversation would be terse if not blunt. There was no exception in this case.

"I am pretty sure I am HIV-AIDS positive!"

Summoning all my energy for a coherent response, I blurted staccato expressions of alarm, and, unable to ask how he knew, just stared at him. I felt like I was going to pass out.

"For weeks now I've been noticing the signs of thrush in my mouth. White foamy spots. I have an appointment for an exam at the county clinic this afternoon. I feel terrible laying it out like this but it's better to, I think."

He was so matter-of-fact, I began to regain my voice. "You're trusting me to deal with this, but it's so, so hard. I'm not going to dig for details, but do you know the source?"

"Pretty sure it was in the southeast. That's the only thing I can figure."

"Okay, guy. You've had some time to live with this. Give me some time to try handling it. Do you want me to go with you?"

"No. Stay here. There's nothing you can do!"

"Get to me as soon as you get tested. Phone me."

That was in the late Eighties. There were still no retrovirals or cocktails. If you got AIDS, you wasted away and died.

Mitch was HIV positive and developing the immune deficiency symptoms of AIDS. But from that afternoon on there was a governing attitude in place. This was not going to be seen as a death knell. It was going to be accepted as a complication, a hurdle, another hoop through and over and around which Mitch would dance his life.

We agreed not to share the news with anyone at Santa Barbara until we discussed it with the rector and novice director and made a decision about when and how the novices should be told. This was a serious consideration because the novice community loved Mitch. It was not unusual for them to invite him to be a lector at special liturgies.

That summer was also a landmark in my own health. Mitchell had to be hospitalized for tests. And that's when Jojo, our spider monkey, savaged the extender tendon of my right index finger. The healing took weeks of one-handed circus directing, while Jennie got a literal advance practicum on being the new right hand in management. The time for a long-contemplated phone call had arrived. With Mitch in hospital and my right forearm and hand in a cast, there was no way I could avoid recognizing my depression. The physician put me on Prozac before very many people had heard of it or any other SSRI drug. I would be on it for about six years. It filled in what I know could have been some pretty deep psychic trenches for about four years.

Now Jennie's arrival was even more of a gift. There was never any doubt that we would maintain our regular workloads and schedules for producing the show. Mitch would even travel until his regimen of medication demanded that he reside in one place. But Jennie immediately realized how important it was to learn what Mitch knew about the business dimension of our circus. In time she could do everything he could do, except sew. And eventually she even managed that, pulling out our sewing machine to reconfigure the backyard canvas.

In the late Eighties, the parameters of our annual touring changed. Covering the bulk of the United States with two cross-country roundtrips each year seemed so excessive that even I could recognize the unnecessary consumption of time and fuel. At first the adjustment would be a division of the country into western and eastern halves, with the winter layover in Grand Coteau, Louisiana. That enabled us to concentrate on our northwestern and Midwestern dates during the earlier part of the tour and the eastern dates after Christmas. Later, a similar arrangement was made for the midyear break to be in Winter Park, Florida, allowing more time on the east coast. But this ability to concentrate on regions of the country meant that we needed more dates in each sector. We increased our appeal for school assemblies, a relatively uncharted population for us even though there were thousands of elementary and middle schools. It also meant mining the scores of college campuses we hadn't ever contacted.

The *National Catholic Directory* listed every Catholic institution in the country by state and diocese. The tiniest school in the poorest parish was there, complete with its principal's name, number of students, phone number, and address. We usually had an advantage with the Catholic school population since our circus was an official work of the Jesuits. Mitch taught Jennie how to use the *NCD* and the myriad college directories. He also acquainted her with the use of our late model typewriter, which had an extensive memory for producing multiple copies of a standard letter. Microsoft was still in the future and we didn't carry a Xerox machine.

To the eyes and budgets of school principals, the nature of our program and our price range made even our cold mailings attractive. The response was heartening. But our material, especially mine, had to be modified for these assemblies. At the beginning, I thought I'd never be comfortable with what I could offer kids as an entertainer. Sadly, I was looking at only half the picture. The kids had plenty to offer *me*. I began to practice what I had been preaching about letting the audience (or congregation) "see you seeing them."

I had long known that when a performer *really* looks at a member of the audience and sees them, the performance is vitalized as never before. Our audiences were literally at our feet, sitting on grass or a gym floor from the edge of the ring curb back. There was no reason not to interact personally with individuals, and we had all developed that reflex on college campuses. Now we needed to hone this skill even with little kids, and it was especially important for me as the show's ringmaster or announcer. Happily, the tonic I had sold to so many of my performing arts students actually worked for the medicine man himself. Once I let the little kids in, their own charm held me until I began to find the material they alone could bring to a circus. When I had learned how to shape and play their own energies back to them, our circus belonged to them too, just as it did to so many college kids who had seen us for years.

*   *   *

Of course we continued to play all the colleges we could but American campus life was incrementally changing. Any circus is a very insular world, public as it seems. It is a small community that has reduced its necessary relationships with the outside world to routine encounters so that it can focus on its intense, often dangerous, internal life. Our circus was no exception and incurred the cost of such insularity. We couldn't detect what was happening to the college scene until it was too late to adjust our connection to it.

It is true that we had been repeating our dates, returning to the same campuses year after year, afraid to lose them if we passed them up. It is also true that we were drawing on past repertoire, restaging our old fables and routines. So maybe we had become "old hat." But there was an attitude change on American campuses as well. The looser, leisure-oriented dimension that had long been part of college life, a dimension seen universally as a vital and fun part of independence and growing up, was being supplanted. Pressure to graduate early, to train for and cultivate an economically sound niche in the "real" world was mounting. In retrospect, it certainly seems that even the finest humanities curricula in the country were being reduced through stern competition with applied disciplines not altogether unlike voc-tech programs.

Programmers in student unions were still booking free acts. We had introduced some of those offices to the concept in 1972. But the number of students willing to give up their noon hour, be tardy for the next history or Renaissance literature class, or talk a professor into bringing a performing arts class to our show—those students were dwindling. The numbers told the tale. Even our favorite audiences were beginning to thin out.

I had a shaking wakeup call about new priorities in the college humanities curricula during a casual conversation with a young Jesuit on a university campus. He had just seen the show, and like a lot of scholastics in those days had a great time and was a little bit proud that this band of brothers he had given his life to could produce something so unusual. He had entered the order with some college behind him and had just finished all his requirements for a master's degree in English, then was to move on to his years of philosophical studies. I congratulated him on completing the English course work. For some reason he volunteered that he had finished that work without having to take a single course in Shakespeare. (He was almost bragging.) I teased him.

"You mean you are preparing to lead large groups of the English-speaking faithful in a very sophisticated ritual that now allows you to improvise prayer, and you haven't studied the most celebrated poet of the western world?"

With not so much as a blush, he played right into my hand. "Well, man, what can I say?"

I should have been thankful he was at least involved in the language arts.

Difficult as it was, we finally began to recognize these shifts and our marketing continued to address new college campuses and school assemblies. Mitch developed an arresting booth display complete with photos and a sound-and-slide-presentation that he took to educators' conventions all over the country. It was a keen business reflex on his part.

By that time, the skill level of our circus had become impressive. Without a doubt, successive years of expertise and confidence had built on the hard work and talents of those who had performed in the previous seasons. We all taught each other from year to year, and I was the most fortunate of our performers, because I met and learned from all the personalities and talents that came to us.

A trademark device developed early on in the history of our circus was the simultaneous delivery of different sideshow-type spiels or pitches.[50] Typically, the cast would be divided into two or three groups and each group would deliver a very alliterative pitch at the same time one or two other groups of performers would be delivering a different one. Both deliveries were timed to end on a beat at which the entire cast would deliver a unison speech announcing the arrival of the circus. Each group of performers presented each pitch in turn. The result was that they all were responsible for the same total number of syllables and could end together, ready for the unison speech.

This effect was enjoyable because it had the musical rhythms of counterpoint; it was funny because almost none of it could be understood for more than a few seconds at a time. One of the gifts from our later emphasis on school assemblies was our discovery that little kids went crazy at their first hearing of this near-noise. And then they laughed because we were ample proof that grownups could indeed talk nonsense.

"Move right in close, folks! This is the chance of a lifetime! A completely chaotic collection of convulsive capers, a cavalcade of chuckle-coaxers confected with the care and cunning calculated to quell coronaries and quicken curiosity."

Imagine two or three people proclaiming such poppycock at the same time as three others were wrapping their tongues and lungs around an exercise of a different letter of the alphabet.

"Hiya! Hiya! Hiya! Step right up and purview this prestigious parade of preposterously performed pranks pilfered from the pantheon of pantomime, prestidigitation, and pandemonium!"

One of the last seasons that pitch was used, 1989–90, Mitch was pilfered from our private pantheon in the backyard. He had to stay behind at quarters in Santa Barbara. From the office near his bed in the bunkhouse he handled all the booking details and confirmations with the sponsors along our route. But most importantly, he was able to get regular and up-to-date medical care. By this time, he had developed what many people in those years were calling "the look": the drawn and emaciated face and body associated with AIDS patients. The launch of that season, with the annual opening performance at Santa Barbara's Our Lady of Sorrows Parish, was a sad leave taking.

Especially for me. The half of me who cared for people when I was gruff, who screamed at folks I was prone to "let off the hook," who remembered details when I was distracted, who could change a tire on a freeway shoulder in

---

[50] As a boy, I had memorized this style of delivery attending sideshows at the West Coast Shows and Craft's Twenty Big Shows carnivals.

less than ten minutes and a fan belt in fifteen, who heard my confession and knew there was already enough penance in the day ahead of us—that half was not going to be there mile in and mile out. The happy-go-lucky kid who knew he was a terrible driver tooling around Missoula—and then became our very best driver—was going to be parked.

Jennie assumed all the on-site sponsor relations, assembly seating, and concession management. She thought clearly and made decisions when I found clear thinking and decisiveness impossible. And when we were extremely shorthanded, she became an onstage assistant, something she had never bargained for. Best of all, she did everything well.

For the season of 1990–91 two nonperforming friends volunteered to travel with the show. They were not so much compensating for Mitch's absence as helping expand our booking and promotion. The hope was that there could be more advance planning in the business dimension of what had too long been a seat-of-our-pants operation. That season we were nine strong traveling with four pickup trucks each pulling a trailer. We opened in Saint Louis and headed directly to the east coast. The mid-season break was in Winter Park, Florida. Routing would then take us south to Key West, then back north and westward home to Santa Barbara. That's what was supposed to happen.

I remember the first half of the season going quite well. The road operation was smooth enough and I knew there was a steady contact with Mitch back in the office. There was a dimness in my own life, however, and I know part of it was lonesomeness. My closest confidant wasn't there. But there were other out of focus perspectives. I was angry. Political postures by church authorities and ruthless policies were trotted out as mandated by moral law and even revelation. Nothing new.

I had been steaming over women's issues in the Catholic Church for a number of years. Not ordaining them—depriving them of a sacrament solely because of their gender— was bad enough. But a male hierarchy's legislation of the care women took of their bodies equally bothered me. Church positions on contraception and abortion seemed illogical. If the intent behind the so-called rhythm method was acceptable, why wasn't the intent behind any other method—especially ones that really worked? If nature aborted, even after implantation, and if the church approved abortion, as a secondary, unintended effect, (e.g. in ectopic pregnancies) then perhaps the act of abortion wasn't in itself evil. Those were *only* logical inconsistencies. The human and pastoral considerations ignored by church regulation appeared treacherous to me.

On top of all such controversies, one more had begun to blindside me because it hit so close to home. My best friend was dying of AIDS and we were expected to condemn homosexual activity. That's how we were supposed to love them: condemn what they were programmed to do. I had long been angered over the selective use of medieval metaphysics in such cases. In the treatment of act and potency, what I recalled and understood of Thomistic philosophy held that a being was more perfect the more it was actively being what it was. In *act* it realized itself. I couldn't make that align with accepting that some people were homosexual but when they acted in accordance with who they were they were evil.

Everyone at the grassroots level in the Eighties knew that significant Catholic theologians were aligning the Church with the more intelligent voices of the medical establishment: homosexuality was more of a tendential condition than a choice. Even in the mid-Seventies the Catechism of the Catholic Church posited such a condition. But the tap dance around the source of such a condition would be long-lived. It will continue until scientific evidence overwhelms the entrenched deductive reasoning of the hierarchy. Perhaps one day medicine's microscopes will replay the miters out of their chromosomal biases just as Galileo's telescope freed them from Ptolemy.

A guy doesn't live with such doubts gracefully, especially when what meager grace he has comes from his loving relationship with a whole bunch of men and women who are affected by such abandonment and persecution. But I was called to be graceful and therein was my difficulty. I couldn't dance the dance beyond the level of a charade.

I knew I was torn and not just because of my thinking. I had let myself doze at some key switches.

In my life on the road I did not have to adhere to the discipline of Jesuit spirit and rule. The spirit of the mission, broad as it was, kept me and I felt compelled to keep it. But while I was juridically a Jesuit priest, it would have been a stretch to conceive the life I led as religious. I fully and lovingly considered myself a member of the Society of Jesus, a companion of Jesus. Ask me about being a Jesuit; ask me to break bread with you in the memorial sacrificial meal the master left us as the way to remember him? I was all yours. But the half-day to half-day, even daily practice of formal prayer, celebration of liturgy, or awareness of rule? I was not there.

Nonetheless, I was as present as I could be to the daily workings of a ministry that absorbed my attention, my energy, and my passion. Not only was the show large, it was healthy. The performances had quality. The community life appeared to be supportive of individuals.

We landed at Rollins College in Winter Park, Florida, and I held the fort while others took the Christmas break till the end of January. The highlight of that break would be a visit from Mitch. He knew I was spiritually and psychologically ragged. It was so good to have someone around who knew how I ticked. I hoped I was as healthy for him as he was for me. It is not easy when you are in your thirties, as he was, to be categorically certain your body is about to fail you completely. It is not easy at any age, and my reflex of course was denial. Mitch would not tolerate that. In many ways, he was still so much of my own health.

The lowlight of that break was a visit from the California provincial, Paul Belcher. Paul had called me in early December very concerned over reports he had received about my behavior. These reports concerned my sexual misadventures, use of alcohol, and my voiced opinions about church teaching. He wasn't so much angry as he was frightened. Reviewing for me how public a figure I was, he actually said, "This could be deep shit." His fear startled me. I had for some years known there were plenty of folks around, some of whom loved me, who did not think I should be a Jesuit. Some were gentle. There were others who cared profoundly about the integrity of Catholicism and its priesthood who also did not think I should be a Jesuit. Often these people were not gentle.

None of this was new. The difference at hand was my superior's legitimate concern and his insistence that I arrange to methodically examine my situation in some kind of prayerful discernment. That was Jesuit-speak for a retreat. When he left Florida, he left me with homework: scheduling the when and where for such a retreat.

One month after Christmas we were back in the trucks and headed for Winter Springs, Florida and points south. We unkinked, listened to the music, smelled the smells, and got with our rhythm. But within the week, the California provincial was leaving messages for me because of a specific threat of serious negative publicity about me and my attitudes and behavior regarding church discipline, sexuality, and doctrine.

I was a quipster in the ring and out. Usually I could be circumspect, or at least count on privacy and off-record status for some risky turns of phrase. "If the Holy Spirit could work through Mary's womb and ovaries, why couldn't he have worked through Joseph's penis and testicles?" That was commonly followed by a testy remark comparing ignorance about the existence of the ovum to the ignorance about the earth's orbit. I even found a way to connect sex and strawberries. "Of course natural law reveals that sexuality is intended for procreation just as eating is intended for physical sustenance. Is scarfing down strawberry shortcake sinful?" All easy stuff. Straw men—some in unimportant miters. What wasn't easy was perceiving that records had been kept about my thoughts and actions.

*   *   *

Eventually the gifts of two simultaneous insights surfaced. First, I realized I might bring some amount of damage to the Jesuits, especially my province, the family I had loved so long. I could in no way tolerate such a possibility. Second, I looked in the mirror and saw a serious wrinkle I had never noticed before and had trouble recognizing as mine. That wrinkle was an aspect of my personal truth: I had not lived as a Jesuit for some while. The short version of a long story was that I had not kept the rules and the rules had not kept me. It would be impossible, of course, to discover which part of that negative process was the more causative. Was I already "out" of the order and so stopped observing my order's discipline? Or did I forego that discipline and then find myself "out" of the order? Either question now seems moot. What is striking is the readiness with which I detected the illusion I was living. The timing was adroit. My guard, whether because of depression or anger or fatigue, was down. Things clicked almost automatically. I was not a Jesuit.

All of this awkward adjustment was taking place as we rolled through the late winter and spring of 1991. There was a constant volley of phone messages between provincial headquarters and assorted phone booths in truck stops, rest areas, and student unions. In the most impersonal places via cold payphones I delivered very personal details and hard-won insights. I can now distinguish awkwardness from pain in what I experienced. After all, the process was taking place in the context of a life in a circus. I was in the middle of the country with responsibility to a staff and to our sponsoring clients. Everything was in proportion to keeping us on the road. I answered questions about my beliefs, my statements and my conduct. Detailed questions. Posed clinically. Answered clinically. I don't remember emotion.

There was perhaps a subconscious replay of my soul's movement when I was five years old: it was time to get on with life, even if it meant leaving a part of life behind. Move on. When I was seventeen, I completed an expensive four year private education at Bellarmine College Preparatory and I remember nothing about how it ended. I moved on. When I was thirty-eight I spent a few hours visiting my biological mother for the first time in over thirty years and left her, knowing she would soon die. I moved on. If there were immediate emotional reactions, they couldn't have been dramatically painful. The events happened and the ensuing process really did seem automatic.

The emotions surrounding my departure from my order would emerge later, unexpectedly. They would be about individual Jesuits with whom I was close, but who would have to seem somehow "other" when I was no longer a Jesuit. On two such occasions, I received what I consider responses so tailored to me that I hold them as paramount examples of Jesuit pastoral care. The first came from a longtime friend who had been my superior at Santa Clara University when the circus was born. I wrote to Leo Rock about how huge an event my leaving the Society seemed, but that I hadn't registered it emotionally. In a loving letter, he wrote "Remember, Nick, we don't change who we are because we sign our name to a piece of paper." A more startling, if more deft, note of advice was jotted on a card from my old juggling teacher, Bill Cain: "Well, there's always that *tantum quantum*, you know." I'd never dreamed of applying that central principle to the Society of Jesus itself.

Easter of 1991 saw us camped at Brebeuf Preparatory in Indianapolis and we were due at Ball State University in Muncie April 5. During that week, a miscommunication between Mitch and our new on-road business staff resulted in havoc. Of course Mitch was apprised of my conversations with the provincial. He also knew I was thinking about leaving the Jesuits. He didn't realize I had made a final decision. I sensed anger. For the first time in our relationship, I feared that anger. Somehow he wrongly concluded that I was too disturbed to continue. He had actually agreed to end the tour, planning for us to disband in the mid-U.S. and recoup. Without my knowledge, the same plan had been communicated to performers. As damaging, Mitch had already been cancelling dates.

There was no way I was stopping the tour. But the misinformation took its toll all round when the business staff and three of our performers left the show after the Ball State performance. It took steady phoning for the next week to save the cancelled bookings and to convince Mitch that we were rolling with the reduced show. For advice and support, I called Jens Larson, our Roman rings star who had already made his mark with commercial circuses. He was doing off-season work as a messenger in San Francisco. I wasn't ready for his reply.

"Well this clearly means I need to meet up with you and help fill out the show. I can ship my balancing table and rigging ahead. Where will you be in a week?"

Not only that. He knew when he would have to leave us and agreed to contact another of our alums, the superb mime Eric Wilcox, also in San Francisco, to help us finish the tour.

The support I didn't have was Mitch's. He faxed me a terse message: "You can't leave the Jesuits. You need them too much."

If there ever was a road test for Prozac, it occurred during the next eight weeks of my life. With a braver than ever Jennie, two very loyal performers who stayed with us, and two loyal alums who rewound their own lives to help us, we logged forty-four stops in thirty-one cities, scattered across thirteen states. Finally, we dragged our heavy equipment and heavier hearts into the Santa Barbara High School gym on May 31.

Mitch was still keeping the schedules so he was there just after we arrived and was still half a basketball court away from me before he gushed, "If I'd known you had already made your decision, I never would have said what I did in the fax!"

Vintage Mitch. We had both been through some kind of hell, but there was a far different and more intense warmth in that one remark. There were still two more performances in the season. There were also hours of conversation to catch us up to wherever we were. But two things were already abundantly clear: I had lost the Jesuits, and Mitch was vanishing, physically, right before my eyes.

*   *   *

That decision to leave the Jesuits had just about fallen into place. I felt that it was ratified when the provincial ordered me in March to bring the show through its final weeks and then report to his office in Los Gatos for reassignment to another ministry. That couldn't happen. Even had I been able to still think of myself as a Jesuit, I knew I would be closely monitored for the rest of my life lest I again become a "loose cannon." Besides, there was no other work I could possibly imagine that would be as fulfilling and alive for me. I would wither and die. I knew it. As importantly, I knew that I could no longer stand the tension between identifying myself as a member of the Roman Catholic clergy and privately rejecting so many policy and doctrinal positions of the Catholic Church. That, too, would wipe me out.

As a result I had for months begun to re-imagine the circus itself. Obviously, it would no longer be a ministry of the province. It would relocate, continue its touring, and I would direct it and perform with it. I would sign my name differently, but I knew the family I was leaving behind would somehow be in my heart. It was a strangely resolute coldness I felt, but I could own it. I would also ask the province if I could own the equipment it had so generously provided. Both my superiors and I assumed that the show's independent bank account would suffice to get us back on the road.

The chill of such determination was definitely tempered by an unexpected phone call I received in the shop at quarters.

"Nick Weber, this is Mike Buckley. How's my you?" That was his trademark.

"We-ell. I guess I'm okay, Mike. How are you?" I knew instantly he knew everything.

"Nicholas, I want to talk with you. I know you're in trouble. When can we meet?"

"Mike. I can't leave here. I have people and animals to take care of and I'm rehearsing."

"I understand. I can be there tomorrow. What time?"

I was stunned. It was the same open-armed readiness I had experienced in Berkeley.

Initially, when I determined that I was to leave the Jesuits, I didn't count on a personal, loving trip by Michael J. Buckley, my past rector and always watchful friend. He had been on my case long before I returned home to Santa Barbara.

It was all too much. Here was this guy I met thirty-five years before when he began his stint as a high school teacher as I was finishing mine as a high school student. Now he was taking time out from the schedule of a professional scholar to help me. Again. He had flown from San Francisco to Santa Barbara, then rented a car to get to our quarters in Santa Barbara. No surprise that he didn't hesitate a second to literally cross through a circus ring for the first time in his life to get to me. The embrace was all. He was on a rescue mission for a fellow priest.

"Nicholas!"

And the old crimping of my lower lip signaled the onset of tears.

"Michael. Another crisis."

A feeble, trembling smile on both sides.

Over lunch, he led me through a replay of what needed to be discerned. He was a Jesuit steeped in the best of methods.

"As I see it, the *Exercises* are in order. Serious discernment is the measure of the moment before you make a decision."

I could tell he had heard I had made a decision, but he was as stubborn as I.

"I have talked to Paul about postponing any decisions by him until after you've made a serious retreat."

"Mike, why are you putting yourself through this?"

"Because Nick Weber is good people." Of the lines I will never forget, that is paramount. Promise.

He knew I was set to go out on another tour. He advocated a mid-season revisit of the *Exercises* before making the final decision. He had obtained the provincial's approval for such a scenario, but significantly, "without any promises."

I knew, however, that there were already enough political arguments in position at the provincial level to separate me from my life with the circus. Furthermore, I was out of practice and unable to trust that I wouldn't be distracted during the compromise of an eight-day retreat. I knew I would bring to such an effort overwhelming concerns. I would be preoccupied with the mission to which I had given half my life, and with the outlook for Jennie, our nationwide sponsors, and the young people waiting to be trained. My loving respect for Mike fed an unfair cowardice. I wasn't man enough to outrightly refuse his offer. I told him I would have to let him and the provincial know when I had time to think about it. That was dishonest; I already knew what my answer would be.

Because I had no intention of being reassigned, and because I was not seeking the mandated appointment with the provincial, I knew I was in flagrant disobedience. I did not need to complicate things for my rector by being too visible to the novices. So the entire circus operation kept to its own training quarters, a hillside across the ravine from the main buildings on the property. I gave up my room in the administration residence. And everyone housed and ate and worked at the rehearsal site. Darren Peterson of the previous year's cast once again generously stayed on with Jennie and me. We would rebuild and regroup for a three-person show to leave in August.

In early summer 1991, Mitch entered a Santa Barbara AIDS hospice. So much of our lives had been spent saying goodbye to people. At least that's what ordinary folk would have called it. We taught all our friends and sponsors and hosts the usual formula for farewell that show folk use: "See you down the road!" In most cases, it would mean seeing the same beloved faces right in that same spot on that same road in a year. In those years, no one knew "whether" about an AIDS patient a year down the road, never mind "where" and "when." We wouldn't let ourselves say it, but we both felt frightfully unsure whether we would see each other again.

We were also frightened of our own emotions. I think that was a defect he contracted from me, but I suspect he was far too bright to think he could shut out feelings. Whatever the source and the cause of such pseudo-Spartanism, we agreed not to celebrate this leave-taking, not to say goodbye. There was to be no final dinner. The provincial had just about ordered me to take Mitch to dinner, and there was official disapproval when he found out I had not.

The night before we pulled out, I visited the hospice in downtown Santa Barbara. It was right across the street from the site of each year's opening performance. I learned something of what his routine would be in hospice, and he asked questions about details of the new show. Our avoidance of any of the big questions was tangible. But they didn't get asked. We hugged, said, "See you down the road," and I left. I didn't hear the front door close, but I didn't dare look back.

*   *   *

We left Santa Barbara having completely reconfigured the show. With its characteristic generosity, the California Province signed the vehicles over to the Council Players, Inc., d.b.a. the Royal Lichtenstein Circus. There would be three of us in the company. A platform stage between the prop and animal trailers was designed. The band organ was permanently mounted in the rear of the prop trailer behind side-mounted flap doors created to reveal it immediately to the right of the show. The ring was on the ground level for the larger acts. The concession stand was retained, but the manufacture of cotton candy and popcorn took place in the front end of the prop trailer and the product passed through a window directly to the concession stand. Everything had been streamlined to accommodate the work and performance load to only three people: Jennie, Darren Peterson, and me. By this time Jennie was a seasoned right hand.

The route took us through southern California then over through Arizona, New Mexico, Oklahoma, and up to Saint Louis University High School. It was still summer so our friends Carlo Gentile and Kevin Curdt were back in their hometown to give us a hand as we underwent another sudden personnel change. Darren announced he had to leave us. With the help of Carlo's little brother Nick, we improvised a performance at Saint Louis University High

School, which had sent several alumni to the show over the years. True to tradition's form, yet another of its graduates agreed to join on and train to fill out the three-person version as it headed east and southeast to a winter break in Florida. Chris Cuddihee began learning the rolling globe, rola bola and hoop juggling while we were camped for a few days at the Circus Flora quarters in Saint Louis. A diligent student of circus skills, he also dove into the difficult regimen of learning setup, teardown, animal routines, and of course the trick of making cotton candy. He really did save that '91–'92 season.

When serious family illness took Chris back to Saint Louis early in summer 1992, Jennie and I began a long series of yet more improvisations. Carlo Gentile came in to help get us to David Pinto's shop in Kalamazoo, where once again we retooled for a summer and early fall tour. Even then we knew that route would land us at Dr. Mark Wilson's small zoo in Belleview, Florida. We hired a small troupe called "The Circus of the Kids." Eventually one of our pickups failed us and we could no longer afford major repairs so a rented U-Haul van pulled the prop trailer.

When a second pickup failed as well, we began regularly double-jumping, backtracking on a move to pick up a unit left behind. We began to hire relief school bus drivers in districts we played to drive a unit to our next lot. It was a far cry from our salad days when everything and everyone ran perfectly on schedule. By the time we pulled onto the zoo property on Highway 441 south of Ocala, Florida, we had undergone an inglorious but brave struggle to keep the last performances of that tour as sparkling as they could be. I knew that I could not have asked for a more supporting partner than Jennie had been. I could have asked for one, but I'm convinced one didn't exist. Jennie had the market cornered.

We helped our friend Dr. Mark with regular zoo chores to offset what our animals added to his workload and feed bill. The zoo sat on the property of the Market of Marion Flea and Antique Market. An agreement was reached with the Market to permit parking next to one of their warehouses in exchange for weekend shows. Sadly we were not allowed to operate our food concessions because the market had their own franchise, including cotton candy. We did try to pitch what souvenir stock we had left. One of the show's loyal friends, an artist, drew coloring book pages and illustrated some simple magic tricks and my paper tree routine. These we bound in a cover to sell and somehow made it through the winter.

A mutual friend of Dr. Mark's and ours, Brent "Cheeko" Dewitt, visited us and the zoo. He is a superb and authentic "Punch and Judy" man. At that time he even had a perfect little Punch man's dog, named Toby. Cheeko was also an accomplished ring clown whom I had first seen on the Great American Circus. Together with Cheeko we planned for an east coast tour beginning in February 1993.

Just recalling such a decision now is a shock. After losing so much, and having endured such a continuous series of failures in spite of all our efforts, how did I see my way to risk yet another crippled and crippling tour? Unlike Oedipus and Hamlet I managed to survive long enough not only to recognize the hubris, but to uncover its masquerade. There is a dazzle, glint, and sparking glamour about circus. But in the tawdry pedestrian and essential mechanics that support such an undertaking there is a more subtle disguise—one that passes for reality, responsibility, and the honesty of earth. When I began to fall for that illusion I don't know.

The agreement was that Cheeko would present three of his acts and Jennie and I would present the magic and animal acts. By this time, any semblance of the parable content in the show was slim. There was some poetry, to be sure.

Cheeko pulled his house trailer with a motor home that carried his equipment. Jennie and I were down to one pickup. We needed to find a van capable of pulling the prop trailer. Such a van would be modified as living quarters for her while I lived in the forward sleeping compartment of the animal trailer. Our roomy house-trailer would be left behind since there was no truck or driver to pull it.

A chaplain for the national race car ministry, Father Phil DeRea, used his influence with the Hertz Penske organization, which generously donated a used van. It was this vehicle that I began customizing, crudely. A bunk for Jennie, a sink, cook-stove, and electric. All those accommodations were added while we were touring. The first stop was Jacksonville for shows in a Kmart parking lot. Lots of rain. Lots of show time cancelled. Lots of time to finish remodeling the van.

We headed north again, into Georgia, up through South Carolina with a stop at Furman University where our dear friend Chaplain Jim Pitts must have realized what we would soon have to admit: the life of our little circus had run its course. And then it was up into Virginia where another dear friend, Reverend David Tetrault, the Episcopal circus chaplain, would have had the same insight. We managed to make it all the way up into Baltimore by July, where we found ourselves camped at Saint Ignatius parish not only for a performance but for a catch of breath while we looked for work.

Summer had arrived weeks before, and with it the end of regular school calendars. So we were busy looking into the parish networks, parks services, and, as luck would have it, public housing projects, such as those in Baltimore. I had met a coordinator of several of these towering lower income units and suggested that if we were allowed concession privileges we could just about give performances away. We knew the population density would provide us with crowds. But I explained that we were a liability and very vulnerable. We were insured, but we were the quintessential attractive nuisance: animals, only three employees, lots of exposed equipment. We would need security.

I was assured that would be no problem since the projects maintained their own police force. So on a verbal agreement, we provided advertising, scheduled three such dates, and breathed a little more easily. There was at least some work.

It was almost dusk when our rigs arrived at the first project and pulled onto the playing field assigned to us. An ice cream truck was just making its last sales of the day on the site before driving off. The tall buildings that were home to the next day's audience were on the surrounding hills looking down on our three humble vehicles. Kids out for a last adventure before ending their day outdoors (or beginning the first adventure of the night) were all over those surrounding hillsides. Those who came down to talk to us, some with parents, knew nothing of what we were doing. There had apparently been no advertising posted. There was recognizable resentment on the part of many that we were allowed to move onto their playing field. We saw nothing resembling a squad car nor anyone resembling an officer or even a rent-a-cop on the beat.

On a misguided impulse, Cheeko and I decided to get a jump on the next morning's setup and put up our four sets of bleachers. When we broke for cookhouse, the kids got a jump on the bleachers. Kids playing on the bleachers are always a bane for traveling entertainers. Injuries on the seating systems are a common plague and liability. But these kids were inventive. They discovered that the planks had spring in them and were natural trampolines. Their own circus act continued until the first board cracked. Then we knew we had reason to be on the alert. Certainly no one else was on the alert in our protection or defense. Roping off an area behind the menagerie trailer, I brought out the horses and dogs and fed and watered them. The kids were respectful and kept their distance. I knew that inner city kids tend to give animals plenty of room. Many of them inherit from their parents an instinctive fear of all dogs. I've always found that sad, but that night it was an advantage.

We were outnumbered of course, and we were virtually surrounded. So when we saw a kid jump out of the back of Jennie's space in the van, we went into cancellation mode. Jennie bravely went up to the nearest building to call the Baltimore police. She could make decisions. No more waiting for housing authority rent-a-cops.

They pulled in. Although we complied, filing a report was not necessary. Our dogs were nowhere near as frightening for those kids as the sight of a patrol car. That gave us cover to tear down the seats and load the animals. By now word had spread through this community towering above us that there was to be a free circus the next day. But word also spread that the circus people had called the police and now the circus was moving off. It was one of the very few times we made an audience collectively angry, and I honestly didn't see that reaction coming. I thought we were simply resented for "squatting" on their playfield. And we were. But now we were resented for frustrating them. It was a no-win.

Word was communicated to the officials at the next site that such conditions were unacceptable. We fared better. Nonetheless it soon became evident that the new hosts were more interested in the TV coverage our appearance brought them than they were in us. We completed our performance and moved to another site, this one closer to the inner city. Meanwhile, there was no income. A lost performance and trickling concession sales did not bode well for the days off we were going to need to mine future work for ourselves.

At this third site, a longtime officer in the Circus Fans Association of America joined us, our good friend Pete Adams. Usually quiet, with calm eyes you knew were taking in everything, he was as gentle and guiding as a father confessor to a circus would be.

"Hi Nick. How's it going?" Then so gently, "This is a very different kind of venue for you guys. Does it work?"

"Well, it's all gratis except for the joint and no one's even buying floss. We lost the first date." I'm pretty sure he could tell we were down and struggling with discernment about our next move.

Even when things were really bad, Jennie could manage a chuckle at the absurdity of it all. When she was introduced to Pete there was almost bravado in her voice. "Pretty sad, eh? We can't even give it away!"

Pete listened to us and heard the resolution to turn ourselves around and head back south. Cheeko had been in on all the conversations and was usually upbeat. Now he seemed reticent.

Finally it was Pete who admitted that we lacked what every show depends on. "I don't think you have much choice without a front end. You depend on schools and this is the wrong time of the year for you." He watched and enjoyed our performance, then fed us, pitched in with the teardown, and got us on our way. I could feel he was as sad as we were. But he left us with the most valuable gift possible for folks who have made a paramount and painful decision: loving assurance that they have discerned correctly. He was a very serious circus fan, a professional, and he knew the business much more intimately than I did.

We headed for a "Kampground of America" outside of Williamsburg, Virginia, returning to the neighborhood of our longtime fan and knowledgeable source of support, David Tetrault. We agreed to pay our KOA rent by performing for our fellow campers. It was a chance to settle our nerves and settle up our business concerns so that Jennie and I could get the show back to Florida, and Cheeko could head north to meet up with his friends, the Earl Family, who owned Roberts Brothers Circus. David and the Furman chaplain, Jim Pitts, were both in touch with us during this last stand with every type of support they could muster. Like Pete in Baltimore, they extended to us a kind of circus-real and road-tried existential ministry of "decide and be at peace."

When I got a desperate last minute itch of an idea, it was Cheeko who said it best.

"Take it on in. Don't even think of trying out Myrtle Beach on the way south. Why dig the hole deeper? Take it on in."

And so we did.

*   *   *

We didn't need our atlas to find our way back to the animals' new permanent homes at the zoo. Just before we got back to our friends at Belleview, though, we noticed a haven for folks like us, halfway between Ocala and the Market of Marion: Campertown. That's where the van and soon-to-be empty animal trailer would be parked, and where Jennie and I would set up a temporary home for ourselves.

Right away, we learned of stirrings at another zoo far to our west in Arizona.

Always creative, but always communally sensitive, Jens Larson let me know of his coming wedding on January 15, 1994. He and his beloved circus-savvy painter and artist, Maggie, were to celebrate their union at the Phoenix Zoo. Jens knew I was flat broke and not working. He offered me a flight ticket. He also knew that I was paying storage rent on a Santa Barbara commercial garage jammed with old show equipment. He wanted to help here as well. He would rent a truck out of Phoenix. I could drive to Santa Barbara, retrieve the equipment, and head home to Florida. There was no way I could not accept. And then our dear and mutual friend, Cheeko, made it easier yet: he would be at the wedding, and would accompany me over to Santa Barbara and back to his home in Sarasota, Florida.

That was Jens. Inclusive. Generous. Personal. My wedding gift would be a poem. I knew words were valuable to him. The words I wrote were underwritten by my faith, which in 1994 was non-institutional but vibrant. I felt very comfortable with God and those we loved.

"FOR JENS AND MAGGIE"
After the crossword and the personals, both always fresher than the headlines,
And after the second cup of morning coffee, the one that really has the flavor,
God sat back in heaven's kitchen and just—well, wondered.
Not about "time" or "how long" or "when" or "ever"
Or the other mirrors used to vanish the present.
Nor about the "power" or "glory" or "might" or "being"
Or the other mirror polishers.
And certainly not about "responsibility" or "worth"
Or "honor" or "debt" or "guilt."
God just sat there and wondered about—well, risk.
The risk of trusting dreams to the frightful "maybe" of "not yet";
The risk of holding out even a divine heart to human hands
That just might be upside-down;

And above all, the risk that the Dream-Gift, the Galaxy called Galaxies
Will only be seen as the nightmare of a nameless enemy.
The risk, God knows, is love's touchstone in the Dream,
And love, God knows, must bravely wait upon freedom.
Will then, God waiting-wonders, the might-be-inside-out eyes find the Love Dream?
God knows.
Because God risked moving toward the kitchen window and gazing out.
At first the usual homophonic hum and galactic glaze: static.
But over there, smack in the monochromatic middle of the desert, there is focus.
Within sight of the saguaro, the yucca, and even a petunia, there is a brightness.
Amid the smells, roars, grunts and growls of the more extravagant designs,
There is a mirror.
Humble, but brightly efficient, the glass is held by a woman and a man.
It is real glass, they know, and therefore fragile.
So their grips are definite:
His the grip of a trained circus acrobat risking
The just-right marriage of man's muscle with God's Gravity;
Hers the grasp of a finely tuned painter risking
The intricate wedding of woman-wonder with Provider's Pallet.
It is brightly polished, they know, so their grasps are loving.
The mirror, God sees, is held in a gift-grip.
What each holds, each gives.
Hence the luster.
Hence the danger.
Hence the risk.
Confidently, God draws close to the glass, face right smack in front of the mirror.
No trumpets or harps anywhere.
Just the humbly-held, single breath of a careful painter and her acrobat.
And when God finished looking into the mirror, the wonder was complete.
God would well-risk another day at the office.

*   *   *

Whether or not Mitch knew of the wedding celebration for Jens and Maggie, we had kept my participation and my trip to California under wraps so I could surprise him. Then he surprised me by being in the hospital when I arrived. By this time, his mother Irene was staying near him in Santa Barbara. She told me what she knew of the hospitalization and that he was on his way home that evening. Cheeko and I agreed to return later after finding some dinner.

It was a surprise, and Irene had kept mum. She answered the door and went to tell him he had guests. At that moment I knew in a flash this surprise could be an emotional implosion. My bright dancer clown and handsome musta-chioed manager could only shuffle into the hallway light. Motion was a project in itself for this shrunken, stooped, and unshaven wisp straining to train his eyes on the front porch. For both of us, tentativeness was palpable. For him it was by now a way of life; for me it was enough to stop history. When his eyes found my face they couldn't find me. He had never seen me without a beard and long hair.

As nervousness and awkwardness often have it, even with intimates, some motion of humor brought my face a grin. Once he saw that, we truly found each other again. The distance between my two front teeth shattered all other distances. We found our place in the left-off narratives of our shared and now separate lives, and for a day exchanged the chapters that had run separately. We complained, laughed, ate, and worried. Everyone in that hospice community thawed for me the cold concept of *appreciation*. At dinner, I complimented a young teenage kid on how solicitous he was about Mitch's needs at table.

"Oh, I have to watch out for Mitch. He's my model!" Lucky kid.

*   *   *

And so back to Ocala with Mitch stories to warm Jennie's heart. Writing fiction. Animal chores at the zoo. Weekly phone calls to Mitch from the zoo office. And then February. A different kind of phone call. Brain lesion on top of the pneumocystic pneumonia. Brilliant, creative doctors defeated. Three weeks at the most before an almost certain, hardly conscious, vegetative life.

"I want to die. I am ready."

Increased phone calls. Mitch had always been a spiritual man. There were better moments when we both suspected he could be a mystic. His perception was too intense and broad for mere sensitivity to explain.

"I have two days. My family is here with me. I think everything is in order. Will you call tomorrow morning?"

"Of course!" It was clear he knew he was about to die.

"It's today. I know. I won't be here tonight."

"Mitchell, I'm not handling this very well."

"No one is. I don't have it all together either. But it's for sure."

And I believed him, and we were both right. But how do you say goodbye at the end of such a phone conversation? Then, how do you even lay the phone down? How do you breathe?

Faith? We hadn't addressed it, but we both knew that we both knew he was going to heaven to be something like an angel watching out for us. Tony Kushner had taught us that long before.[51]

Typically the comfort zone within which I dealt with matters of faith rescued me. Sorta. My mind was firing thoughts in complete, silly, uppercase sentences: I AM GOING TO HAVE THE LAST WORD HERE. I WILL FAX HIM AT THE HOSPICE.

---

[51] Cf. his two-part 1992–92 play, *Angels in America*.

I only remember the first and last parts of the fax. How I remember them. They alluded to two other deaths—one of a spider monkey, the other of the most famous character ever portrayed on the English-speaking stage.

I have always been surrounded by people who believed they had a right to imagine what heaven would be like. Most of these people were also comfortable imagining that animals went to heaven. And why not? Consequently, when Dr. Wilson had found Jojo dead in his zoo cage, apparently of stroke, everyone, including Mitch, imagined that our long-armed pal went on ahead to help prepare the proverbial "place for us," taking his cue from Jesus.[52] For Mitch and me, that meant Jojo would have the celestial coffee on when we got there. That's where the fax began.

Dear Mitch,
And tell Jojo it's gotta be regular coffee. None of that designer flavored stuff!

But at the end, all humor gave way to the huge sense of loss overtaking me in a cluttered veterinary examination room. I resorted to an iconic image, Horatio with his best friend Hamlet dead in his arms.
Goodnight sweet prince,
And flights of angels sing thee to thy rest.[53]

Who can gainsay Shakespeare? But I could never again say aloud nor write those two lines without extreme emotion.

Mitchell died. That afternoon. He had known. I had known. And all the animals I was taking care of knew of the pain. That's because I turned off the fax machine and went out among the rows of cages and howled. Literally. For an hour. I even tilted my head back. Yes, toward the sky—heaven. I wailed sound I had not known I could produce. I could feel some of the pain leave. I would calm for a moment and then catch the placid stoic glance of one of our horses and erupt screaming again. Surrounded by tigers, pumas, and monkeys, I was alone in a place where howling was okay.

Then it was over. On the way back to Campertown I stopped at the Publix Market to pick up steaks, some white zinfandel for Jennie, and bourbon for me. It was time to party because Mitch had made it. Of course he joined us, as only he could, because he knew neither of us could possibly make it out to California for his memorial.

A year later, time—right on time—had worked its wondrous perspective.

---

[52] "I go to prepare a place for you." (John 14:2)
[53] V.i.348–349.

M. J. K. Anniversary One

A cold morning kindles the memory of a year past
When your warmth left us on a warm evening.
How then we strove to trust
  that love could be trusted
  to be freed and kept.
But I, for one, gave up;
  grasped tight the love trusted
  held and clutched and wept.
I howled, even skyward
  as though it was only
  my loss, not your gain.
Forgot, even blotted
  all but "He is stolen."
  and "What right such pain?"
Now I, and all, give thanks
  for love somehow trusted
  free and shared and sung.
We shout, again skyward
  sure that you have gained
  what we have just begun.

While I hadn't managed to gainsay Shakespeare, I did manage to regain my voice and some grasp on what I took for reality. That reality included what was left of my traditional faith.

Then I went on a long, long journey over a fifteen-year span.

I worked as a restaurant prep cook, zoo attendant, traditional white-faced circus clown on large tent circuses, and as itinerary director for a Jesuit lecturer. Meanwhile Jennie's own trek took her through years of work as a restaurant line-cook, circus dining department director and finally manager of her own restaurant. By 2001 I had performed in all forty-eight contiguous states and written and acted in three solo shows. Thanks to a connection with long ago San Francisco stage manager Michael Bartel and his talented wife, Ellen, I was able to devote the best part of seven years to an encore of high school work. Finally, at the age of sixty-seven, when I retired in Milwaukee, I realized that for the first time in my life, I had lived in the same building for more than three years. I had definitely stopped migrating.

I had definitely not stopped my journey.

Back in 1996, during my second season with Carson and Barnes, Dad and Mom and I got together for lunch after a performance near Willits, California. The usual easy ribbing between Dad and me picked up where it had probably left off years before. When we said goodbye, Mom gave him a very special eye.

Mom and Dad as I now remember them.

It always meant "slip the kid some cash," and the wallet opened on cue. It was always embarrassing. As a family we didn't stay in touch, so maybe we needed to give and receive more while we were in arms reach. I only remember receiving, and mightily hoping that the excitement I had in seeing them carried my love.

In early 1998 I was touring a one-man performance of the works of Gerard Manley Hopkins and stopped off in Willits again, but this time Mom was hospitalized. In the spring I began my tour with the Kelly Miller Circus and Mom ended her tour of a life that was one of the brightest gifts in my life. But because my mailing address had changed, I didn't find out for weeks. Then for ten years, Dad and I only talked on the odd holiday phone call.

It took some time but Dad and I caught up with each other. In mid-May of 2008, I answered the phone and heard my family nickname for the first time in ten years.

"I'm looking for Nickie Jim Weber."

"This is he."

"This is your niece, Jenny, in Salt Lake!"

Then Amtrak got me to my dying father's bedside. He was ninety-two. Since I had last seen my father in that Willits motel room, my brother John, the youngest of us, had died. Then, Dad had moved to join my sister and brother-in-law north of Ogden. Now, all my anxiety over how I would act and what protocol was expected fell away. I moved into the room and caught his eye.

"Hello, Dad. It's Nickie Jim."

All of us there were convinced that through the haze of morphine and the weakness of dehydration and starvation, he did know me. There was a faint smile and two faint words.

"Oh. Yes."

And I, the clown, actor, priest, softie, held the heavy equipment operator's hand, the outdoorsman's hand—the hand that once held my baby hand, and wiped and spanked my ass. My sister was on the other side of the bed holding his right hand. It felt good. My brother-in-law, John, and my late brother's two boys, Nick and Mitch, were also in the room. Occasionally one nurse or another would come in with the blessing of a morphine dose. It was clear they enjoyed getting a dose of Nick Weber's dying humor and charming gratitude in the bargain.

"Oh thanks, Babe. Thank you sweetheart."

Decades before, as a little kid, he had charmed another lady, Sister Carmelita of Saint Teresa. He was beginning the trek he was now finishing and Sister explained the ashes of Ash Wednesday. She remembered his reaction and wrote to him when he graduated from high school in June 1933.

My dear Nick,

I was telling you all about Ash Wednesday, how the priest would put ashes on our foreheads in order to remind us all that we were dust and into dust we should return someday. Anyhow my instruction had a terrible effect on you for you went home dreadfully troubled and told your mother that you were not going to school the next day because Sister said you were going to turn into dust.

One who prays for you,

Sister Carmelita of Saint Teresa, SND

There were three Nick Webers in the hospital room. Only one counted during those last two days. Sue and I and Nick and Mitch waited round the clock with Dad. But he found us wanting in our watch and in some minutes when not one of us was in the room, he surrendered. His heart stopped; the Timex wristwatch above the hand I had been holding ticked on. Time had given him ninety-two years of perspective and then left him behind. It always does that. That same watch is now ticking on my wrist. It did not stop. It reminds me I will always be catching up, even to where Dad was when time left him behind.

When I hitched that ride on the planet from the corner of Plumas Street and the Colusa Highway, I was alone. I came from nothing I can possibly remember. That was my alpha point. In what I know is a departure from Teilhard, I expect that my omega point will be the same. No one will ask me if I want to enter it either. I am determined to resist the illusion, achieved by decades of consciousness, that my accustomed awareness will perdure. It won't. What will remain is what I have left behind in the conscious awareness of others. Memory, yes. But in a few cases where the memory might be healthy and challenging and productive, an action or project might just be able to improve some unnoticed corner of society.

Meanwhile? It's imperative to spend plenty of time with people who can see better than I can. Those will include folks much smarter than I am, who know how to tease from history the best of its secrets. They will include folks braver than I am, who will coax me to share more of my own history in the high-risk project called love. And they will include folks who can forge from our language the bridges over which I can trade their stories for mine.

I believe all that. And I believe it will get me to the end of the season.

Photo: Brad Reynolds

And before we say goodbye,
May we ask a very special favor?
Before you fall asleep tonight,
Would you spend two or three minutes
Just trying to—imagine—
This whole world at peace?
Take care of one another
And thank you very much.[54]

---

[54] Throughout the last five years of performances, I ended the show with this request.

Cast Chronology
The Royal Lichtenstein Circus

1971 (Summer)
Steve Aveson
Rosemary Hart
Gary Brill

1972 (Summer)
Bill Cain
Mike Moynahan
Mike Sparough

1972/1973 Tour
Barton Goldsmith
Mary Hildebrand
John MacConaghy
Carlo Pellegrini

1973/1974 Tour
Steve Saiz
John Salazar

1974/1975 Tour
Steve Aveson
Dana Smith

1975/1976 Tour
Tommy Crouse
Kevin Duggan
Mitch Kincannon

1976/1977 Tour
Kevin Duggan
Gary Gitchell
Mitch Kincannon

1977/1978 Tour
Jim Jackson
Ken Kaye
Mitch Kincannon

1978/1979 Tour
Stevie Coyle
Mitch Kincannon
Larry Ryan

1979/1980 Tour
Stevie Coyle
Mitch Kincannon
Larry Ryan
Philip Wellford

1980/1981 Tour
Stevie Coyle
Steve DeSaulniers
Mitch Kincannon
Chris French
Ed Glad
John O'Laughlin
Steve Vacha

1981/1982 Tour
Steve DeSaulniers
Jens Larson
Bob Lee
Nanci Olesen

1982/1983 Tour
Jimi Difillipis
Peter Griffith
John Hadfield
Jens Larson
Dan Trainor
Eric Wilcox

1983/1984 Tour
Linus Ackerman
Joey Colon
Nina Gray
John Hadfield
Paul Hadfield
Mitch Kincannon

1984/1985 Tour
Joey Colon
Andrew Hale
Keith Hughes
Howard Fireheart
Mitch Kincannon
Tim Latta
John Teeples

1985 Tour
Bob Coddington
Dom Ferry
Stefan Fisher
Mitch Kincannon
Jane Mitchell
Eugene Pidgeon Jr.

1986/1987 Tour
John Bollard
Jody Ellis
Mitch Kincannon
Peter Lees
Kelly Robertson
Mary Ellen Sellars
Jackie Shannon

1987/1988 Tour
Kevin Curdt
Leslie Hill
Mitch Kincannon
Joe Reichlin
Doug Rodman
Jules Vyner

1988/1989 Tour
Kevin Cloughley
Kevin Curdt
Carlo Gentile
Sam Lowry
Jeff Luoma
Jennie Madrigal

1989/1990 Tour
Nick Brill
Kevin Curdt
Carlo Gentile
Enrique Lopez
Jennie Madrigal
Jennie Martin
Joe Reichlin
Matt Reichlin
David Shaheen

1990/1991 Tour
Beverly Kerr
Jennie Madrigal
Eric Mason
James McCann
Darren Peterson
Joe Reichlin
David Shaheen
Billy Tomber

1991/1992 Tour
Chris Cuddihee
Circus of the Kids
Sean Fitzgerald
Jennie Madrigal
Darren Peterson

1993 Tour
Brent Dewitt
Jennie Madrigal

Acknowledgements

There are persons and groups of persons without whom this account could never have been realized. Some of those names overlap another list: those without whom it simply *would* not have been written.

In the group of stark enablers, must come the California Province of the Society of Jesus, some outstanding mentors, superiors, and collaborators such as Michael J. Buckley, Terry Mahan, John Clark, William Rewak and Tennant Wright, Ed Fassett, the Jesuit community of Santa Clara University, Queen of Peace Jesuit Novitiate in Montecito, Peter Filice, Gordon Bennet, Robert Walsh, and Bob Shinney. So must the Santa Clara County Council of Churches, Thae Murdock, Trinity Episcopal Church of San Jose and the First Unitarian Church of San Jose, the families of Semmes and Mary Jones, John and Peggy Rose, Patricia Puskarich, Joe and Millie Schweitzer, August and Muriel Wolf, John and Rosemarie Pastizzo, Patrick and Catharine Stewart-Roache, Nina Marucci, the Williams Toy Theater, Don and Irene Kincannon, Carlo Pellegrini, Juanita Madrigal, David Pinto, Ray and Shirley Michele, and Tom and Jean Sheridan. Long ago support from the theater department of Santa Clara University and students John Baker and Mary Hildebrand should be coupled with that given by Creighton University, and Jesuits Don Doll and Jonathan Haschka. Likewise, Thad Seymour and Rollins College as well as the Jesuit Novitiate of Grand Coteau should be mentioned for their generously providing winter quarters in the Eighties. Generous hospitality came our way from Regis College in Denver, Loyola University of New Orleans, Xavier University in Cincinnati. Our patient and loveable livestock would want appreciative mention to be made of Dr. Mark Wilson, DVM and Uncle Donald's Farm who gave them a home when The Royal Lichtenstein Circus was liquidated. Little Sisters of Jesus, Jo and Priscilla, the Geary and Barbara Byrd circus family, Fathers Jerry Hogan and Phil DeRea kindly enabled and enriched the latter years of my clowning and then Mike and Ellen Bartel, Sister Virginia Honish and Professor Tim Grandy welcomed me to another city and chapter of my teaching career: Milwaukee's Divine Savior Holy Angels High School.— Twenty-two years of cross-country tours playing one-day stands must suggest dozens of others who deserve mentioning here, but over that period, no one person had time to take notes. Here, let me take the time to say, "Thank you" wherever this finds you.

Writing is more private than growing up, going to schools and running a circus. Fewer knew it was a process in progress but they were nonetheless vital to it. I first heard "You have a book in you" from fellow travelers to the Serengeti. But neighbors Bill Olson and Don Nelligan made it stick and got me writing. My first efforts were graciously read by Sally Gramling, Mary Beitzel, and Mike and Ellen Bartel. Others who read the first draft were my sister, Susan, who let me know what I got right, Bob Kaiser, who shared his superb instinct for journalism, and my shotgun from three years on the circus, Kevin Curdt, who has been non-stop in his encouragement. My sleuthing proofreaders were Barbara Gratton and Jim Henderson. Technical assistance came from Gay Donahue and Timothy Ryan Goss. I owe most of the improvements in this decidedly superior current version to my editor, Stavra Ketchmark.

CPSIA information can be obtained
at www.ICGtesting.com
Printed in the USA
FSOW01n2051050617
35057FS